DRYING OUT

DRYING OUT

SAM HUMPHREY
Joel Rabe

Inspirit Alliance

DRYING OUT

More Stories from my Career
as a Commercial Diver

sam humphrey

Joel P Rabe

Copyright © 2023 Inspirit Alliance
Copyright © 2023 samuel c humphrey
Illustrations © 2023 Joel P Rabe

All rights reserved
sam humphrey 2023
Joel P Rabe 2023
Inspirit Alliance 2023

No part of this book may be reproduced, stored in a retrieval system, or transmitted in any form by any means; electronic, mechanical, photocopying, recording, or otherwise without express written permission from the publisher.

First Edition

ISBNs: Paperback: 978-1-959239-13-0
Hardback: 978-1-959239-14-7
e-book: 978-1-959239-15-4
Library of Congress Control Number: 2023909412

Cover design by: sam humphrey
Interior illustrations by: Joel P Rabe
Photographs by: sam humphrey

Printed in the United States of America

Contents

Introduction   xiv
Preface   xvi

Traveling Man   1

A Fish Out Of Water   21

Back In The Drink   45

Hurricanes - Good For Divers - Bad For Everybody Else   65

Dam It - Not Again!   135

There Are Old Divers And Bold Divers   155

Desiccation   183

I Am Not A Mole, But I Am In Tunnels   217

Thoroughly Dehydrated The End Of It All   269

Afterword   293

Introduction

Let me introduce myself, or Re-introduce as the case may be. My name is sam humphrey. You may already be familiar with me if you have read the first volume in this series – WET PAY. That book is filled with stories from the first half of my career in Commercial Diving. This book is filled with stories from the second half of said career. My original plan just included one book, but I had too many stories to tell for a decent sized book. I didn't want to publish some super thick book that would scare away readers. After talking with my son, we decided that a two-volume set would be the way to go. Here is Volume Two.

This volume is just a continuation of the first book. It starts where that book left off – in the middle of my dive career. It is the year Two-thousand-and-one. I have just decided to quit working for Norwesco Marine. They are going through a name change because of the state of their safety record and a change in majority ownership. I have started working with other companies more often and am looking for a company that I can work with more regularly, or maybe find an alternate career – not commercial diving, but still around water. I am still married to the Brasilian and have two children with her, although our marriage is on rocky ground – very rocky.

The same caveats still hold true for this volume: These are my stories told from my memory. You may recognize the stories or the characters in them differently from the way I remember them. That does not make the story any less true, it just shows my point of view. As in the previous volume, I will not be using any proper names of the people I worked with. You may think you recognize them – or not – but that doesn't necessarily mean the character is who you think it is. In the same way that each of us has a different take on how an event takes place - each of us also has a different take on what we see in people. We remember people differently. I may like someone that you cannot stand. I may dislike someone you adore. It all depends on our own personal experiences and perceptions of the people we work with. You may read one of my stories and know who I am talking about, then say to yourself "that is not how I remember that person." We are all biased by our own personal experiences. Just remember I am not wrong and neither are you. Like I said in WET PAY: There are three sides to every story: yours, mine, and the truth.

Also, just because this is a new volume doesn't mean commercial divers have changed. We are still a rough-and-tumble group of foul-mouthed party animals who work hard and play hard. This book will reflect that in the language used and the Political Incorrectness of the people in these stories. If that bothers you, don't read the book. If you are reading this book because you liked the first book, then that is not a concern. I hope you enjoy this book as much as, or more, than you did the first.

Thank you again,
sam humphrey

Preface

If you have read the first volume, you know how I came to be in this world, or maybe not "how I came to be," but at least where I came from and how I got into commercial diving. If you didn't read the first volume and you don't know anything about me, here it is in a nutshell:

I was born in Moscow, Idaho; first and only son followed by three sisters – two born in Germany, the third born in Japan. My family moved back to the Spokane area in the mid-sixties. I graduated high school, joined the U.S. Navy to become a diver but that didn't pan out. I learned about a commercial dive school operated by Highline Community College in Midway, Washington – a small town half-way between Seattle and Tacoma; hence the name Midway.

I spent three years at that college going through a two-year program because of a waiting list. I met lots of good people there. I worked several jobs while going through that program. including, but not limited to; diver support for the Marine Biology class, Hyperbaric Chamber Operator at Virginia Mason Hospital in Seattle, and self-employed dock cleaner in the Puget Sound area. I also prep-cooked at a Mexican restaurant in Bellevue, and worked at the Toys-R-Us at the Southgate mall. You do what you gotta do to get by.

I did some volunteer work for CAN-DIVE at the nineteen-eighty-six World's Fair in Vancouver, BC. I worked in the Gulf of Mexico for American Oilfield Divers. I married my first wife when I returned to Spokane from the south. We got divorced a year-and-a-half later. After that my career more or less took off and I continued working as a commercial diver - mostly in the Pacific Northwest on dams and bridges. I predominantly worked for one company, but also worked with several other companies over the years. In this second volume, I have quit working with the previous company and am working only with other companies.

That should give you an idea of where I came from and how we got to where we are at the start of this book. If you have not read the previous book and want to know more about me and my career, please do read WET PAY. I hope you enjoy reading it as much as I enjoyed writing it. The same goes for this volume.

This book is dedicated
to all the good Divers, Supervisors,
LSTs, Techs, and Tenders
I have worked with over the years.
Whether or not you are mentioned
by name or nickname in this book,
know that I enjoyed working with you.
I am sure you know who you are.

*water provides everything
without water
we have nothing*

Traveling Man

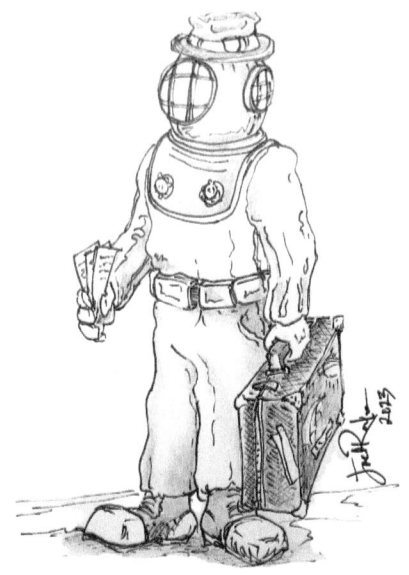

I spent the early part of the summer (two-thousand-and-one) working on a month-long job repairing pilings under the Seattle ferry docks with the company based out of the Bellevue guy's garage. Duck Fart joined me on that job. The Marine was the main Supervisor and I was the assistant supervisor. We had another tender that worked with us rounding out a four-man crew. There was a lot of diving to do, so we needed three strong divers. Duck Fart had turned into a really good diver and worker.

I made a practice of carrying around a set of Dive Safety Manuals and Emergency Procedures. We were doing a lot of jobs for government entities – like the City of Seattle, Seattle Metro, Army Corps of Engineers, WSDOT, MDT, ODOT – and they all required mountains of documentation and paperwork. As per my normal operating procedures, I always made sure the standby diver station was set up and ready to go. I also made sure every diver had a functional and filled bailout bottle. You'd be amazed by how many divers still didn't put much importance on those two things.

The Marine was one of them. He was always so anxious to dive that he thought we should start diving as soon as the main diver hose was ready to go. When I first started working with him, he would get very irritated that I wouldn't let him get wet until all the standby gear was set up and ready to go. By the time this Seattle ferry dock job had rolled around, he was used to it and just let me do my thing.

That happened to be very lucky for us and the owner of the company. OSHA doesn't make a practice of inspecting every single job site, but they do have the right to make inspections whenever they want to or feel it is necessary. They send an inspector who looks to make sure all your documentation is in order. The inspector also looks at all the equipment, the equipment set up, the work environment, employee dress - everything.

By now we had to have all our pressure vessels tested and inspected regularly and the documentation for that had to be on the worksite. We were required to have the resumés and *all* the required certifications of each member of the crew on site. You know, things like CPR certs that had to be renewed every year, proof of dive school graduation, OSHA safety certs, etc. It was a lot of paperwork, so I made a practice of keeping a file of each diver I liked to work with and kept them with my Dive Safety Manuals. Each employer also kept a file on each employee at the home office.

Our divers are accessing the water through an access port in the middle of the car holding area on the dock. We are very visible to the public. Below the dock, and out of the public's view, we have a small section of boat dock we are using as a dive platform. A tender is working from it to support the diver in the water. It also gives the diver a place where he can get out of the water and take his hat off for a break without having to come all the way up to the top of the ferry dock. We have a small aluminum work skiff under the ferry dock to move our dive platform around and shuttle work supplies back and forth. The crew working on the topside of the ferry dock is in direct view of all the foot traffic getting on and off the ferries. From the vantage point of the foot traffic, all the public can see is the dive control station, the radio operator, the standby dive rig, an umbilical going through a hole in the dock, and a single tender helping the radio operator out.

One morning, about half-way through the job, a random man walks up to Duck Fart and starts asking questions. Duck Fart knows not to answer any questions or talk about the job to random people, but, rather, to send them to the supervisor for answers. He points me out. We get lots of questions from the public when we do jobs in public areas. This stranger comes up to me and starts asking me questions about the job. I tell him that I am not at liberty to give him any details on the job, only that we are doing some service work for the Ferry system. He pulls out his official government-issued OSHA ID that shows he is a certified OSHA inspector. He informs me that he needs to see our documentation and he wants to see it *ALL*. He also wants a tour of our worksite.

On top of that, he wants me to go through the dive station with him detail by detail to make sure we are doing everything to OSHA and WSHA standards. He won't let us dive until he sees all this stuff. I am happy to comply. I have to pull the Marine out of the water while all this is going on. The Marine is not happy, but he has to defer to the agent's demands. He doesn't want to have anything to do with this interrogation, so he stands off to the side with Duck Fart and the other tender while I deal with this government agent.

I go through everything with the OSHA agent. I show him all our safety manuals, emergency procedures, and emergency contacts. I show him all the documentation of each member of our crew. I show him that we have the proper equipment and everything is set up according to OSHA and WSHA standards. I show him that each crew member has the required PPE (personal protective equipment) including, but not limited to, life jackets, gloves, safety-toe boots, etc.

When we finish the show and tell, he looks at me and says everything looks very good. He discloses to me that this wasn't a random inspection. His office had been called by a "concerned citizen" who had said we were running dive operations on the Seattle ferry dock without a standby set up. I assure him that we had everything set up just like today from the start of the job, which we had. He smiles and says he is glad for that. He does give us one hit, though, that he says he wants remedied by the next day. That is that I do not have a current CPR card for one of the members of the crew. That member of the crew is me. I have a copy of it in my file, but I had left the actual card in my car, back at the dive company owner's house. I assure him I will make sure to have it on the job site after that.

I thought about that visit all that day. I had decided that the "concerned citizen" had to have been someone who worked for a competing dive company. Whoever had made the call to OSHA obviously knew something about how dive stations were supposed to be set up if they had said we were lacking the standby diver. They were either hoping we would get shut down, maybe even run off the job, or they just wanted to hassle us. Sometimes the competition between dive companies could be quite fierce; especially in the Seattle area.

We finished that job up a week or so ahead of schedule. That made everybody happy except for the guys on the crew. Some people just never get enough work. The WSDOT was so happy that they actually gave us a couple more little jobs right after that. The jobs were small enough that they didn't have to go out to bid and could be given to whoever WSDOT thought best. Duck Fart, the Marine, and I celebrated a job well done by getting really toasted at a bar in SeaTac where we were staying at a motel.

*   *   *

I started working more and more with this guy out of Bellevue. He seemed a little more up front about what was going on with his company than some of the larger dive companies had been. At most, he only ever had two dive crews, but normally he only had one crew working. He was getting ready to retire, so he didn't go after work like he had in the past. He had enough work to keep one crew fairly busy though, and that was good for me. Because he didn't have loads of work, he had a little trouble hanging on to employees.

The crew that he was using consistently now, included the Marine as supervisor/diver, and me 'n' Duck Fart as the Divers/Tenders. We all got along really well and worked well with each other. That made the jobs enjoyable. This was more like the close-knit dive crews that I had started out working with at United Marine Divers back in the late eighties. It felt good and it was fun. We did lots of small jobs all over western Washington and Oregon. It meant a lot more out of town travel for me, but at least I still got home for most weekends.

Most of his work was in the Seattle and Puget Sound area. That was fine with me. My sister lived just south of Seattle near Des Moines and my best friend from high school was living just north of Everett by this time. I had several friends in the Seattle area so I always had a place to crash. If I went on jobs that were more than a week, I usually stayed at a hotel. On any job more than an hour out of the immediate Seattle area, the owner paid for our hotels. He didn't just give us our per diem, he actually paid for the hotel. We had to pony up for our meals, but I figured I had to eat whether I was working or not. The hotel bill was always larger than what our union-mandated per diem was, so I was ahead of the game - in that regard anyway.

On top of working with that guy, Vancouver, the older brother of the owner of Norwesco, wanted to start his own dive company. We had talked about it several times before. I knew I could get him the work in Montana. The management there at MPC - now PPLM - had told me more than once that it didn't matter to them what dive company they hired, they just wanted the divers they liked. Those divers included me, Kalispel, Blanchard, Boston, the Mouth, Duck Fart, Vinegar Flats, and a couple others we liked to work with. One of the PPLM engineers out of Butte, Montana kept a little black book with all the diver's and tender's names he had worked with. I am sure he had some sort of scale in his little book that he ranked us on too. Every time I had a new crew member, I would see that engineer writing in his little black book.

I told Vancouver that the hard part would be finding other divers to work for a new company they had never heard of. He asked if I thought the new company should be involved with the union. I told him that it *had* to be. That was the only way he was going to get good reliable divers to work for him in the Pacific Northwest. Vancouver had made a deal with some company from the Midwest to open an office in the Pacific Northwest, but it didn't last long. That company didn't want anything to do with the unions. They must have thought they could come in and underbid all the local companies by using non-union divers. Hah! Not likely. Once-in-a-while non-union companies would win a bid in the northwest, but the Seattle or Spokane union would go after them and force them to hire local divers and tenders. I think that usually ended up costing them more than they thought it would, so they rarely out bid local companies.

Meanwhile, I worked for just about all the union dive companies in the northwest that year. I did a lot of different jobs all over the place. I didn't work for the Norwesco group anymore, they had changed their name and were now majority owned by Big Load. I had a hard time working for a company that I felt was responsible for my friend's death. I didn't like working with Big Load and he was becoming more of a presence at that company. They had a big safety hit on their record with the death of the Texan and the other guy. After they changed their name, they had a clean safety record. Kind of a rotten deal, but that's how it works. Besides that, the original owner and I didn't really see eye-to-eye anyway.

Things weren't working out with the Brasilian and me either. We filed for divorce for the third time in the early spring. She had taken a trip to Brasil alone to "find herself." She left the kids with me. That was fine. My family helped take care of them while I was working. I made a point of being home every weekend. When she got back from Brasil, we filed for divorce. It was finalized in the fall of two-thousand-and-one. Even though I hated being away from my kids, I felt much better spiritually. I moved in with my dad and his wife right after filing for divorce. I lived with them for about two months. After that, I moved in with my step brother. He had a basement bedroom and bathroom that I rented. He had just gotten divorced, so it worked out well for both of us.

* * *

Vancouver married a woman who lived in Corvallis, a small town south of Portland, Oregon. He was trying to convince her to help him finance and start a new dive company. They invited me over to her place for dinner one weekend so she could talk to me about the viability of a new dive company in the Pacific Northwest. I told her there was always room for a new company. I also said the company would need to treat the divers well if they wanted to hang on to good divers. In the dive industry, reputation is the most valuable commodity. The way a dive company gets a good reputation is by having good quality employees; that is hard-working, responsible, knowledgeable crew members.

They asked me if I would help them start a new company. I told them I couldn't help financially, but I could bring my experience, knowledge, and a couple clients to the table. Over that weekend we had decided that we would all be equal owners. I had suggested to both of them that it might be best, on paper at the very least, if Vancouver's new wife was the majority shareholder. I suggested a fifty-two percent share to Corvallis and a twenty-four percent share to both Vancouver and myself. That would make the new company minority owned and give us an advantage when bidding jobs. We hadn't carved anything in stone at that point. It was all just ideas and talk.

A few weeks later, Vancouver called me up and said he had bought a large tandem-axle enclosed trailer. He wanted my help in setting it up as a Dive Control station. I thought that would be fun. I told him I would be happy to help. He and his wife had rented a small commercial garage and wanted to start acquiring dive equipment. Vancouver had always been good at finding deals. He got the trailer for a really good price and he had bought some dive equipment that had been purchased new by some others that dreamed of starting a dive company. They hadn't had any luck and had used their equipment only a couple times. Vancouver basically got new equipment for half price. Good on him.

I stayed at Corvallis' house while I helped Vancouver work on the trailer. He bought all the supplies we needed. I laid out the trailer like I thought it should be and he looked it over. He was satisfied with the layout, so I put it together that way. The trailer was twenty-four feet long – huge. It was seven feet tall on the inside, which was nice because you could stand up in it even if you were six-foot-seven or eight. Not that any of us were, but a few divers I knew were well over six-foot tall and this would be great even for them.

I put the Dive Control station in the front eight feet of the trailer. That left the back sixteen feet for all the dive hoses, compressors, welders and other machines and equipment we would use on a job. The trailer was large enough that it would end up being a self-contained Dive Station for any diving we would do that didn't require a boat. Ninety percent of inland diving doesn't require a boat. Both Vancouver and I had enough experience diving inland that we had a good idea of how to put together a very good dive station in a trailer. Honestly, we didn't need a twenty-four-foot trailer, but it *did* give us lots of extra room. I installed tie-down points on the floor and low in the walls of the trailer that would work well for both the equipment we would be using and my motorcycle. That way, if there was room in the trailer and we were going on a longer job, I could easily bring my bike along with me.

I worked a fair amount over the summer and fall, so didn't have all the free time in the world to work on Vancouver's project. Once-in-a-while if I was working on a job close by, I would spend my little free time working on the trailer. As far as I knew, Vancouver and Corvallis hadn't even got the dive company thing all sorted out. I did keep in touch with them on a regular basis to keep abreast of the situation. The main thing Vancouver asked when I talked to him was when PPLM might need more dive work. I told him they typically did the majority of their work in the late summer and fall. There was a fair bit of annual work they required in the spring. I also told him that I knew they were planning a fairly large project at Holter Dam for the spring of two-thousand-and-two. If he wanted to get in on that, he had better get the company paperwork done. I let him know I would help him however I could.

    I ended up having a pretty good year, even without working for the same company I had in the past. The guy from Bellevue kept me pretty busy. There was no more fiber optic work. The "five-year's worth of work" that Pirelli-Jacobson said they had never materialized. The Fiberweb project in the Gulf of Mexico went away too. What happened? Cell phones. That is what happened. Fiber optic cables were still the best and most reliable method of data transmission, but cell phones and wireless were *so* much less expensive. Several companies had launched hundreds of satellites, phone companies had set up cell towers everywhere. It just wasn't cost effective for telecommunication companies to invest in fiber optics anymore. Yeah, cell phones became available in the late eighties, but they weren't really affordable and reliable until the late nineties. Now, just after the turn of the new millennium, everybody was getting them. It was cheaper to get a cell phone than it was to get a landline.

*   *   *

    Vancouver gave me a call in the early spring of two-thousand-and-two. He and Corvallis had gotten the company all set up and ready to go. They had decided not to bring me in as a part owner. They said "Thanks for all the volunteer work you did for us. We will treat you very well. You will be our main supervisor." Great.

    I replied "That's fantastic for you two. Thanks so much you guys. You don't have any work, though. Give me a call when you do. See you later."

"Wait, wait, wait; that's why I'm calling. PPLM called and said they'd give us a chance to show them what we could do. We got the job to clean the trash racks at Madison Dam. Are you available?" Vancouver asked.

Hmm. Sure, I'm available. I asked if they had all the insurances they needed. I asked if they had signed on with the union. What wages were they planning on paying. How was travel pay going to work. I asked him all that stuff. I was not very happy with them for cutting me out of partial ownership without talking to me about it. I kind of felt like he had stabbed me in the back. I didn't say anything about that to either one of them, though. I decided I would work for them just like I worked for anyone else. If they got a job and put me on it, I would do the best I could for them.

Vancouver told me when we were supposed to do the work at Madison. I was available. He said he would drive the trailer over and be the supervisor. I would be a diver. Oh, and by the way, did I know of anyone who would work with us? We still needed a three-person team and everybody he had called was busy. I found someone, a semi-regular with the company I used to work for.

We went to Ennis. Vancouver put us up in a hotel. He paid the bill and gave each of us twenty-five dollars every day for food. We all ate together anyway; just like all our jobs in the past. The job went the same as it ever had. PPLM was happy with the work and said they would see us on the next project. That was good news for Vancouver and his wife, Corvallis. The trailer worked very well as a dive station. Its only drawback was that it was *so* long it was a little difficult to get into some of the places we would work.

* * *

The big job at Holter Dam started in April. Active Diving and Marine Services out of Corvallis, Oregon got the contract. Good work, Vancouver and Corvallis. They had asked me to run the project. Vancouver said he was too busy to go on this one. He would be spending his time bidding other jobs. That sounded good to me. I wondered who else was going to be on the job. He didn't know. He wanted to know if I knew anybody who might be willing to work on it. I told him I'd ask the guys I like to dive with. After a couple days, I gave Vancouver a list of names to call. He called me back and had informed me he had a full crew ready to go and we needed to be on site Monday a couple weeks out.

Then he asked if there was any way I could get to Corvallis and pick up the dive trailer? I told him my sixty-four Chevy pickup wouldn't pull that trailer. He told me not to worry, they had bought a newer used Ford diesel to haul the trailer. Oh, and by the way, did I have a place in Spokane where I could store the truck and trailer? Really? I told him I could find a place. I talked to my dad – he lived on eighty acres just west of Spokane. My dad told me I could park it out on his property.

I rode my motorcycle over to Corvallis and picked up the trailer. I loaded all the dive equipment and other tools and machines we might need. The purpose of the trailer was to have a complete dive outfit on each job. We had two three-hundred-and-fifty-foot dive umbilicals – one with video. We had a breathing air compressor, two K-bottles of air and two K-bottles of oxygen. We had dive radios, pneumo gages - everything we needed for a proper dive station. We had a welder with both welding and burning leads. It really was a nice set up and easy to work out of.

The back door of the trailer opened down and doubled as a ramp like on a toy hauler. Since we could lock everything up, we didn't have to break anything down when we finished diving at night. That made for really quick set up and break down times on the job. That effectively gave us more time for actual diving. The clients really liked that. Out of an eight-hour day, it was very easy to get seven-and-a-half hours of diving no matter where the job was as long as we could get the trailer there.

Anyway, the job at Holter Dam was starting in April. My crew would be Illinois, who had worked on Holter Dam a year and a half ago with me and Puppy Dog Eyes. The third member of the crew would be Spider, with whom I had worked in the Gulf of Mexico on the Fiberweb project. Two good workers. That would be great. This should be a good job. Illinois and Spider didn't know each other, but I was fairly certain they would get along fine. Hmmm.

I got to Wolf Creek early Sunday afternoon. PPLM wouldn't let us stay in the little house at the base of the dam. They weren't as accommodating as MPC had been. I had talked to a woman in Wolf Creek that had a little three-bedroom house for rent. She normally rented to fishermen on a nightly or weekly basis. She was ecstatic to have us there for two or three months. We paid her weekly. The other two guys showed up later that night.

Illinois had a college friend who lived in Helena. He had a two-bedroom condo and his roommate was moving out. He might need another roommate later in the summer. I had talked with him about moving into his place after this job was over. I was planning on moving to Montana anyway, so I brought both my motorcycles with me on this job. They both fit in the dive trailer along with all the dive gear. It just took some creative packing to get everything in. I should say here that one of my motorcycles was a ninety-four Honda Shadow Eleven Hundred and the other was a ninety-nine Ural Patrol – the one with a sidecar and powered sidecar wheel. Montana was a great place for both of those machines.

Illinois and I had spent a lot of time in Wolf Creek on that other job and a couple little ones in between that job and this one. We were well-known in this little town. We had breakfast every day at the Oasis - the bar we used to frequent last time we were here. The building was split in half with the bar on one side and the restaurant on the other. They were happy to see us in Wolf Creek again. After breakfast, we drove the truck and trailer up to the dam.

The dam used to be used as a bridge across the Missouri River by the public, so it couldn't be blocked. After Nine-Eleven though, access had been closed off. Almost all the dams in the U.S. had been required to limit access to the public. Now there were high chain-link (cyclone) fences all around the dams. This was good for us, especially on this job. The job was going to last two to three months. Now we could set up the dive station in the middle of the dam and leave it there until the job was finished.

The scope of this job was to replace the rusted-out trash racks; similar to what I had done at Rainbow Dam a few years earlier. The main difference here was that *all* the trash racks were going to be replaced with new sections. There would be no repair of bad sections. That made the job a little easier, not any shorter though. We would burn the bolts securing the old trash racks and replace them with new hardware. There were a few support stanchions and crossbars that we had to burn out and bolt in new frame and support pieces.

We worked with a crane almost every day. The crane was hired by PPLM independently of us. It came from a crane company that had worked with MPC for years. They were great to work with. We had worked with them on many projects for MPC over the years. They only had a couple crane operators and the one they sent was the one that had worked with us the most. That was very good for us because we could put a speaker from the dive radio in the cab of the crane and he could hear right from the diver what the diver needed. Communication was very good on this project.

The bottom of the trash racks were just over forty feet deep. With the elevation here, we had to add a table for the decompression schedule. Forty-plus feet put us on a fifty-foot table; add one for elevation and that put us on a sixty-foot table. That meant we had a dive time of only sixty minutes when the diver worked towards the bottom. Ten feet up from the bottom, we were running a fifty-foot table which gave us one-hundred minutes of dive time. To say the least, time was of the essence. There was a lot to do under water and I didn't want the diver waiting on anything from topside. The tenders needed to think about what was going on and anticipate what the diver would need. That was common practice on all the construction jobs I had ever been on. Things did tend to work a little slower in the Gulf. Spider had never been on a construction job before. His only experience with commercial diving had been the Fiberweb project. On that job we followed the trencher. The diver did not make the pace of the job, so it was quite a bit more relaxed than the typical construction job. Spider had a hard time getting used to this.

I guess in Spider's head, he looked at all dive jobs as relaxed. Somewhat like school, just relax a little and tend to the diver. Or like the jobs in the Gulf he had been on – the tender just held onto the diver's umbilical and sent him what he needed when he asked for it.

Up here, I needed him to step up his game. I don't think he liked the pace of the construction job. After a few times of him dragging his ass, I started to get short with him. I even got on his case a few times and told him that he needed to work faster and have everything the diver would need ready for the diver before the diver went in the water. He had a hard time getting that through his head too. One time, after I got on his case, he asked me why I was being such an asshole on this job. I wasn't like this at all on the Fiberweb job. I explained to him that it was a different type of project and that we were on a limited bottom time with limited divers. On the Fiberweb project we had lots of divers, so never worried about running out of dive time during the work day.

Illinois had a real problem with the pace of Spider's work. When I was diving, I think they argued quite a bit. In the northwest, we didn't really have an order of rank. Yes, I was the supervisor and in charge of the project, but the other two members of the crew were equals. You would think the crew member with less experience would defer to the one with more, but that didn't always happen. As a whole, divers tend to have strong personalities and are not good at stepping aside or backing down from conflicts.

When Spider was in the water, his sense of urgency didn't improve any. He took his sweet time doing the work and ended up not getting a lot done on his dives. He was comfortable in the water and a hard worker. He just had no sense of time management. Illinois wanted me to swap him out with someone else. I didn't. I couldn't really. By the time Spider's work practice had become bothersome, we were more than halfway done with the work. Also, I couldn't find a replacement because everybody I knew was working on other projects. I didn't look too hard, though. I figured I would whip Spider into shape. Tenders and new divers needed to be molded into good divers.

Of course, after work the first week on the job, I went to the Wolf Creek Cyberstop to see if they still made Chocolate Malts. They did. The girl (woman) behind the counter was a different woman than the woman who had helped me a year-and-a-half ago. She was still a redhead, but she seemed shorter and had a much more athletic build than the other girl. I came to find out she was the owner of the little shop and the previous girl had just been an employee of hers. I asked if she still made sack lunches that we could take with us. She said she did.

She also published a monthly news journal that covered what was going on in the Wolf Creek/Craig area. Craig is a little town about ten miles north of Wolf Creek. It is super popular with fishermen as well. Anyway, she asked what I was doing in Wolf Creek and I told her we were doing some repair work on Holter Dam. She said that sounded interesting and wanted to know if she could come up one day and take some photos. She wanted to do a little article for her journal that showed what was going on at the dam. I told her that would be fine. I informed her that we started at eight a,m. and finished by four p.m. every weekday. I also said that if she wanted to see us diving, it would be best to show up at least a half-hour after we started and also at least an hour before we finished for the day.

A couple days later she showed up around noon with a camera and notepad in hand; just like a real reporter. She asked what she could take photos of. I told her there were no trade secrets here, so she could take photos of whatever she thought was interesting. She also wanted to interview me. She asked all sorts of questions about what we did, how we got into diving, how much diving was done around the inland states. Stuff like that. I answered all her questions to her satisfaction, I think.

A few days after she had visited the dam. I went into her café for a chocolate malt, like I did almost every day after work. She made the malt for me and then asked if I could read over the article that she was writing about the dive project. I told her I would gladly do that. I helped her with some definitions and descriptions of the photos she took. I helped make sure she didn't write anything incorrectly. After I finished helping her with that article, she asked if I would mind proof-reading some of her other articles. I told her I would be happy to help. I started going there after work to help her out a little bit before dinner every night. What else was I to do? Drink beer and play pool at the Oasis like we normally did? A few nights later I asked her out to dinner. She accepted. I took her up to Craig on the motorcycle and we ate at a little restaurant there.

I wasn't going back to Spokane every weekend. My ex-wife would only let me see my children every other weekend and she even made that difficult. On the weekends that I wouldn't see my kids, I stayed in Montana. One Friday night I asked the owner of the Cyberstop if she wanted to go drinking and dancing at a bar. There was a fun place just north of Helena called the Silver City Saloon. You could get there on dirt roads from Wolf Creek in about half-an-hour. It was a perfect ride on my sidecar rig. I asked her if she was game for that. She said she was.

We went to Silver City and had a great time. The bar there served dinner – like most in Montana – and it was good. We closed the bar down and I took her back to her place on the dirt roads all the way. I didn't have to worry about any cops pulling us over that way. I did have to watch out for wildlife though! We started seeing each other on a regular basis after that.

The Job was going well. We had to co-ordinate the movement of the old trash screens and the new trash screens with what we were doing in the water at the time. We had a flatbed trailer that would be left on the top of the dam we could load the old rusted trash screens on after we pulled them off the dam. When it was loaded, we would have a semi take it away. The driver of the semi would take the trailer off the dam and down the little hill where he would leave it while he hooked up to another trailer that had the new sections on it. He would drive that up to the dam and leave it there until we had removed all the new pieces on that trailer and replaced them with the old sections. It took us a few days to unload and load the trailers, so we saw the driver about once a week.

We finished that job in early June. Spider had decided he didn't want to be a commercial diver and applied to the U.S. Border Patrol for a job. I never heard from him after that. I hope all is well with him. Illinois already had more work lined up with another dive company. He liked to work and did not like sitting at home. As soon as he saw the end of a job in sight, he started making calls looking for more work. I always waited until my current job was completed before looking for another job. I liked my time off.

At the end of this job, I needed to decide where I was going to live. I wanted to move to Montana. I had talked to Illinois's friend in Helena. I had also talked about my plans to move to Montana with the owner of the Cyberstop. She told me that she had two empty bedrooms in her house and had two bathrooms also. She would happily rent one of the rooms to me if I didn't mind living off the grid. Her place was about ten miles of dirt road out of Wolf Creek. I thought about it a very little bit and accepted her offer. I never paid any rent, but I did end up marrying her a couple years later. Who would have thought that might happen? I'm still happily married to her twenty years later.

Vancouver and Corvallis were actually happy with the way my living arrangements worked out because the majority of their dive work was in Montana. I could park the dive trailer in Wolf Creek and it would be much closer to the work we did for PPLM. They saved a bunch of money on fuel for the truck since it didn't get driven back and forth to Spokane any more. They ended up getting almost all the work for PPLM over the next couple years. They had a second smaller trailer outfitted with a dive package that they kept in Oregon for the jobs they got west of Idaho.

* * *

A Fish Out of Water

I was still working mostly for the guy in Bellevue. Vancouver's company – Active Diving and Marine - was new, so he had trouble getting work in Washington and Oregon. Most of his dive work came from PPLM so it was rather limited. In the summer he asked me if I would consider being a DSO. A DSO is a Dive Safety Officer for the Army Corps of Engineers. The ACoE requires a DSO on *all* their dive jobs. The DSO's responsibility is to keep an eye on the dive company. They cannot interfere with the work or the diving unless someone was actually in danger. They are just there to report the progress of the job and the performance of the dive company. They are also there to make sure the dive company does not try to pull a fast one or cut any corners on the job. You would be surprised how often that kind of thing happens.

I told him I would be happy to do it as long as I got paid a decent rate – at least diver's pay – and he paid me through the union. I wasn't about to work for no benefits. He told me they would pay me Superintendent's pay through the union and I would get the per diem as required by the union. He and Corvallis also told me they would re-imburse me for fuel to and from the job site. That works for me.

I had to get certified by the ACoE to be a DSO. I didn't have to take any classes for it. I just had to file a bunch of papers and give them copies of my dive logs and dive certifications. Another of their requirements was that a DSO have at least five years of working on and around the rivers in the Pacific Northwest. Also, I wouldn't be allowed to be a DSO on jobs done by any company I had worked with in the past five years. That meant I couldn't be a DSO for the Norwesco Marine group – even after their name change. I also couldn't be a DSO on any jobs the guy from Bellevue got, or the company in Portland I worked with once in a while. That was okay though, because there were several other companies that regularly got the ACoE work.

It turns out I was way overqualified for the job. The ACoE said they would be happy to have me as a DSO. Before this, DSOs were employees of the ACoE who had gone to a "training course" in Florida where they would be introduced to the equipment used in commercial dive operations. They also had to learn how to read and use the U.S. Navy dive tables. Now, so much dive work was going on all over the northwest on so many of the ACoE dams that they didn't have enough people to fill the positions.

Vancouver had seen this hole in the work force and figured he could supply people to do it. He was correct. He asked me for a list of names of who I thought would be qualified and also interested in doing that kind of work. The list wasn't very long, but I gave him the names of people who might be interested. He got two or three others along with himself certified with the ACoE.

I started doing some of that work. Actually. in two-thousand-and-two, I did quite a bit of that work. One sad thing was that if I was doing that, I couldn't go on dive jobs. Another sad consequence of the job is that now all the divers look at you as the enemy. They think you are there to spy on them and report any unprofessional behaviour. They view you as sort of a Police Officer. That was not the case at all. The good thing about it was that I made more money doing that than I did when I was diving. I also got introduced to the owners and supervisors of the companies I hadn't worked with. There was a *lot* more paperwork to that job though. In fact, that job was *all* about the paperwork. I had reports to fill out and I had to make copies of all the dive companies paperwork. It's a good thing it paid well, otherwise it wouldn't have been worth it.

Shortly after Vancouver got that part of his company going, another guy started doing the same thing. That would have been okay because there was plenty of work for them both. Problems arose about a year later when they started trying to underbid each other. It would have been fine if they hadn't gone into a bidding war. After that it seemed like every time I went on a DSO job the pay was a little less than it had been on the previous job. Then they started cutting my perks – the travel pay, the per diem, the fuel re-imbursement. After a while it wasn't worth it for me to do that job and I let Vancouver and Corvallis know that I wouldn't be available for that work anymore. I explained why and they accepted my decision. The sad thing about the whole situation was that Vancouver and the other guy could have agreed on an acceptable wage and the ACoE would have paid it. There was plenty of work to keep them both busy. Greed; it blurs the vision, I guess. I would still run dive jobs for them whenever they needed though.

* * *

Vancouver and Corvallis were having trouble getting divers to work for them. Most of the guys I had worked with at Norwesco wouldn't work with them. I asked Kalispel, Vinegar Flats, the Mouth and some others, but none of them would. I think the owner of Norwesco was pissed at his brother for starting a competitive dive company. I know he was pissed at me for taking the Montana work away from him. Even though the managers and engineers liked some of the guys still working with that group, they didn't like doing business with the management at Norwesco – or whatever their new name was. I don't *know*, but I think the Norwesco owners probably told the divers who worked for them that if they ever worked for Active Diving and Marine, they would never work for their company again.

In the spring, PPLM had the regular work on the dams in Great Falls plugging leaks in the dams there. Illinois was willing to work with us. Blanchard was working with some company in California that wanted to open an office in the Pacific Northwest. Puppy Dog Eyes was going to college. Duck Fart and Vinegar Flats weren't comfortable working with us. The Mouth wasn't available. Hope wasn't diving anymore. Shit.

I had the dive trailer already in Wolf Creek. I headed up to Great Falls early Monday morning. Illinois met me at the Rainbow office. Vancouver had called and said he was sending a kid from Western Washington over. He was new to us, but had gone to dive school in Canada and supposedly worked quite a bit up there. Vancouver said he was a good, hard-working guy who was also good in the water. Yeah, man. We'll see. I'll test him out and see how he really does.

By this time Illinois and I had been working together over two years. We knew each other's routines. We were probably a little hard on new guys. I knew Illinois didn't put up with much crap. Hopefully this new guy would be alright. Otherwise, Vancouver would never hear the end of it.

The new guy showed up at the Rainbow shop about a quarter to eight. Very good. He was off to a good start. He was tall – over six-foot, clean-shaven, short hair and in good shape. He looked like he had just stepped out of a Hollywood movie. He had his own helmet and all the required dive and safety gear.

This was the first job of the season for us at PPLM. There was lots of back-slappin' and "hellos" and "how ya' beens" going around. Everybody was in a good mood and looked like they were ready for another round of work with us. They were all nice to the new guy. We got our scope of work and our assigned crew. It was the same few guys that had been working with us for years. We all headed down to the Duck and started loading in our gear. This was the first time some of these guys had seen our new trailer and they were pretty impressed. The new guy didn't know what to make of the Duck. I think he liked it though.

We started at Morony Dam – the farthest from Great Falls and would work our way back. We were going to work on at least four of the dams. We might be here a month or more. It would be nice to have some fairly steady work for a change. The previous year had been a little slow. Lots of growing pains getting a new company going. We rode with our gear in the back of the Duck - as usual – all the way to Morony Dam. It was about eighteen miles and took us about forty-five minutes in the Duck. The weather was nice, so it was a comfortable ride.

When we got there, the PPLM guy drove down the bank and into the water – like he always had – and we motored up to the right-side spill gate. I think the new guy was a little freaked out with the whole routine. He handled it well though. Once we were moored to the dam, we set up the dive station. The new guy knew what he was doing. He had a carpenter's toolbelt that he wore in which he had all kinds of tools – everything you might want on a dive job. Illinois and I teased him about it and called it the Bat Belt. It seemed like every time we needed a tool, no matter what it was, he pulled it right from his belt. It was a little comical, but very nice. I liked working with a guy who was prepared to do his job. He worked hard and did a good job. Illinois wanted to dive first, so he did. I dove the new guy second. He did a fine job. Granted we were only sealing leaks, but he followed directions, took advice, and did the work without complaining.

The PPLM crew noticed how clean he was. They had also said that the secretary (administrative assistant) had been making googly-eyes at the new guy all morning. She had made some remark about him looking like a movie star so we all started calling him Hollywood. I think that embarrassed him a little, but he took it in stride.

We were at Morony Dam for three days. After that we moved back to Ryan Dam. We would finish out the week there and come back Monday to finish that dam. After finishing up Ryan Dam we would move back to Cochrane Dam. From there I don't know what the plan was – that was three weeks away. Illinois went back to his family over the weekends. He had a trailer and had rented a spot at the trailer park in Great Falls for the month. That was much cheaper for him than staying in a hotel all month. Hollywood went back to his home in Washington for the weekends also. He was staying in a hotel for the week. I was staying in Wolf Creek and riding my motorcycle up to Great Falls and back every day. We were lucky with the weather. It stayed pretty nice for us the whole month we were there.

I wasn't doing any of the diving on this project. Both Illinois and Hollywood were capable divers. Corvallis and Vancouver had decided to pay me Diver's Wet Pay for supervising. That was nice of them and I really appreciated it. There was no Supervisor pay in the union. We had a Superintendent pay, but a Superintendent over-saw the whole dive operation and usually multiple supervisors. That's not really what I was doing. Of course, most dive companies wouldn't pay more if they didn't have to. I thought it was great that they paid me the wet pay for being a supervisor. That made Illinois and Hollywood happy because they got to dive every day.

It was strange not doing any of the diving. I missed getting in the water and working by myself on a project. Working under the water was calming most of the time. I liked the sound of the bubbles from my regulator exhaust. I liked the weightlessness of the environment. I liked that you could float down to the worksite like an astronaut. It was like being on another planet. It was a whole different world under the water and it felt like an escape from the real world.

After we finished with the Morony, Ryan, and Cochran Dams we took everything back to the Rainbow shop. We had a few days to finish out the week. The manager of the Rainbow shop – the guy in charge of all the maintenance at all the dams owned and operated by PPLM – told us that the spill gates at Black Eagle Dam were leaking and we needed to seal those gates as well. I hadn't worked on Black Eagle before. They rarely needed more than what the maintenance crew could do from the surface. The wooden batter boards must be starting to rot, or maybe they were just too old. Black Eagle was put in service in nineteen-twenty-seven – one of the newer dams! Actually, Cochrane was the newest Dam MPC had built. It was operational in nineteen-fifty-eight.

MPC had the permits to build one more dam, but the project needed to be started by nineteen-eighty-four. It wasn't, so they lost the permit. The EPA would never grant them a permit for a new dam now. All the greenies were trying to get the dams removed. I guess they'd rather have their electricity come from coal or natural gas power plants. What?! Don't *even* get me started on wind and solar! And nuclear power is even worse. Talk about poisoning and destroying the earth. At least dams created habitats for fish and wildlife.

We couldn't use the Duck at Black Eagle Dam. It was in the city of Great Falls and there were no good places to get the Duck in the water. Plus. the rocks and silt upstream of the dam would really hinder its movement. There was enough room on the south side of the dam for us to park the dive trailer and work out of it. The PPLM crew had a carry deck and a man-basket that we would use to put the diver in and out of the water. The access to the worksite was a narrow dirt road. It was really, really, steep. And narrow, did I say it was narrow? The trailer had to be backed down the access road because there wasn't enough room at the bottom to turn it around. That was a hairy ordeal and took a little longer than I had hoped.

There actually was more work to do on Black Eagle Dam than just seal leaks. We had to do some work on the spill gates that operated more or less like head gates. The main difference being there was no turbine chamber on the other side of these gates. That meant there would be no way of diminishing the pressure change if a diver got sucked up against one of these gates. Also, we would be working at the bottom – which wasn't deep really (only thirty-five feet) but it put us on a fifty-foot decompression schedule – because of the altitude. That limited our dive time to one-hundred minutes. All three of us would have to dive. I was happy about that for a couple of reasons; first, I got to get wet and second, I had never been on this dam before. One of my goals was to dive on every dam owned by MPC (PPLM now). I had already dived on every dam owned by Washington Water Power.

We finished up the work at Black Eagle without any issues. The diving went well. All the divers did well. I was very happy with Hollywood's performance and looked forward to working with him on more projects. Of course, I always enjoyed having Illinois on my crew. He was a good hard worker who had a lot of good ideas on how to get things done in the water. That finished up the scheduled work for PPLM at the moment. On to the next project!

* * *

Corvallis had a son. She had other children also, but her youngest – a son – was not making much of himself. I don't know what the whole deal was. All I know is that he couldn't hold a job – or didn't want to. He was dating a stripper from Portland, and I don't know what all else. Well, I do. I just don't want to say. Haha! Anyway, I know that Corvallis wasn't happy with his current trajectory. She had decided to send him to dive school so he could start working with us on dive jobs. Wonderful. I knew that I would have to deal with this guy after he completed dive school. I had met him a couple times and he just didn't have a very good attitude. He was a spoiled brat as far as I was concerned, but I didn't say anything to Corvallis or Vancouver. Maybe he wouldn't finish dive school. Maybe he wouldn't like the dive industry. Who was I kidding? His mom owns a dive company.

After he finished dive school, he came over to Montana with Vancouver to do a job. I don't remember the job really. All I do remember is I had to tell this kid every little thing. I realize that you learn more on the job about how everything really works than you do in school, but you at least have the basics down when you graduate. At least you *should* have the basics down. I don't think this kid paid attention at all while he was going through dive school. He wasn't very mechanically inclined either. Oh well, he *is* the owner's son so I *do* have to work with him I suppose. Maybe he'll get better. That job only lasted a couple days. We got it done. The boy went home with Vancouver.

The next job I had with Active Diving and Marine was at Hauser Dam just outside of Helena, Montana. Vancouver told me the foreman of the dam wasn't happy that I would be the supervisor on the job. I thought that was weird for a couple reasons. I had worked at Hauser Dam before – several years ago – and I remember getting along with the foreman and the rest of the guys very well. The foreman rode a motorcycle so we had something in common. I also remember getting the job done for him and he was very happy with our performance. I think Vancouver was trying to stir the pot or something. I had been told by the manager up in Great Falls that PPLM preferred it if Vancouver never came back for any of the jobs. They preferred the crews that I ran and preferred me as a supervisor.

Anyway, I went to Hauser Dam with Hollywood and the son. We got a warm reception and the whole dam crew was happy to see me. I have *no* idea what Vancouver was talking about. We met in the old one-room schoolhouse on the east side of the dam. MPC - now PPLM - used it as a conference and lunch room. The foreman told us what the scope of the job was. It seems that they had closed the headgate on the number one unit but water was still flowing through. There was enough water leaking by or through the gate that they couldn't shut the turbine all the way down. They needed to do some maintenance, so they needed to shut it down.

Hauser Dam, like many of the older dams in Montana, has a forebay that is separated from the pond behind the dam. The penstocks – the pipes that water goes through to the turbine chamber from the forebay – are oriented perpendicular to the river flow. The headgates are at the top of the penstocks and are what is used to shut the water flow down. Head gates are basically a gigantic gate valve. Leaks by a closed head gate can have many causes. The gate might not be all the way down. Maybe the gate goes all the way down, but only seals on one side; like the head gate at Cochrane Dam. These gates are made of wood and steel; maybe the wood rotted or the steel rusted out. Maybe the gate isn't sealing along the sides. Maybe the penstock fill valve wasn't closed. There could be hundreds of reasons for the leakage. That is one of the things that makes dam diving so dangerous.

I assured the foreman of the Hauser project that we would locate the source of the leak and decide what to do from there. It depends on what is causing the leak to determine how we will stop it. First things first; is the head gate all the way down? Yes, there is a gage on the head gate shaft that indicates the position of the gate. This one showed the gate to be all the way on the bottom of the gate slot. Okay. Well, we will put a diver in and look for leaks. Most likely is the P-seals have worn or are missing pieces allowing water to flow by. By the amount of water flowing by, maybe even a whole section or two of P-seal is missing. I've seen that before. No problem. We can use two-by-fours or four-by-fours to help seal the leaks; whatever we need to do.

We parked the trailer on top of the dam near the head gates. Because of the orientation of the dam, I cannot see the head gates from where the dive station is set up. Communication is critical on this job. I will dive Hollywood first. The son will be the tender. In fact, the son will be a tender until he shows me that he can work reliably enough to be a diver. Judging by his past performance, that may be quite a while. I will supervise. If a second dive is required, I will make it and Hollywood will run the dive station.

We used the umbilical with the camera on it so we could see what the diver could see. Cameras are great because many times the camera can show more than what the diver can see. Also, the dam crew will have a better idea of where the leaks are coming from if they can see them. The son had never worked around leaks like this before. I told him that we needed to be vigilant in the tending of the diver's hose. Since I couldn't see him, I would be relying on his abilities as a tender. I told him that under *no* circumstances was he to give the diver slack unless I told him to. He assured me that he understood this.

The plan was for Hollywood to go down one side of the gate looking for leaks as he dropped down. Then he would move across the bottom looking for leaks. From there he would leave bottom and come up the far side searching for leaks as he came up. These were the most likely sources of the leakage. If he didn't find any leaks in that search, he would then start at the top of the gate and move across it from side to side and move lower with each pass looking for any leaks. We would take care of the leaks once they were found.

While Hollywood and I set up the dive station, the son was running around the dam with a camera taking photos. I told him that he needed to stop being a tourist and give us a hand setting up the dive station. He retorted back to me that his mother had asked him to take photos of the job, so he was doing his job. I told him that he could take all the photos he wanted after we were set up and the work was done. I re-iterated here that this was a potentially very dangerous job and he needed to pay attention, listen to me, and not put dive hose in the water unless I told him to. Yeah, yeah, he replied he knew what to do and do it the proper way. Okay.

We coiled about a hundred feet of umbilical right above the head gate where Hollywood would enter the water. The bottom of the head gate was only eighteen feet, so that would be more than enough dive hose for the job. We did all the checks on the dive gear and Hollywood got dressed in. I helped him get dressed in and watched him enter the water and drop down until his head was under the water. He would wait there until I got back to the radio and the video screen. The dam foreman was watching the video and listening to what the diver was saying. I informed Hollywood that we were ready for him to start the inspection.

Hollywood went down the left side of the gate to the bottom. Everything looked good and there were no leaks. We could hear water roaring through the gate somewhere. I advised him to be very careful along the bottom. It wouldn't surprise me if there were some sort of debris keeping the gate just a little off the bottom sealing surface. He replied that he would be very careful. He looked at the bottom of the gate and said it was sitting squarely on the bottom and he couldn't detect any leaks. He had a piece of rope that we had frayed on one end to use as a tool to look for leaks. He said there had been nothing visible down the left side or across the bottom. Okay, come up the right side and we will see what we see.

   He started moving up the right side. I told the son that the diver was leaving the bottom so he needed to come up on the diver's hose. He gave me a thumb's up. Hollywood kept moving up. Shortly after that, the son yelled to me that he couldn't come up on the dive hose. He thought it was fouled – that is caught on something under the water. I relayed to Hollywood that the son thought he might be fouled. At that same moment Hollywood informed me that his umbilical was going down towards the bottom middle of the gate. He was only five feet deep, but he couldn't come up any more. Okay. Well, you're fouled man. It happens. We will get you freed up and out of the water.

   I told Hollywood to carefully follow his hose to the site where it was fouled. Most likely it is just caught on some of the angle iron framework on the head gate. I told him to pay close attention to the umbilical he had in his hand and reminded him that we hadn't found any leaks yet. It was possible that there was a break in one or more of the timbers making up the gate. He assured me he would be careful. He followed his hose back down to where it was stuck.

   I was watching his progress on the video. He was doing fine. At the same time I saw his hose going into a rectangular hole in the center of the gate, Hollywood let out an agonizing yell. Then he started screaming "I'm Stuck! I'm Stuck! I won't be able to get out of here!"

"Calm down, calm down, man." I said over the radio. "We will get you free. Tell me what you mean by 'I'm stuck' please." I could tell by his voice that Hollywood was scared. I don't think he had ever been fouled like this before. I asked him if he could move around any. He replied that he could.

By "stuck" he meant that his umbilical was going through an opening in the gate and he couldn't pull it out. Okay. I could see the hole. It was large; four-foot wide by about a foot high. Water was gushing through it so fast that it was white and I could hear it roaring through the diver's comms. It was about ten feet below the surface. It was a bad situation, but one we could deal with. I told Hollywood to remain calm and relax a minute while I went over to assess the situation from where the tender – the son – was. I told him I would be right back and to just be sure that he didn't let any more umbilical go down the penstock. I went over to see what the situation looked like where the son was.

When I reached the tending area, I couldn't believe my eyes. There was only one loop of umbilical on the deck – that is about eight feet of dive hose. That meant that about ninety feet of dive hose was in the water. What the Hell?! I specifically told the son *not* to put dive hose in the water unless told to do so by me. I had also told him that the deepest depth the diver would be going was twenty feet so he wouldn't need more than twenty-five or thirty feet of hose in the water. I had told him that by no means should he let more than thirty-five feet of hose in the water. Obviously, he hadn't been listening to me.

I asked him why he put so much umbilical in the water. He replied that the diver kept pulling on it, so he figured the diver needed more hose. "*Holy Fuck, Man!!* Didn't you *Fuckin'* hear me when I specifically said *NOT* to give the diver *any* umbilical unless I said to. We are dealing with leaks here. That means *sucking* water. Sucking water will take anything nearby with it. Do you not *understand* that?! I was livid. I wanted to pound that guy's face into the concrete deck. He had put my diver in way more danger than he should have. I was so pissed I could hardly contain myself. I knew that wasn't helping my diver though, so I calmed down. I took a few deep breaths and explained to the son what we were going to do and he better *damn well* do it. I explained to the son the diver's situation. I told him that I was going to have the diver pull his umbilical out of the hole. As the diver pulled on his hose the tender was to pull the slack up onto the deck. I told him to keep a good strain on the hose and pull it out of the water as he could. I returned to the dive station.

When I got back to the radio, I asked Hollywood how he was doing. He told me he was okay, but wasn't sure we could get the hose out of the penstock. He had been pulling on it to no avail. I told him not to worry. At the very worst we would have the dam close their tail race gate. That would stop the flow of water through the penstock and then we could get him out of there. That process would take a couple hours though. He groaned at that. Then I told him we were going to try something else first to get him out quicker. He was all for that. I told him to straddle the opening with one foot above the opening and the other foot below. Then he was to grab the umbilical as close to the opening as he felt comfortable and pull it out of the penstock. I also told him that he would get less tired if he used his legs rather than his back and arms to do the pulling. Then I asked him if he was comfortable with that. He was.

He started pulling on his dive hose. He could get some out. He said it was a pretty hard pull, but he could get it out of the penstock this way. Good. I told the son to start coming up on the umbilical. It was a slow process but it was working. It took them about twenty-five minutes to get all the umbilical out of the penstock. Hollywood heaved a sigh of relief after he got the last bit removed. I let out a sigh of relief as well. I asked him if he could give us a little visual inspection of the rectangular opening so we could determine how to repair it. He complied. We both saw a screw shaft about four feet above the opening. I told him it looked like a miniature head gate. He agreed. The dam foreman let out a little laugh.

"What's so funny?" I asked.

He told me that was the penstock fill gate. It was what this dam used instead of a fill valve. He said they must have forgotten to close it before lowering the gate – obviously. I just shook my head. Really? You've got to be kidding me. There was a handle on the top of the head gate that operated the fill gate. I told the dam foreman that I would bring the diver out of the water, then they could shut the little gate. After that, if we needed to, I would send the diver down to check for leaks. He agreed to that, but said he doubted there would be much leakage. They hadn't had any issues in the recent past. Okay.

I pulled Hollywood out of the water. He stayed in his dive suit, but took everything else off. We waited for the dam crew to close the fill gate then check for water flow. That took about half-an-hour. When they had finished their tasks, they told us that there was no significant water flow through the penstock and turbine chamber. As far as they were concerned, we had completed the task. Sure, whatever you say. I filled out the paperwork while Hollywood and the son secured the dive station and got the truck and trailer ready to go. I had the foreman of the dam sign the necessary documents and gave him his copies. He said he was happy with our performance and glad nobody had been hurt. He also said he was impressed that I kept my cool during the stressful situation. I told him that if the dive station were set up correctly with all the necessary equipment there was no reason to panic.

I took the truck and trailer back to Wolf Creek and both Hollywood and the son headed back to their respective homes. I called Corvallis and Vancouver and had a little chat about the son. They assured me they would have a talk with him when he got back home. He didn't go on the next couple jobs I did with them.

* * *

The last job I did with the son on my crew was at Cochrane Dam. It was in the late summer. There was some work to do on the dams just outside of Great Falls. As usual, PPLM had work for us to last the whole week. We had work on Morony, Ryan, and Cochrane Dams again. The only task we did that week that sticks out in my memory, though, was sealing the Cochrane Dam head gate; you know, the one we seal with the CP hose. I drove the truck and trailer up to Great Falls. Hollywood and the son met me there. None of the jobs required the use of the duck. We got to leave the dive equipment in the trailer so set up and break down was quick.

When Corvallis called me for the job and told me who the crew would be, I asked if she had talked to her son about his performance on the job. She answered that she had. Then she told me that he would be taking the role as supervisor. He would be doing all the paperwork. He would be running the radio - basically running the dives. She was hoping that I would teach him how to do all that stuff and make sure he did it properly. Lovely. Of course I would make sure he did everything properly. Our lives depended on it. I tried to explain to her that she couldn't magically make her son a supervisor, though. It took a lot of experience to make a good supervisor. She said she understood that, and was hopeful that I could teach him what he needed to know. I just bit my tongue after that. I talked with Hollywood about that and told him that we needed to keep a good eye on the son when the other of us was in the water. He agreed.

The son was all over the dam with his camera while Hollywood and I were setting up. I told him that a good supervisor would know how to set up a dive station and would give his crew a hand. We had to have the Lock-Out-Tag-Out signed before we made our dive – that was usually the first task completed by the dam crew. It took them a while to get that all taken care of. We would get our dive station set up while they were taking care of the LOTO. After it was done, one of us - or all of us - would walk with the dam operator as he showed us how everything was turned off or closed and locked in the shut-down position. One of our crew would need to actually witness the LOTO. One of us had to sign the dam's documents too. That was usually the supervisor.

When we had everything ready to go. I walked the son through the dive station. I made sure all the valves were properly lined up and everything was ready to go. I showed him everything; pointing out the position each valve was supposed to be in. I also explained why the valves were in those positions so he would, hopefully, understand how it all worked. Hollywood was not comfortable making the dive, so I would do it. I put my hat on line. We did all the checks and we were good to go. Now all we had to do was sign the LOTO and we were clear to dive.

The son was all excited that he would get to sign off on the dam's documents as the supervisor of the job. I didn't care who signed the actual paper, but I wanted to walk the tag-out just so I knew it was done. I trusted the PPLM guys to do it, but, you know, I wanted to see it with my own eyes. If the supervisor was somebody I trusted – like Blanchard or Boston – I would take their word for it and not have to see it for myself. But, the *son*? No way, no how. That guy wouldn't have a clue what he would be looking at. I told the PPLM guys that our whole crew would walk the tag-out with them. They didn't mind. They were all about all the workers being comfortable with the situation.

After we had taken care of the tag-out, I got dressed in to my dive suit. I had double checked that the regulator on the K-bottle for standby air was properly set. I double-checked the valve line up on the manifold. I checked that the volume tank between the air compressor and the dive station was full of air – it acts sort of like a bladder tank giving the diver a good amount of air in case the compressor quit. That way the diver wouldn't be out of air as soon as the compressor stopped. A good supervisor would have the standby air on before the diver had any idea the system had shut down. We had a sixty-gallon volume tank in our system. That was enough air for a normal diver at thirty feet for about fifteen minutes.

Our volume tank was "full" when it had one-hundred-and-eighty psi. We never ever planned to breathe that tank down below a hundred-and-twenty psi. The Superlite Seventeen needs a minimum of one-hundred psi to breathe properly. I had our compressor to cycle on at one-hundred-and-thirty psi and cycle off at one-hundred-and-eighty psi. There were about five gages on the manifold and piping that indicated the air pressure going to the diver. I know this is a lot of technical stuff that you don't really care about, but it is pertinent to the story. Just stay with me for a minute.

I was on top of the trash racks. I had everything I needed to make the dive. Hollywood was there with me to tend my dive hose. A couple of the PPLM crew were also there to lend a hand if we needed it. I let the son know we were ready for him to start the compressor so I could start my dive. He started the compressor. I put my hat on and did one last comms check before entering the water. The son assured me we were all set and he was ready. I climbed down the ladder inside the trash racks. I grabbed the CP hose from one of the PPLM crew and headed down to the bottom of the head gate. Everything seemed fine and the task was going along like it always did. I got to the bottom, stuck the CP hose in the corner and the water pressure sucked the hose into the gap. The water flow stopped and the task was completed. I left bottom. So far, my total dive time was about seven minutes. It would take me about three minutes to reach the surface.

When I reached about ten feet, it felt like I was out of air. I took another breath and definitely sucked the last of the air out of the hose. I called to topside and asked what my air pressure was. There was no response. "Hey! Topside! What Is My Air Pressure?!" I yelled through the comms. Still no response. I was just about to open my bailout bottle when I got a whoosh of air through my regulator. I could breathe normally again. Just as I got the air back, the son came over the radio and said that my air pressure was one-hundred-and-sixty psi just like it was supposed to be. Hmm.

I went to the ladder and climbed up and out of the trash racks. Hollywood helped me take off my hat and when I did, all the PPLM guys started clapping. They were also laughing and saying that I could hold my breath longer than anyone they had seen. I didn't know what they were talking about. I took the rest of my dive gear off and asked Hollywood what they were all talking about. It seems that just before the son had started the compressor, he had closed the valve that lets the air go to the dive manifold. He didn't open it back up after he got the compressor started.

There had been enough air in the volume tank for me to just about complete this task at seventy-some feet. It was nice for me that I had enough air to stop the leak and get off bottom, because if I had run out of air *before* placing the CP hose, it would have been challenging to finish the job. My head probably wouldn't have been in a good place. As it was, I was just angry with the son, again. I got dressed back into my work clothes. I helped Hollywood break down the dive station and told the son that he needed to help. He gave me a funny look and was about to say something, but he didn't. He bit his tongue and helped out a little bit.

After everything was loaded up and secured, I asked Hollywood to give me a minute with the son. I got him away from everybody and had a little talk with him. I told him that he needed to wake up and that no matter what position he was working on a dive crew, other people's lives depended on his work. I told him he needed more experience in the dive industry before he became a supervisor. I also told him he would *never* be a supervisor on *any* job I was on again. He didn't say anything, but I could tell he was fuming. He was not happy at all.

We finished out the week without any other issues. I demoted the son back down to tender. He informed me that I couldn't do that because his mom owned the dive company. I told him that I had way more experience than he did and I would be running the jobs. If he didn't like it, he could leave. I told him the guys on the PPLM crew made better tenders than he and they hadn't even been to dive school. He huffed, but stayed. He didn't work any better. He just went back to taking his photos. I just shook my head. Unbelievable.

I called Vancouver to give him an update and let him know that we had finished all the tasks for PPLM for that week. He asked if everything was going all right or if we had any issues. I told him everything was fine. I told him we had a little issue – I didn't say what it was – and that I had taken care of it. He said he wasn't so sure about that and informed me that Corvallis wanted to talk with me. She wasn't around at the moment, but wanted me to call her later.

I went back to Wolf Creek with the dive package. Hollywood and the son went on their merry ways back home. When I got to Wolf Creek, I parked the trailer in the same spot I always had. I went into the Cyberstop and talked to my girlfriend. I told her Corvallis wanted me to call her that evening. I had been talking to my girlfriend all week, so she knew what was going on. She asked if she could do anything for me and I told her I could really use a Huckleberry milkshake. She happily made me one. I relaxed a little and drank the milkshake. It was delicious as always.

I called Corvallis. She asked me what had gone on that week. I told her. She agreed that was not good but stated the valve was just a little mistake and everybody makes mistakes. I told her mistakes like that kill people in our line of work. She thought I was being overly dramatic. She also said that her son was going to be the designated supervisor on all the jobs he went on whether I liked it or not. I would just have to learn to deal with it. Uh, yeah, no. If I was not going to be the supervisor on her jobs, then I wouldn't work for her anymore. She said she was sorry to hear that. Then she told me that Vancouver would be coming over to take the trailer back to her house in Oregon. Fine and dandy. I really didn't mind at that point. Vancouver had been acting really strange the past few months and I was ready to not continue working with them. I had still been working with other dive companies anyway. I never worked for Active Diving and Marine again.

* * *

Back in the Drink

Did I stop working in Montana after I stopped working with Active Diving and Marine? No. As I've said before, the engineers and shop managers at PPLM didn't care what dive company was doing the work. What was important to them was what divers were doing the work for them. They had heard that I wasn't working with Active anymore and were actually relieved because they didn't like dealing with Vancouver at all. When they had more work to do, they called me up and asked me who I was working for now.

In January of two-thousand-and-four, my girlfriend in Wolf Creek - with whom I was living - asked me where our relationship was headed. I told her I didn't know, but I wanted to stay with her. Then I asked her where she thought our relationship was going. She said she also wanted to stay together and maybe we should take the next step. On Valentine's Day I asked her to marry me with one stipulation – we get married in two weeks on the last day in February which happened to be the twenty-ninth. It was a leap year. She said yes. We got married at her - now our - cabin and had a reception in Craig to which we invited everybody from Wolf Creek and Craig – a whole eighty-some people. It was tons of fun and we are still going strong.

Blanchard had been working for a company from California. He always needed people. I told him I could help him get work in Montana for PPLM if he wanted. He was interested. I had also been contacted by a guy based out of Boring, Oregon who owned a dive company. I had been a DSO on several jobs that he had done for the Army Corps of Engineers. He seemed to know what he was doing. After not working for Active anymore, I called him up and told him I was available for work.

Boring was glad to hear that. He had quite a bit of work on Army Corps of Engineers projects on the lower Columbia River. Blanchard's company was also getting work on ACoE jobs, most of them east of the Tri-Cities, Washington. The ACoE had different districts and each district had their preference for the dive companies they hired. I had plenty of work now.

After working with Boring on a few jobs, I was ready to recommend him to PPLM. He was happy to get the work, but it was by no means enough to keep him going. He still needed to keep bidding all the other work he had been bidding in the past. He knew that. He did appreciate having one more client though. I worked several jobs in Montana with him after that.

In the summer of two-thousand-and-four the Bureau of Land Management had a large project to do at Canyon Ferry Dam on the Missouri River just east of Helena. It was going to require a lot of diving. The tail race needed a lot of concrete repair and restoration under the water. That sounded like a fun job and it was very close to my home. I kept an ear out for which company won that bid. Shortly before the work was to start, I learned that a company from Seattle got the job – Global Diving and Salvage. I had never worked for them. I had been a DSO on several jobs they had done for the ACoE on the Columbia River though, so I knew many of their regular employees. I decided to give them a call to let them know I was available for work.

I called their office and told them who I was and where I lived. I got the normal response of "Yes, okay. Send us your resumé and we will be in touch." That was the brush off. I knew that any paperwork I sent to them as an unknown would be filed in the circular file as soon as they received it. Still, the best way to get a dive job was to go to the office in person, shake some hands and let them see you. I wasn't going to Seattle anytime soon and I surely wasn't going to make a special trip just to go to their office.

A couple friends and fellow divers were slated for that job and they had told me the date of the first walk through. A "walk through" is the introduction of the work site and job scope to the company that is awarded the job by the client. It is usually the first time that the owners or directors of a company and their managers and dive supervisors get to really see the worksite and are shown what needs to be done. Before this point there is a lot of work – research, calculating, engineering - that is done on paper and in meetings. Details of what exists and what needs to be done are sent to the companies doing the bidding. They don't need to actually *see* the project to make the bids.

Anyway, what that meant for me was that the important people from Global would be at Canyon Ferry Dam on that day to set up the actual start date of the job. It would be a good place for me to meet the owners, managers and supervisors who would be involved with that job. Illinois was going to be on that job and he had informed me of when and where this meeting was going to take place. That would be at the downstream side of Canyon Ferry Dam.

Canyon Ferry, like all other dams since Nine-Eleven, was fenced off with high chain-link (cyclone) fencing topped off with razor wire. The access gates were all locked and you had to have a code to open the gates. Canyon Ferry Dam had a speaker system at each gate that enabled you to talk to the operators of the dam. You could tell them who you were and what you wanted and they would decide whether or not to open the gate for you. They didn't open the gate to just anyone – especially someone like me whom they had never heard of before. Tours of the dam were guided and set up through an office at the top of the dam. Neither of those methods would let me near the Global people I needed to talk to. I had another plan.

There is only one road going to the access point to the downstream side of Canyon Ferry Dam. There is a campground with a boat launch right there at the bottom of the dam. It is a very popular place for fishing. There is public parking right outside the fence that guards the lower part of the dam. I knew that would be where everybody from Global would be parking and exiting their vehicles. I got there about a half-hour before the meeting was set to take place.

I was sitting in my truck, waiting for people to arrive. I didn't have to wait long. Most people in the dive industry are conditioned to arrive at least fifteen minutes early to anything having to do with work. Often times this spills into our social lives as well. About twenty minutes before the meeting was to start, I saw several cars drive down the road and park in the same lot I was parked in. I got out of my truck and watched the other people get out of their rigs. I went up to the guy closest to me and introduced myself. He informed me that he was not the person to talk to. He pointed out another man and told me he was one of the owners of the company and who I should talk to about working on this project.

I promptly walked over to the man I had been directed to. He was in a conversation with another man. I stopped by them and made eye contact, but didn't interrupt them. After a bit, the owner of the company asked me if he could help me with anything. I replied that yes, he could. I introduced myself, told him that I lived nearby in Wolf Creek and would like to be involved with this project. He had heard of me, but had no personal experience of my work ethic. He told me to send all my paperwork into the main office. I told him I would do that and thanked him for his time.

The man standing next to the owner introduced himself. He was the main engineer on the project and would be the superintendent of this project. Then he introduced me to another fellow who would be the main supervisor on the project. I had heard of this supervisor, but had never met him. He was rather stand-offish, but that was common in the dive industry at first introductions.

I asked the owner of the company if I could join them on their walk through. He refused, which was not a surprise. I worked for other dive companies and he had no idea if I was really looking for work or if I was a spy from another company looking for ways to take the job away from him.

Overall, the meeting went well and I was happy with the introductions. I went home, got my paperwork together, and sent it all into the main office in Seattle. The actual work was scheduled to start in two weeks. I called the superintendent - whom I had met at the dam - the following Monday. I introduced myself on the phone and told him I was ready to go to work on the Canyon Ferry project. I informed him that since I lived in the area, he would not have to pay me any per diem and that would save him quite a bit of money over the course of the job. He told me he would let me know if he could use me, but at the moment, the job was fully crewed up.

That was disappointing to hear, but not really unexpected. Shortly thereafter Illinois called me up and asked if I had been hired for the Canyon Ferry project. I informed him that I had not. I wasn't too disappointed, because I had just been called to do a short job for the guy out of Bellevue. It turned out to be only a week of work, but that was better than a poke in the eye with a sharp stick.

Illinois called me over the weekend and asked if I had heard anything from Global about their job in Montana. I told him no, I hadn't heard anything. He thought that was strange, because he had been talking to both the superintendent and the main diving supervisor. Both told him that they could use another topside hand. Illinois told them that he was pretty sure I would be happy to work topside as well as underwater. Whatever was needed is what he told them I would do. I hadn't heard from either of them.

Sunday evening, after dinner, I got a call from the superintendent. He told me that there was a position that needed to be filled on the Canyon Ferry job. He said it would be topside only and that I might be required to run back and forth from the job to Helena during the shift. Then he asked if I was willing to do that. I responded that I would be happy to do the job, depending on the pay and the re-imbursement of fuel expenses. Then he informed me that this was only a work as needed type position. Some days they needed more people than other days. He said he would tell me Friday afternoon every week whether I was to work the following week or not. I was okay with that. I also told him that if I wasn't assigned permanently on the job and another better job came along, I would be taking it. He didn't say anything about that. I told him I was in the union and expected tender pay at the very least. We haggled a little bit. He reiterated that I wouldn't be doing any of the diving and would only be doing topside work on the beach. Most likely I wouldn't even be working on the dive barge.

I knew how dive jobs worked. I knew that once on the job, I would be moved around to where ever I was needed. I stood my ground and said tender pay was the minimum I would work for and I expected my hours to be reported to the union like they were supposed to be. After a bit he said that would be fine. He also said that they had bid the job out of Missoula, so *all* the pay would be paid at the Montana union scale. I figured as much and told him I was fine with that. I'll bet none of their Seattle employees knew that they were working for a reduced rate. At that time, Montana was about eighty percent of what eastern Washington paid, and eastern Washington was about ninety percent of what the Seattle scale was. That means *all* the guys who were out of the Seattle hall would be working for about seventy-five percent of their normal pay. Their first check would probably be a shock to them and their wives! He told me I needed to be on site at eight in the morning. I assured him I would be there.

I got to the worksite about seven-thirty on Monday morning. Nobody else was there yet. I looked over the set up. There was a barge anchored out in the middle of the river not far downstream from the dam. The actual worksite was on the beach right next to the parking area. There were a couple Conex boxes on the site. There were several piles of construction materials and some equipment on the site. None of it was fenced in. I thought that was a little strange, but it was Montana. We didn't have much in theft from construction sites around here.

At about a quarter-to-eight, people started showing up. I was looking for anyone I might know. I saw Illinois and went over to talk with him. He showed me the layout of the site. The superintendent arrived right at eight-o-clock. He introduced me to the main diving supervisor. Only a couple dives had been made – just to assess the bottom and verify what needed to be done. There was a lot of work to do on the beach before the real diving started. They expected to start diving more by the end of the week. I would be working on the beach putting stuff together for the divers to use. I would be working with the daughter of the owner I had met a few weeks earlier. She wasn't a diver and didn't really want to be one, but she liked physical labor.

There was a dive crew of four on the barge – the supervisor and three diver/tenders. Anywhere outside of the Gulf, there was no such thing as a diver who only did underwater work. We all did everything. We rarely had crew members that were just tenders. Sometimes, on jobs like this, the company would hire non-diving crew and they would be paid less than everybody else. They were laborers and not necessarily in the union. That bothered me a little, but as long as they had *nothing at all what-so-ever* to do with the diving equipment and operations, I was okay with it. I understood the company wanting to save money on non-diving personnel to increase their profits. On this job, there were several of these non-diving employees. Those were who I worked with the first couple weeks.

I asked the supervisor if he knew that he was working for Montana rates rather than Seattle rates. Most of the people in the Seattle union didn't like working in eastern Washington because the payrate was lower, so I had a hard time believing that they would work for even less here in Montana. He told me that as far as he knew, he was being paid Seattle rates. I chuckled and shook my head. I told him that I had been told we were working for the Montana rates. He had not received a paycheck yet so didn't know for sure. I asked him if he had inquired about the dive pay before he took the job. He answered that he had not; he just assumed it would be Seattle rates. I told him that usually all the Montana work was out of the Spokane office, so the very most he could expect were Spokane rates. He shook his head and told me I was wrong. Okay. Whatever you say, dude.

A week later, when the supervisor and all the other Seattle employees got their checks, everybody was upset. Their pay was quite a bit less than they were expecting. The supervisor brought his check stub to me and asked if I thought it looked correct. I looked it over and it was correct according to the rates out of Missoula. He was livid. I didn't say "I told you so," but I wanted to, real bad. Instead, I just smiled to myself. You should always ask what the pay is going to be before you accept a dive job. No matter what the company says, their profit is *the* most important thing to them. They will take money from where-ever they can get it. One of my pet peeves about that is Per Diem. All government jobs pay per diem as laid out by the federal government. There is a schedule that you can get from the IRS that shows what government per diem is paid for every place in the U.S., and many places where Americans typically work; like the Cayman Islands, Mexico, and Canada. Sadly, we rarely receive that per diem because the unions have their own rates. I have tried and tried to get the unions to mandate that companies pay per diem according to the federal guidelines to no avail. That is one thing the companies just refuse to do. I could go off on that subject here, but I won't. I'll just stop by saying it's a form of accepted thievery perpetrated by the dive companies.

At lunch the whole dive crew was saying they had to do something about the pay. The supervisor said they would all stand together and tell the company that they would walk off the job if they didn't start getting paid the Seattle rates. I asked them if they had signed any documentation to get on the job. They all said they had, but none of them remembered what it was they signed. I suggested it was their agreement to work for Missoula rates. They all laughed and said "No Way!"

The supervisor talked to the superintendent about it and found out that they all *had* signed a document stating that they accepted the Missoula rates. The supervisor was pissed, as were several of the other employees. That night over dinner at the dam bar, several of them – including the supervisor – said they were going to talk to the main office and if they didn't get the Seattle pay, they were going to walk off the job. They never got the Seattle pay and none of them walked off the job either. They knew they would be replaced. It's very hard to get divers to stick together over things like that. Blanchard once told me "The only thing you can get two divers to agree upon is how bad the third diver is!"

Often the crew on the dive barge would need an extra hand. When that happened, I was the one to go. I was happy to do that. After the first couple weeks I spent about half my time working on the beach and the other half on the barge. The superintendent wasn't very good about telling me on Friday whether or not I was working the following week. Never did he seek me out, nor did he ever leave a message on my phone. I would have to find him and ask him. Once-in-a-while he would say yes, I would be working the following week. Mostly though, he would say he would give me a call over the weekend. If he didn't call, I wasn't working. Okay, whatever. What a weird situation, I thought. Well, nothing else was going on at the moment, so I let it be.

A couple times during the week, the superintendent would tell me I wasn't needed the next day or two. A couple of the weeks I only worked three days. That was weird, but okay. I mean, I was cheaper than the other diver/tenders because I wasn't being paid per diem, but I wasn't running the company or the job. If I wanted to work, I would just have to deal with it. That didn't give me any reason to guarantee that I would be available when they needed me though. I didn't get the feeling they were too worried about that.

Boring had a job coming up in mid-August that he wanted me to go on. I told him that I was currently working with Global, but if I was free, I would definitely be available for the job. I told him that it was week to week with Global and I would prefer a better commitment. His job would be at least six weeks, but probably more like eight or nine, all said and done. He asked me to keep him updated. He would have to supervise the job if I couldn't, but he said he would really prefer to have me on the job as he had a lot of other business to take care of. I appreciated that and let him know that.

I worked for Global at Canyon Ferry all five days of the week before Boring's job was to start. At the end of every day, I asked the superintendent about being permanently hired on. He wouldn't commit to anything. I told him that I had an offer of another job in the Seattle area, but I would rather work in Montana. He would just nod his head indicating that he understood what I was saying. I told him that I needed to know by knock-off on Friday at the very latest so I could let the other company know whether or not I was available. Yeah, yeah, okay.

Friday morning after our tailgate meeting, I asked the superintendent about my status. He responded that he would let me know by the end of the day. Fine. I worked the rest of the day as usual. At the end of the work day, I looked all over for the superintendent. He was nowhere to be found. I asked the supervisor if he had seen him and he said no, because he had taken off after lunch to return to Seattle. Great. Just fantastic. Fine. I would try and call him to get an answer to my question. I called three times. I left three messages. On the third message I told him that since I hadn't heard from him, I figured he didn't need me to work on Monday. I told him that I was taking the other job and thanked him for the opportunity to work with him on the Canyon Ferry project even a little bit.

*   *   *

I called Boring late Friday night and informed him that I was available for his job in Seattle. He said that was fantastic. He told me the job was in Lake Sammamish. It included videoing the sewer pipe that ran along the edge of the lake just off the beach. Most of it was in fifteen to twenty feet of water about fifty to seventy-five feet off the beach. I'll bet most people living on Lake Sammamish don't realize there is a main sewer line right off their docks in the lake. This is the same sort of sewer line that I had worked on with Brazil in Lake Washington back in ninety-eight. On this job we were also going to replace the hardware just like what we replaced on the pipe in Lake Washington.

I knew this job was going to be at least six weeks, and most likely more like eight. I loaded my Ural sidecar motorcycle into the back of my truck along with all my dive gear and drove to Bellevue; Overlake actually. Boring had rented a condo in the Villa Marina complex just south of Marymoor Park on the north end of Lake Sammamish. The condo came with a boat slip. Boring had a ski boat for us to use as a water taxi to the worksite. He rented a couple Flexi-Floats that we pinned together to make a twenty-by-thirty-foot barge. The dive station was set up in a Conex on the barge. His plan was to leave the barge at the dive site every night. We would use the ski boat to get back and forth between the barge and the condo. That was excellent.

Boring didn't pay us any per diem for this job. Since we were basically in Seattle, the union didn't require him to pay it. I didn't mind because he was footing the bill for the condo *and* the fuel for the ski boat. He even bought us dinner once-in-a-while. It was nice to be treated this way by a dive company owner.

Boring wasn't on the job every day. He popped in about once or twice a week to see how we were doing. I was supervising and had two other diver/tenders working with me. They were both regulars for Boring, but neither had enough dive experience that he felt comfortable having them supervise a whole project. They were both capable divers and knew enough to be good radio operators and run dives. It took more than that to be a good supervisor though, and Boring knew that.

I got a call on Tuesday from the superintendent on the Canyon Ferry job. He asked why I hadn't shown up to work on Monday morning. I told him that I hadn't heard from him on Friday even after leaving several messages on his phone, so I figured I wasn't needed. I reminded him I had told him I had upcoming work. He said, okay, that was his mistake, but he was hoping I would be available for work on the Canyon Ferry project. I told him that I had committed to this other project and when it was done, I would contact him to see if he could use me on any projects he had going on.

Illinois also called me on Tuesday. He asked how long the project on Lake Sammamish was going to take. I told him, I wasn't sure but it was slated for six to eight weeks. He advised me to be sure and keep in touch with the superintendent from the Canyon Ferry job, because - apparently – he had decided he wanted me on the project. Too bad so sad, he didn't tell me that and now I am on this project making more money than the supervisor of *that* project. I did think it was funny – funny odd, not funny ha-ha – that I, from Montana, was working in Seattle while all these other guys from Seattle were working in Montana not even an hour from my front door. Diving jobs. You just never knew how they were going to play out.

The job in Lake Sammamish was fun. It was easy. I got to dive almost every day. I ran a regular dive rotation so we each got two dives every three days. The job consisted of videoing and swapping out nuts on fixed bolts. Once-in-a-while an angry homeowner would come out and yell at us for having an ugly barge anchored in front of their house ruining their view of the lake. We always told them we wouldn't be more than a couple days and if they had a problem with it, they could call King County and all would be explained to them. Other times we would be working close to private docks and young women would come out in bikinis to splash around in the water or suntan on the docks. They would usually ask us all kinds of questions. A couple times we got invited to parties and waterskiing. We couldn't take part in those activities while we were working. I went home to Montana on the weekends, so never took part in those activities. I don't know what the other guys on my crew did.

The job did last just eight weeks. It ended up being a really good job. It was fun, the crew was good, and the water was clean. You really couldn't ask for a lot more on a dive job. It was fresh water, so there was not much in the way of fish and life to see under the water. For the most part the weather was good. There were a few rainy days, but, hey, it is Seattle – where people don't tan; they rust! Ha-ha!

The last week of the job, when I *knew* it was going to end, I called Illinois and asked him how the Canyon Ferry job was going. I figured it might be winding down. He told me that Global had been awarded a whole bunch of extras and the job was going to last a fair bit longer – probably at least until Thanksgiving. He said he was fairly sure more people would be needed to work there. For one, some guys get bored working on the same job for more than a couple months. For another thing, Global had several other jobs going on and would want certain personnel to work on those other jobs. Also, winter was coming and lots of people from Seattle didn't like winter conditions much and would rather work in warmer climes. He suggested I call the superintendent. I told him I was planning on it.

*   *   *

I did call the superintendent of the job going on at Canyon Ferry in Montana the weekend I got home from Seattle. He said that yes, they had a position for me, and yes, it would be a diver's position. He also reminded me that the job was paying the Missoula rates. I reminded him that I lived in Wolf Creek, Montana and was fine with the Missoula rates if that was how the job was bid. He also reminded me that I would not be getting per diem. I reminded him that I had suggested that to him when the job first started because I lived right there. It only took me forty-five minutes to get from my front door to the job site. He told me to show up Monday morning. I thanked him and told him I would be there.

Usually, I liked to have a little time off in between jobs. Especially this time of year – the end of September, early fall. It was prime motorcycle travelling time for me. The weather was usually pretty nice and it wasn't tourist season. People were back in school and others had taken their summer vacations already. But, a job this close to home I just couldn't turn down. It is not very often that you get a good job right off your doorstep when you don't live near the ocean. I would gladly take this job.

I showed up at the Canyon Ferry work site Monday morning. Illinois was there. Some other workers I was familiar with were there also. The superintendent was different. He was a long-time Global employee who had gotten into an argument with the owners a few years ago and worked for other companies for a season. He worked a job with me at Hebgen Dam during that time. It was good to see him again. I was glad that he was the superintendent because he was a little more communicative with me than the other guy had been.

When I got out to the dive barge, I was shown what was going on. The project had been expanded quite a bit from what was originally planned. Originally, only the tail race guide walls were to be reconditioned. Now the whole floor of the tail race was to be refurbished. That was more than twice the original work added – meaning the job was now about three times as big as the original scope. Wow. We would be here for quite a while longer.

There was a lot of underwater concrete form building to do and then a lot of concrete pouring to fill those forms. Before all that, though, we had to remove bad concrete and loose debris from the tail race. After that we would drill holes in the river bottom and put anchor bolts and rebar in them, then tie a lot of rebar into place. Looks like we were about to become underwater iron workers for a bit. That was one of the things I liked about diving – we got to do all the different jobs done on a construction site – jackhammering old concrete, welding, burning, drilling into rock and existing concrete, setting anchor bolts, tying iron, fitting forms, pumping concrete, and finally removing the forms and temporary support structures. That is what I was looking forward to on this job. It was going to be fun and it was going to last at least a couple months.

I worked with a lot of people I had never worked with previously. I also worked with some that I had worked with before. I worked with some that I had watched working when I was a DSO. I made some good friends and some really good connections. It was good to reconnect with a couple of guys that I had worked with a few years ago – like the new superintendent. He was living in Issaquah when I first met him and he was still living in Issaquah now. So that is how I will refer to him. I don't know where he was originally from. We both had been in the dive industry for quite a while so we had a lot of common friends and coworkers.

There was so much work to do that we were working ten-hour days. We also started working six days a week. That was a lot of overtime and the money was great. It also meant that the guys from Washington who had been going home on the weekends really couldn't do that anymore. That meant they were all around for the weekends now. That was fun. The local bars were happy, because the crew started spending more money in them. Hallowe'en was on a Sunday that year. The Oasis in Wolf Creek was hosting a Hallowe'en party on Saturday with a costume contest and everything. They did that every year, but this year I brought a bunch of my dive buddies to the party. Illinois, Issaquah, the owner's daughter, and a few others joined us. Wolf Creek is about half-an-hour north of Helena, so we told everybody if they wanted to drink, we would put them up in Wolf Creek so they wouldn't have to drive back to Helena drunk. We had a great time; lots of dancing and partying. None of us won the costume contest; a pair of the locals did. We didn't care. We were having too much fun drinking and dancing.

There were some intense work days – especially when we were pouring concrete. Concrete doesn't really get "poured" under water. It goes from the concrete trucks into a concrete pump which pushes the concrete through Tremie Hose. The end of the tremie is either stuffed into the concrete as it forms a mound on the bottom - that way the cement and aggregate won't get separated as it flows through the water - or it is attached to a port on an enclosed form. On this job we had a form that had a top. On the top we had ports that we attached the end of the tremie to. There were also marker vents so we could see when a section of the form was filled. Because the concrete was running through a tremie, the aggregate had to be fairly small to help keep the hose from getting plugged.

Sometimes, though, the hose would get plugged anyway. You never knew where it would get plugged, but you knew it would. On pouring days we had several people spaced along the tremie hose with four to eight pound short-handled sledge hammers. You could tell when the hose got plugged because it would jump and get really hard. When that happened, we would start beating the hose (ha-ha, I know this sounds lewd, but I don't know how else to word it) with the hammers like madmen. Beating the hose would loosen the concrete plug and allow the concrete to start flowing again. We tried to keep the hose as short as we could to reduce the frequency of the stoppages. If we couldn't dislodge the plug and the concrete hardened in the hose, it would have to be thrown away. That hose was not cheap either, so we did what we could to keep the concrete flowing. Those were quite stressful and physically demanding days. We always felt good after a successful concrete pour though.

It snowed on us several times on that job too. To me that was no big deal. I had been on many, many jobs with snow, ice, and adverse weather conditions. I think most of the crew on this job had worked in the snow before too. Most weren't used to how cold it could get in Montana, though. We didn't really have any issues with the water in the river freezing because it was moving all the time. Our equipment, however, was a completely different story. The water temperature was getting pretty chilly too. We talked the company into getting heaters and a hot-water system for the divers.

Hot-water systems are great for the diver. Some dive companies don't like to use them because most of the systems run on diesel and that is an added expense to the job. Plus, the hot-water system isn't cheap either. The thing is, a warm diver works a lot better and longer than a cold diver. If you think about it, a hot-water system is well worth the extra expense. The job will probably get done faster. It will definitely get done better – because the diver is more comfortable and has warm hands. Cold divers have a hard time keeping their minds on the task at hand. A hot-water system consists of a hot-water suit – which is a wetsuit with perforated hose running through it, an extra hose tied into the diver's umbilical for the hot water to flow from the heating unit to the diver, and the water heater. We typically set the water temperature between a hundred-and-five to a hundred-and-twenty degrees Fahrenheit. By the time it gets to the diver, it's probably around ninety to a hundred degrees; depending on the length of the umbilical and the air and water temperatures. It is like working in a hot tub. It is much healthier for the diver too.

We finished this job in mid-December. Most of the crew went home after the water work was done. A few stayed to break down all the equipment, pack it up and load it on a couple flatbed trailers. Since I lived close by, I was one of the crew who stayed to load up the equipment. This job had a slow start for me, but ended up being a really good job and made for a really good Christmas. It also got me working with Global, which I didn't know at the time, would be really good for my future career. It's funny how things work in the dive industry.

* * *

Hurricanes - Good for Divers - Bad for Everybody Else

The Brasilian ex-wife had taken my two children to Brasil to live in January of two-thousand-and-four without telling me. I was not happy about that when it happened, but that is another story to be told in a different book at another time. Because of this my new wife and I planned a trip to Brasil to visit my kids and show my new wife all around Brasil. We arrived in Brasil just before Christmas two-thousand-and-four so we could spend that holiday with my children. The Brasilian disappeared while we were there, so my wife and I had my children for almost two months. We traveled all over Brasil and had a great time. More stories for another time. Anyway, we got back to Montana in mid-February two-thousand-and-five.

Shortly after getting back, I went to work for Boring on the Columbia River. We did several projects there and a couple in Montana. In mid-June, he called me up to go on another job in Montana. That was normal. But when he arrived and we started the job he told me things were changing. He had quit the union and would no longer be reporting our hours and paying the fees to the union. He was now a non-union company. He would still pay the union wages though. I told him I was happy that he would be paying good wages, but if he wasn't in the union, I couldn't work for him anymore. I depended on the union for my health insurance, life insurance, and retirement. I had been vested for over ten years, so I didn't want to just throw all those built-up benefits out the window. He was not happy to hear that. That was the last time I worked for him. It was also the last job Boring did for PPLM.

I did a couple little jobs with Blanchard and one or two with the guy in Bellevue. In May or June – can't really remember – Issaquah called me up and said he had a job in the Gulf of Mexico that he needed people for. I told him I wasn't interested. I told him I'd had enough of Gulf work to last my lifetime. He actually called me two or three times and each time I told him no thank you. He tried to tell me it would be completely different from the other jobs I had been on in the Gulf. Yeah, yeah, I've heard all that before. No thank you.

In August I went to a Bar-B-Que at Blanchard's place. Every summer Blanchard would have a big party where he would roast a whole pig, hire a band, and invite his family and all the divers he worked with. It was always lots of fun and usually lasted for three days. The reason I mention this is because at this particular party, the Coeur D' Alene Kid showed up with another kid from Caldwell, Idaho. They cornered me and started talking about Global's job in the Gulf. I told them I didn't want to hear it. The funny thing was that not as many people were at this party as I had expected. The Coeur D' Alene Kid told me that several of them were working on this SAT job in the Gulf and it was a great job. It was kind of funny – funny strange, not funny ha-ha – that the Kid was here, because I hadn't seen him on any dive jobs since the thing on Deer Island a few years ago. Blanchard had told me the Kid was taking a break from diving to get his head clear. I thought that was good. The Kid must be ready to get back to diving now though.

When the Coeur D' Alene Kid left me to go talk to Blanchard, the kid from Caldwell started in on me. I call him a kid because he didn't look old enough to drive – but he was. He had been to dive school, but he didn't really want to be a diver. He wanted to be a welder. I found out later that he was a *really* good welder and had been a welder for several years. He had read the advertising and believed the hype from the dive schools and thought he could make a ton of money as an *Underwater Welder*. Yeah, Ha! Ha! That always makes me laugh when people tell me they want to be a diver and make loads of money. It doesn't work that way. He discovered that after his first job out of school and decided he still wanted to be a welder.

Later on that evening, both of them got on me again and told me all this wonderful stuff about the job. The Coeur D' Alene Kid said he was a SAT Diver on the job. SAT is short for "Saturation" and it is a type of diving where divers are pressed into a pressure chamber. When they need to dive, they enter a pressurized diving bell which is lowered to the work site. Typically SAT divers remain under pressure in a living chamber – where they eat, sleep, and live - for four weeks at a time. Divers are advised to take four weeks off before going back into SAT after decompressing. Caldwell was a designated welder on that job. They said they were working on a foreign boat that was more like a cruise ship than a dive boat. They told me they had five-star European chefs preparing the meals and a steward crew of all females from Poland. Yeah, yeah, now I *know* you're telling stories. No! It's *all* True! They swore. Fine, fine, you can tell Issaquah to give me another call.

Monday, a few weeks later, Issaquah gave me a call. We talked about the job. He told me everything the kids had told me at Blanchard's party was true. He said it was four weeks on, four weeks off, twelve hours a day, seven days a week. I would be paid a day-rate that worked out to a couple dollars an hour more than what the union pay for a tender would be. Global would pay forty hours per week union benefits. This position was a deck position and we would see where it goes after this first hitch. He said he could really use me in regular rotation. He also said the job looked like it would go on for at least five years. Oh, My Gawd! I had heard all this kind of stuff before and it was *never* like it was described. I'm really not interested in it, I told Issaquah. After a little more jibber-jabber I caved in. "Fine," I said. "I'll give you four weeks – one hitch. If it's like you say, I'll go into the regular rotation. On the other hand, if it's not, the four weeks is what you get." He was happy with that. "When do you want me to head south?" I questioned.

"Can you fly on Wednesday?" he asked me.

"Huh?! *THIS* Wednesday?!" I exclaimed.

"Yes, this Wednesday. There is some training on the beach you need to go through before we get you on the ship. We will fly you down there, put you up in a hotel, send you to the training, and if you pass the classes, we will put you on the ship for a four-week hitch. That will start the following week, so this first hitch will actually be four-and-a-half weeks. All at the agreed upon day rate."

"Okay," I replied. "Just e-mail me the info and I will be there." I thanked him for the job and told him I would let him know what I thought about it all after the hitch was up. He said that would be great and told me they would e-mail the details of the hotel, the training classes and the plane tickets – which would be e-tickets. I had never used those before. He told me just to print out the ticket from the e-mail and show it to the airline attendants at the counter. They would know what to do. Alright, sounds good to me. Looks like I need to talk to my wife.

I talked to my wife about it and she was not happy that I would be gone for four weeks and not coming home on the weekends. She agreed that the money would be nice. She also thought it might be nice for me to have a job with an actual schedule that we could plan around. I told her I wasn't sure that I would do more than one hitch. What Issaquah was telling me about the job conditions and living situation was very close to what I had been told before and it never was like I was told it was. I told her I would let her know what it was like as soon as I knew.

I packed up my bags for a month-long job. After talking with Issaquah, I knew I would only be working the deck. I didn't pack any dive gear. I packed only what I would need to be a good tender; knives, spud wrench, and a couple other things. I also packed my favorite deerskin work gloves. I fit it all in one check-in bag and a backpack. When I flew, I always packed the minimum I would need for a few days into a backpack that I carried on to the plane. You never know whether or not your checked baggage might get lost or whatever. I wasn't about to be left without a change of clothes and bathroom necessities.

I flew into the Alexandria, Louisiana airport. Normally, the crews were flying in and out of New Orleans, but some hurricane had hit the Louisiana coast pretty hard just a week or so prior to my arrival. It had done quite a bit of damage to the area. It was all over the news. It had caused several of the people working for Global to need some time off to take care of their houses and families in the area. I would find out a little later how bad the damage really was and how much this hurricane – Hurricane Katrina – would affect the dive industry.

For now, I just had some training to get through so I could go off shore.

A limousine – an actual black limousine with a chauffeur in a suit, little hat, and everything - picked us up from the airport and drove us to a training center just south of Lafayette. The training center had a bunkhouse where we would be staying during the training. There were eight bunks to a room. Wonderful. They also had a cafeteria where we would be dining – breakfast, lunch, and dinner. Yeah. "Oh, this isn't like all the other Gulf jobs you've been on." I remembered Issaquah saying. Huh, so far, besides the limo ride, it was *exactly* like all the other Gulf jobs I had been on. I was not excited about the outlook of this one.

The sheets were clean anyway, and the room didn't stink. All the walls were painted white. At least the place was clean. Dinner was served promptly at six p.m. The cafeteria – they called it a galley, I guess they wanted us to get used to offshore nomenclature – was pretty nice. It was clean too, and the food was very good. Okay, things are looking up. Breakfast would be served at seven and classes would start at eight in the morning. We were told that the administration didn't recommend we leave the "campus" but we weren't locked in or anything. After dinner, a couple of us took off on foot, looking for a half-way decent bar – that meant cheap beer and decent music.

We found one less than a mile away. Perfect. It had a couple pool tables, decent music on the jukebox, served both beer and hard liquor, and wasn't expensive. Nice. We stayed until about eleven or so. None of us got plastered, we just had a few drinks and played a lot of pool. It was a Wednesday night and the place was not very busy. We walked back to the training center and were in bed by midnight.

Everybody was up in time for breakfast, which was pretty tasty. They had eggs to order, choice of meats, cereals, and fruits. I had no complaints. The class started promptly at eight.

The instructor talked about water safety and how to get into survival suits in the water. He talked about how to get out of helicopters that had made water landings and flipped upside down. We had to take a quiz before lunch to show that we had been listening. Lunch was sandwiches. Okay.

After lunch we were asked to get into swimming trunks and meet at the pool. It was a large outdoor pool with a shallow end and a larger deep end. There was a pile of orange survival suits by the shallow end. At the deep end was a tube frame thing with six patio-furniture chairs fastened to it. Each of the chairs had a four-point seat belt that we were told was what we would find on the helicopters. This training was called HUET - Helicopter Underwater Escape Training – and was mandatory for anyone taking helicopter rides out over the Gulf of Mexico.

Everybody had to go through both "training stations" at the pool. At the shallow end of the pool, we had to grab a survival suit and jump into the water. Then we had to get into the suit, zip it up and float around in it for a little while, both on our backs and on our fronts. After we had shown that we were comfortable with that, we took off the suits and put them on the deck, ready for the next group.

At the deep end of the pool, we sat in one of the seats attached to the tube frame and strapped in with the seat belts. We were told to cinch up the seat belts, because we would be flipping upside down into the water. Oh, so this was going to be like a carnival ride! Joke all you want; this is serious business. Yeah, it looks like it. As soon as all of us were strapped in, cinched up and checked by one of the assistants, the set of seats slid down towards the pool and flipped upside down splashing into the water. Just as soon as the rig stopped, we unfastened our seat belts and swam to the surface. There were two guys in the pool with SCUBA gear to help if anyone freaked out and couldn't get their seat belt undone. All of us got our seat belts undone. We all passed the class and were done for the day.

That evening was a repeat of the evening before. We had dinner, went to the bar – this time a couple more classmates joined us – where we had a few drinks and played some pool. It was Thursday night – Ladies Night – so the place got fairly crowded around nine. Most of us left about ten and headed back to the training center.

The next couple days – Friday and Saturday – we had more training. There were several more certifications we all needed to work offshore in the Gulf of Mexico. We all did fine and passed all the classes. Saturday afternoon, after we finished the class and got our certification cards, a van picked us up from the training center. We were taken to a fishing resort in Cocodrie. This was one of the places on the Louisiana coast that hadn't been damaged too bad by Hurricane Katrina. The helicopter port was still serviceable. There was a motel at the fishing resort that Global had rented. There was a restaurant and a bar there also. This place usually serviced tourists, but the hurricane had knocked out tourism in that area for a while.

The rooms weren't bad and we only stayed there one night. We were taken to the heliport the next morning. At Cocodrie we met more of the crew from Global and other companies that were working on the Boa Deep C, that had already gone through the training and already held the necessary certifications to work offshore. All in all, there were about twelve of us going out to the Boa. A couple of the new guys were a little nervous about the helicopter ride. You know how helicopters fly, don't you? – by beating the air into submission! Ha-ha!

The van dropped us off at the heliport. We signed in and had to get weighed along with our bags. The helicopter could only carry so much weight. My bags and I were on the heavy side, but not so heavy that I couldn't fly with my group. I had to sit in the front seat next to the pilot though. That was great for me. I had only been on a helicopter once before, so this flight was a lot of fun. The flight was fairly long – over an hour. It was fun seeing the oil rigs and boats on the water. From the air, you could see the currents and different water visibilities as we headed offshore. I had never seen that before. It is a completely different view than what you get on a crew boat. It was a *lot* smoother ride too!

The pilot called the ship when we got close to it. Then he circled it before making his approach. I saw a small square deck on the bow of the ship that had a big yellow circle with a yellow H in the middle of it. That had to be the landing pad. It didn't seem very big from my vantage point. The ship was going up and down with the waves. This was a little nerve-racking for me. It was my first-time landing on a floating vessel from a flying vehicle. The pilot did a great job landing us though. He was watching the up and down movement of the landing pad and set the chopper down nice and lightly, not a bump or anything. I was quite impressed.

Some of the ship's crew grabbed our bags and guided us down a couple ladders and into a reception area on the deck below the helicopter pad. We were met by a taller woman with an athletic build and short, dark brown hair. She spoke English very well with an eastern European accent. The ship was very clean and smelled like Pine-Sol. The woman introduced herself and called our names from a list she had on a clipboard. As each of us answered, she gave us a clip-on badge and three magnetic name tags. She also gave each of us a packet of papers which she went through with us, page by page. It included the layout of the boat, our crew designations, our cabin assignments, our lifeboat stations, and the rules and regulations of the ship. There were several documents we had to initial and sign, then give back to her. When she was done with us, she pointed us to the ladder going down and welcomed us to the Boa Deep C.

I threw my bags over my shoulders and headed to the lower decks. The first thing I did was find my berth. I found it and it wasn't very big. My cabin was on the outside bulkhead, so I had a porthole. That was awesome. The room had only one bunk against one bulkhead and a desk up against the other. There was a wardrobe against the same bulkhead as the desk. At the foot of the bunk was another little room with a head, sink and shower in it. The floor was heated in the shower room. This was the nicest berth I had ever had on a dive job. Later I found out we weren't hot-bunking (sharing the bunk with the opposite shift) and I just couldn't believe it. I had this whole cabin and bathroom all to myself. We even had a satellite phone in the cabin. Wow!

After dropping my bags off in my cabin, I went to Dive Control. There was a small SAT system in the middle of the deck just aft of a moonpool. A moonpool is a hole in the middle of the deck of a ship. They can be any size. This one is about twenty feet by twenty feet. The diving bell from the SAT system was lowered into the water through this moonpool. The SAT system on this boat consisted of one large – but not very large – pressure chamber and a smaller pressure chamber attached at the aft end. The larger chamber was twenty-five feet long and ten feet in diameter. Much larger than a normal DDC, but much smaller than contemporary SAT systems. The smaller chamber was twenty feet long and ten feet in diameter. The system was owned by Global Diving and Salvage and they called it SAT-One.

The inside of the larger chamber is split into two sections. The forward section takes up one-third of the chamber and is called the Transfer Lock (TL). It has a shower, sink, and toilet in it. It is also where the diving bell attaches – or Locks on – to the habitat. There are hatches that separate each section and also allow the bell to be separated from the rest of the chamber. The aft two-thirds in the larger pressure vessel are called the Main Lock (ML). It has four bunks in it and a small table at the foot of the bunks.

The smaller chamber locked on to the aft section of the main chamber is a Hyperbaric Rescue Chamber (HRC). It has four bunks in it. It is also divided into two sections. The smaller section containing a toilet, sink, and shower is on the aft end and called the Entry Lock (EL). The HRC is used to press a dive team into the chamber and also used to decompress a team out of the system. Sometimes the dive team would be pressed into the system using the diving bell. On the side of each, the ML and the HRC, is a small access point called a Med Lock. It is used to press food and supplies into the chambers and take garbage and other stuff out of the chamber. There are also four little six-inch viewports on each chamber. There are several cameras mounted inside the system so the topside crew can monitor the dive teams.

Dive Control was inside a Conex on the main deck to the port side of the SAT chambers. The Conex was split in half with Dive Control and the LST (Life Support Technician) panels in the forward part. In the back half of the Conex was a desk with a computer, a coffee pot, and supplies for the deck crew. On top of that Conex was another Conex that housed the heating, cooling, and water systems for the SAT system. Breathing and atmosphere gases for inside the chambers (also used for the divers when they are in the bell and when they are actually diving) was supplied by racks of gas stored a deck above and forward of the moonpool.

I met the dayshift dive supervisor, the Life Support Tech (LST), the SAT Tech and the rest of the deck crew – four guys besides myself. Since I was the newest member of the dive crew, I was designated the "Betty." The Betty is the crew member responsible for getting the food, clothing, dive gear, bedding, and everything else the divers inside the chamber need. As the Betty, I was responsible for taking care of all the needs of the divers. I reported directly to the LST. On some crews the Betty is also the assistant LST. That wasn't the case really on this system. Typically, the Betty was the greenest tender on a SAT job.

I thought that was hilarious, because I had just about twenty years in the dive industry by this time. That was more than double the time most of the other deck crew had in the industry. Global didn't have any tenders fresh out of school on this job though. Most of the deck crew was made up of divers. The divers in SAT were guys that had been diving for more than ten years. Some of Global's divers had been in SAT before on a project or two off the west coast. Global tried to crew the whole job with their employees from the northwest. They needed so many people, though, that they had to hire some Gulf divers. Some of the jobs *had* to be filled by Gulf guys, just because SAT diving wasn't done in the northwest. Jobs like the SAT Supervisors, SAT Techs, and LSTs were all filled by Gulf hands. Global was training their own guys to fill these positions though.

Global had started crewing this job up in May. It had taken them a month or so to get all their equipment set up on the Boa Deep C. There were some growing pains getting the Gulf divers used to how things were done in the northwest. Since the majority of the crew was from the northwest and all the Superintendents were from the northwest, the crew was expected to work like we did in the northwest. Most of the Gulf divers had a hard time with that. In the beginning it was like trying to mix oil and water. My first hitch on the ship, we went through several Gulf divers. There were a few personality clashes, but it was mostly that the Gulf divers didn't like being expected to work on the deck if they weren't diving or pressed in SAT.

I liked my duties as the Betty. The job was very easy. I was getting paid better than any other tender in the Gulf I am sure of it. It was kind of a joke on the deck that I was the most experienced and highest paid Betty in the whole of the Gulf of Mexico at the time. For some reason, most of the other deck crew didn't want to be the Betty. It must have been more of a psychological thing; the position of Betty being the bottom rung on the SAT ladder. I'd rather do that than hump hoses up and down for the divers though. In doing my duties as the Betty, I got to go all over the ship. I had to go to the galley to get the diver's food. I had to go to the laundry for the diver's clothing and bedding. I had to go on the computer to send and receive e-mails for the divers. When I didn't have any Betty chores to do – which wasn't often – I helped the deck crew with their job. Time really flew by for me.

After I had been on the job for three weeks, Issaquah asked me how things were going. I told him he had been correct. This was the best job in the Gulf of Mexico I had ever been on – not counting the Cozumel job back in ninety-nine. The accommodations were fabulous. The food was fantastic. The ship was clean. There were about twenty females on board at any one time. It was nice to have women on the ship because the behavior of the male crew members was much better than when it was an all-male crew. Being the Betty, I had quite a bit of interaction with the female crew. They made up most of the steward crew. They did the actual laundry. They did the food prep and the galley clean-up. They cleaned our berths, bathrooms, and all the corridors on the ship.

One of my LSTs, who was from Gilroy, California, taught me a lot about being an LST. He also liked to keep the divers as happy as he could. One day he got to talking to me about where I lived and what I did during my time off. He told me he had heard that my wife and I had an ice cream parlour. I told him that we did, and during the summer, I helped her run the place when I was home.

After hearing that, he stated that I must know how to make banana splits and specialty sundaes. I assured him I did. He exclaimed that was a good thing, because all four of the divers in the Main Lock had asked for banana splits; cherries, bananas, whipped cream, and all. They had heard that I owned an ice cream parlor. I looked at him dumbfounded. Yeah, I suppose I could do that. It would take me a little while to get all the stuff together and build four of them. He said that would be fine. Okay, off to the galley I went.

When I got to the galley, I found one of the girls working on the galley crew and explained to her my situation. She smiled and said that would be no problem, she just needed to know what I needed to complete the task. I told her I needed three flavors of ice cream – chocolate, strawberry, and vanilla. I also needed maraschino cherries, four bananas, chocolate syrup, caramel sauce, and whip cream. I helped her gather all the ingredients. She got me four dessert dishes and spoons. I scooped the ice cream and assembled the treats. The girl helped me. She also helped me carry the finished desserts down to the SAT system from the galley. I thanked her. I loaded the banana splits into the med-lock and sent them down to the divers.

I am not sure what state the desserts arrived at depth. Ice cream is fifty-percent air and whipped cream is more air than cream. I figured the compression might squeeze all the air out of the dessert. I told the LST that the desserts had been pressed in. I asked him if the divers were happy with them. They must have arrived okay, because he told me the divers really liked them and were very happy with the desserts. The only problem with that was, from then on, banana splits and special sundaes were being ordered on a regular basis. That was okay, I enjoyed making them. I love ice cream. Smiles.

Another enjoyable and cool part of being on the Boa Deep C was that it had an international crew. I can't remember who owned it or where it was flagged, but it was run by a Norwegian crew; the captain, pilots, and a couple of the crane operators. The riggers were from Nova Scotia and Labrador; Canadian. The engineering crew was mostly Spanish; from Spain. They had a woman engineer too. The Steward crew was Polish; including the chefs and sous chefs. The ROV crew was American. In fact, they were Oceaneering. Finally, there was us – the dive crew. We were, of course, American.

Most of Oceaneering's crew were from the southern states – Florida, Louisiana, and Texas. Most of the dive crew was from Washington and California with a couple from Idaho and Oregon. The Gulf guys on our crew were predominately from Florida, Louisiana, and Texas. A couple were from Mississippi and one or two were from Alabama. I was from Montana. Global was paying all our travel expenses. They were flying us back and forth from our home cities no matter where we lived. During our time on the Boa, one of the guys from California moved to Hawaii and Global still flew him back and forth.

The job we were hired to do was to deconstruct and salvage damaged oil rigs. Hurricane Ivan had come through the Gulf of Mexico in September of two-thousand-and-four. It damaged quite a few of the oil rigs that had been built before the seventies. The oil companies had been ordered by the EPA to take down the damaged rigs and cap the wells to prevent crude oil from leaking into the oceans. There were government-funded programs and insurance to help the oil companies cover their costs for this project – at least that was the way I heard it. There were several government-financed projects to mediate the damage done by Ivan, offshore, onshore, and on the islands.

Anyway, the EPA had demanded the deconstruction of the damaged rigs, capping of damaged and decommissioned wells, and removal of most of the debris. Some of the steel had been allowed to be left on the sea bottom in hopes of creating artificial reefs. The insurance companies had hired several boats with ROV and dive systems on them to do the work. There was a name for the project, I think it was called the Ivan Main Pass Project. It was a major project and I knew of at least three other ships hired to do the same sort of work. The Boa Deep C had been hired by Wild Well Control, who had been contracted by Noble Energy to take care of their wells. I can't remember how many rigs of theirs the Boa was under contract to deconstruct, but it was forecast that this cleanup would take two to three years. It looked like Global was going to need a lot of people for several years. They still had all their work in the northwest to do also.

Issaquah talked to me again and asked if everything was okay with me. I assured him all was well. He explained to me that most of the crew was doing four weeks on and four weeks off. The divers in SAT were doing twenty-eight days under pressure, then would decompress out. The length of decompression depended on the depth. At the moment we were diving at four-hundred-and-twenty feet. That took just under five-and-a-half days to decompress. Decompression could be estimated at one day per hundred feet plus a day. That meant that even though the divers were doing "twenty-eight days on with twenty-eight days off," they were actually doing thirty-three days on with only twenty-three days off. On top of that, Global expected their northwest guys to go on jobs in the northwest if they were needed during their twenty-eight days off.

Issaquah asked me if I wanted to get into the regular rotation. He said they were really shorthanded and could use me to fill a spot. I told him that I liked the job and I was game for going into regular rotation. I had a couple stipulations, though. First; I didn't want to remain a deckhand. I was a dive supervisor and I had a good understanding of all the math and science part of diving. I was more than just a deckhand/tender. I expected to be moved up the ranks. I was willing to get whatever certifications were needed for me to do that. Second; I expected a day off for every day I worked. If they needed me to work more, I might be willing, but I didn't want them to expect me to work during my time off like they did with their other regular employees. He told me both of those provisions could be met.

Then he let me know they had a vacancy in the crew arriving in a few days. He really needed one of the deckhands to stay an extra four weeks. Would I be interested, he inquired. I told him that I was and that I would stay. Then I stated again that I wanted to move up. He asked if I might be interested in becoming an LST. I told him I would. He said he would talk to the supervisors, LSTs, and owners about training me to do that. I thanked him for the opportunity.

After my conversation with Issaquah, I e-mailed my wife and explained to her the situation of the relief crew arriving in the next week. She wasn't happy that I would be staying an extra four weeks, but told me whatever I needed or wanted to do, she would support me. I thanked her, and let her know that I missed her and loved her. That first hitch of mine, I ended up staying ten weeks. It was a long time, but the work was fun and the money was great.

As I said earlier, there were some growing pains mixing the Gulf crew with the northwest employees. One of the things that *really* bothers me is the caste system that exists in the Gulf diving community. The Gulf guys still have their hierarchy descending from Superintendent, Supervisor, to Diver, and down to Tender; with LSTs and SAT Techs off to the side of divers. A couple of the supervisors really liked yelling at the tenders and trying to make them feel like crap. I do *not* like that one little bit. Supervisors don't need to yell at the tenders just to demean them. A tender – or any employee really – works better with positive re-enforcement rather than negative re-enforcement. I do not like getting yelled at either;

especially for no reason. If my performance isn't up to snuff, I will improve better and faster if the issues are explained to me. Yelling just shuts me down and puts me in a bad mood. Treating fellow crew members like crap really puts me in a bad mood too. People need to respect each other no matter where they fall in the ranks.

I explain this because one shift during my second week, I had an issue with one of the supervisors – or maybe he had an issue with me. I had finished all my Betty duties and I was helping the deck crew come up and down on welding and burning leads. I know the importance of being prompt and working quickly. With SAT diving this isn't as important as other forms of diving, because SAT divers have unlimited bottom times – that is the whole point of putting divers in SAT – but we still don't want to waste the divers' time while they are working outside of the bell.

Anyway, it was hot and muggy out. We were working our butts off hauling tools and equipment up and lowering tools and equipment back down to the diver. We were sweating like crazy and nobody was slacking off. The supervisor came over the loudspeaker and yelled "Up on the burning gear! Come on!! Get up on the burning gear! Chop! Chop! Quick like a bunny!!" For some reason that just really ticked me off that day. It probably had something to do with the accumulation of yelling every day all the time. I had just had enough.

As soon as he had yelled "Quick like a bunny!" I dropped the burning lead I had in my hands. I turned and walked – not ran, but walked – to the Dive Control. When I got there, I opened the door and looked straight at the supervisor and told him "You need to be nicer to people. You need to have a little more respect for the crew working the deck. You need to *stop* yelling all the time for no reason. We are working our *asses* off and doing a good job. One more thing, when I hear 'Chop! Chop!' I get the urge to pick up an axe and you do *not* want to see what happens after that." With that I turned around and walked – not ran – but walked out of the dive shack and back to the work station. On my way out of the dive shack, I noticed the LST watching the whole scene and his jaw was on the floor.

After dinner that day I found Issaquah and told him I needed to have a little talk with him. He took me into his office and asked what I needed to talk about. I told him about my little episode out on the deck earlier that day. I stated I knew I had been subordinate and that the supervisor was probably going to talk to him about it. If it meant that I got sent home, I was okay with that decision. He looked at me and burst out laughing. He said scenes like that were left up to the supervisor to deal with. As far as he was concerned, nobody was getting sent home.

"We're on a dive job here," he said, "not everybody has to like each other, we just have to work together." He told me not to worry – I was not going to be sent home any time soon. I thanked him, left his office, and went back to work. I was on the noon to midnight shift – called "Day Shift."

Shortly after that, I started training with the LSTs. That fit in very well with my duties as the Betty. The rest of the deck crew was happy with that arrangement also, as it meant that I would be the Betty all the time when I came out for my hitches and none of them would have to be. Like I said, I didn't really understand the aversion to the job, but it worked out well for me. There were a couple guys like me, divers from the northwest - older than the average diver/tender - that were interested in getting certified as LSTs.

We took most of our LST and supervisor classes together. One of them had worked with me at Norwesco on the Lotto Barge. He had worked for Santa Fe when I was still in high school. He was very smart and my main competition in the LST classes. We always had a friendly competition for top position in the class. Sante Fe was always the one to beat. Another had been working for Global on one of the jobs that I was a DSO on a few years earlier. He was from Portland, Oregon – or close to it.

The more time you spent working in the dive industry, the more you realized how small a community it really was. It has been said that there are only two degrees of separation between all commercial divers – at least in the United States and Canada. I know divers from all over the world though.

* * *

I think it was my second, or maybe my third, week on the Boa Deep C – I can't really remember. There was another hurricane warning in the Gulf of Mexico. A hurricane – Rita - was heading our way aiming for New Orleans or Texas again. The Gulf coast hadn't even begun to recover from Katrina. In fact, Katrina was so recent that its full effect wasn't even known. Its impact on the dive industry certainly wasn't realized yet. The effects of Hurricane Katrina would really impact the dive industry for several years, as we were about to find out later.

The presence of hurricanes didn't really matter to us. The Boa Deep C was dynamically positioned – meaning it didn't need anchors to hold it in place for dive operations. The plan was that we would keep working as long as we could and when the hurricane got close, we would just stop the dive ops and sail the ship out of the hurricane's path. By the time the hurricane got close to us it was a category five. No worries, we just moved position. We didn't see it as it went by – we had sailed far enough away to not be bothered by it. I do remember some really big waves – one was at least thirty feet high. The Boa Deep C was big enough that waves like that didn't bother us too much. That wave did wash over the deck at about four feet high though. It did move some of the equipment around, but didn't cause us any issues. Rita added to the damage that Katrina had done to Louisiana and Mississippi. What Katrina hadn't already flattened and flooded; Rita finished off.

The two-thousand-and-five hurricane season impacted our job in several ways. The main way we were impacted was that both Venice and Fourchon (pronounced foo-Shawn) could no longer be used as ports of entry and exit. Both of those ports had been wiped out – and I mean *Wiped Out* – as in *completely* flattened by Katrina and Rita. Cocodrie was the port that we used for a little while after that. We also used Cameron when we were working on oil rigs further west. Another way our job was impacted was that the hurricanes had damaged many more oil rigs than Ivan. The EPA added all those damaged rigs onto their list of rigs to be deconstructed from the damage caused by Ivan. At that time, it was estimated that we would have this kind of work for the next ten years now. A third way our job was impacted was that all that damage created way more dive jobs. Now every dive company that could work in the Gulf of Mexico, plus a lot of newly created dive companies, were getting SAT jobs. In some cases, people that had no business at all running a dive company were starting dive companies to get their piece of the pie. This meant that the industry needed many, many more divers, tenders, supervisors, and everybody else that made up dive crews.

The pay jumped way up. Tender pay went from seven-dollars-fifty-cents an hour to nineteen dollars an hour. Some companies – like Cal-Dive – offered to pay people to go through dive school with the promise of a new Superlite Seventeen after two years of service. Tenders that never should have been promoted to divers in the first place were being promoted to SAT divers. Lead tenders and deck foremen were getting trained to be SAT supervisors. A process that used to take ten years or more was now reduced to two or three years; sometimes even less. Wet pay jumped way up too. I was appalled. Now we were getting too many new people into the dive industry and not nearly enough were being weeded out. On top of that, guys that *had* been weeded out, or dropped out in previous years, were getting hired back into the industry. All they needed was that piece of paper saying they had graduated a dive school. This was a recipe for disaster as far as I could see. Not to mention all these new young divers got really big heads. I called them Katrina Babies, and as far as I was concerned, they weren't real divers.

You see, to me, a real diver is one who has been in the industry at least ten years. Let me explain. Hundreds and hundreds of people graduate dive school every year. As I've said earlier, the majority drop out within the first year. The work is hard. The schedules are hard on the family and the money isn't all that great. It was good, but there were easier ways to make more money and spend more time at home. The raise in pay because of Katrina took the money issue out of the equation.

Another thing that caused people to quit diving was the long process of tending for two to five years before breaking out as a diver. The demand for divers caused by Katrina removed that issue from the process also. Before Katrina, ninety percent of the people finishing dive school dropped out of the industry in less than five years. If you weren't in the business more than five years, you really weren't in the business – you were just playing at being a diver – or a tender really. You were just a tourist.

Ten years in the dive industry is kind of a tipping point. What happens after ten years is that you now have likely worked your way up to diver and probably beyond. Most likely you are a supervisor every now and again. You know enough people in the dive industry that you can work all over the place. If you have been in ten years, you have proven to the dive companies that you are worth their time and pay. Also, after ten years, it would be harder for you to start a new career.

You have become ingrained in the dive industry. You are now working enough and earning enough that to start doing something else would most likely mean quite a large decrease in yearly income. It is no longer cost effective for you to get a new career. Whether you like it or not, you are more or less stuck in the industry. Now you are a real diver.

Hurricane Katrina allowed way too many people to make too much money in the dive industry too early in their career and they were no longer as invested in the job as divers used to be. Tourists. Many of this new group of divers were just tourists in the dive industry – Katrina Babies. I did not have much respect for most of them. They weren't all bad though. I worked with many new guys that were very good and became real divers later on. But the number of guys who got into SAT for a couple years then dropped out of diving later was astounding. I know many divers think I'm just a cranky old man for thinking this way, but I don't care. What it comes down to is this: if you are a good worker and a good diver, I want you on my crew. If you are a poor worker and a bad diver, I don't want you on my crew and I don't think you should be in the dive industry. I'll get off my soap box now. Ha-ha.

With all this new work needing to be done in the Gulf of Mexico, we thought we would be here at least ten years. That would be fantastic. The Boa Deep C was a great ship to work on. Global wanted to cash in on all the new work too. They bought another SAT system – SAT-Two. It was put on a barge. I don't remember the actual name of the barge, but on the Boa, we referred to it as "the Prison Barge." Some friends have recently reminded me that it was owned by Crowley. I spent a little time on it to help set up the SAT system equipment, but I didn't stay on it. In fact, I never even slept on it.

We called it "the Prison Barge" because that is how it compared to the Boa Deep C. It was a typical dive barge set-up from the Gulf of Mexico. Some of the barge workers were ex-cons too – that is not necessarily a bad thing, but it did add to the reasons it was referred to as "the Prison Barge." It was because of set-ups like the prison barge that I vowed never to return to the Gulf in the first place. Issaquah didn't even suggest that I get assigned to that barge. He knew that if I did, I would most likely not return to the Gulf. He was correct in his assumption too. I don't think the food was as good over there as it was on the Boa either. Regular Gulf of Mexico cooks were hired to work on that barge, rather than the European-trained chefs like we had on the Boa.

The Prison Barge had some cool features though. The barge had a sliding deck that covered the moonpool when it wasn't in use. I think the crew was allowed to fish off that barge. Fishing was not allowed on the Boa. SAT-Two was bigger than SAT-One. I am pretty sure the divers liked it better. The diving bell on SAT-Two was significantly bigger than the bell on SAT-One. I am positive the divers liked that too.

I was glad to see several of the guys I had worked with in the northwest end up as SAT divers. They are good workers and can pass on their good habits to the new divers coming in. SoCal, Duck Fart, the Mouth, and Hollywood all got into the SAT diving. Illinois got into it, but preferred working in the northwest. He only did SAT a couple times. Because of that, his career took off. He became a supervisor and even superintendent on several jobs. I met a bunch of guys from California – both supervisors and divers that had worked with people I knew and worked with outside of the Gulf. I think some of the Gulf divers really resented the influx of inland and west coast divers. Some of them meshed well with us, though, and even did some inland work later on.

* * *

I got my four weeks off after my first hitch. The way the scheduling worked out; I was out on the Boa Deep C over Christmas. That was fine with me. My kids were living in Brasil with their mom and I could see the rest of my family whenever I wasn't working. If I couldn't spend Christmas with my kids, I might as well work the holiday and allow other crew members to spend it with their families.

Global must have been rolling in the dough with this new job. I got a Christmas Bonus – a first for me in the Dive Industry. I also got a Christmas gift bag containing a personalized denim work shirt, a couple t-shirts, and a hoody; all with Global logos on them. That was awesome and very good for morale. All of us on board the Boa got the gift bags that Christmas. This time I spent six weeks on the ship. I worked with a couple different LSTs. That was good, because I got a different point of view on how things were done. I also worked with different supervisors. It was good to see the different supervising styles.

After six weeks on the ship, I went home again. I had agreed to return after four weeks. I went back to the ship as scheduled. The work was enjoyable and the conditions were great. I was getting to know everybody on all the different crews. Global was getting new people all the time. Some of them worked out and some of them didn't. Some of Global's regular northwest guys would do a hitch or two, but not return because Global would assign them to other projects. Every hitch I worked; the superintendent would ask me if I knew of anybody in the dive industry who might be interested in getting on this project. I talked to several friends and co-workers - who weren't working with Global - about the project. I talked to a couple guys I went to school with who had gotten out of diving years ago, but they weren't interested in working away from home for weeks at a time. I understood where they were coming from, but let them know this job was different than other Gulf jobs I had been on.

I e-mailed my wife every day to tell her how things were going. Working on an offshore project like this you get to know your co-workers very well. Also, you are spending at least half your life offshore. It starts to feel like you have two separate lives. On one hand, you have your home life with your family and friends there. On the other hand, is your Off Shore life with your crew – some of whom you get so close to that they feel like family. The company tries to keep crews together that get along well and work well with each other. For the most part, you go offshore with the same people most of the time.

Offshore we have all the same drama and stuff going on that you have at home. People hang out in their little groups. People get along with some better than others. New crew members have to prove themselves – or not, and they get sent home forever. Sometimes crew members due to arrive for crew change get drunk or in trouble with the law and don't make it to the heliport in time to make the crew change. This happened more than you might think, especially after we went back to meeting in New Orleans for crew changes. There are lots of fun memories and good stories just from the one or two days spent there each month or so. Anyway, as I would relate these stories to my wife, we started referring to my life offshore as "Dives of our Lives." For the most part nothing too exciting happened, but there always seemed to be more drama than there needed to be.

For the next year and a half, I worked on the Boa Deep C. The planned schedule was four weeks on and four weeks off. I worked more than that. Much more than that. Almost every time I worked an extra week or two. That year I worked over nine months instead of just six like I had planned. I think Hollywood worked over three hundred days that year. His wife didn't like that and they ended up splitting up. That was sad, but as I've said before this life is very hard on the family. Also, the Boa Deep C only had nine days during the whole year that we couldn't work due to bad weather. I think that was some kind of record.

I became a certified LST along with a couple of the other guys from the northwest. SoCal became a SAT supervisor after doing a fair bit of SAT diving. I worked a lot with another diver from southern California who became a SAT Supervisor. He and I talked about everything and realized that we spent more time with each other in those Boa Deep C years than we spent with our wives. You start thinking about which life is more important and what is more important in life. I decided that my life at home was much more important than the dive life. I still enjoyed the diving life, though. I just decided to stick to my guns and get a day off for every day I worked.

* * *

We worked in the Gulf of Mexico all year around on the Boa Deep C. That meant that we were offshore during all the migrations of the animals in the Gulf; Birds, Bugs, Jelly Fish, Sharks, Rays, and Sea Turtles. There are six species of Sea Turtles in the Gulf waters and they migrate in the spring and summer. All six species are protected and that means we had to keep an eye out for them, making sure we didn't inadvertently harm them in any way. During their migration season the Gulf states would send marine biologists offshore to count and record any turtles we encountered. These marine biologists would get stationed on the Boa Deep C – and most other ships and rigs in the Gulf. They usually stayed on board a few days to a few weeks. All of them that came to the Boa were female and everybody called them "Turtle Girls." When I first got on board, when people talked about "Turtle Girls" I had no idea what they were talking about until a couple of my friends explained it to me.

I have a degree in Biology and at one time had thought about becoming a Marine Biologist. When I looked into it more, I thought a degree in Biological Oceanography would suit me better. I would have had to spend too much time in Seattle or Southern California - maybe Massachusetts – to earn that degree though. By that time, I was already making a good living as a Commercial Diver and knew I wouldn't make as much money as a Marine Scientist. I still have a huge interest in all things Scientific that have to do with the oceans. I am really intrigued by Octopi, Squid, and Cuttlefish.

Anyway, back to the Turtle Girls. I really enjoyed talking with them when they came on board. I learned more about turtles and the general biology of life in the Caribbean and the Gulf of Mexico. A lot of the other dive crew talked to them quite a bit and it seems wages always became part of the conversations. After learning about their actual pay, I realized there was no way I could support my family with that kind of work – even though I think it would be quite enjoyable. One of our divers started dating one of the Turtle Girls and I think they even ended up getting married.

The first time I learned about the Turtle Girls was in the early spring of two-thousand-and-six. A juvenile Green Sea Turtle had ended up in the moon pool. At the time the Diving Bell was in the water at about four-hundred-and-fifty feet. It would be down there another six hours or so. All of us on deck were checking on the little turtle every fifteen minutes or so hoping it would swim down and out of the moon pool. That's how it got in the moon pool in the first place; by swimming under the boat and coming up through it. We thought – or at least hoped – that it would find its own way out. After several hours it looked like it was getting really tired and it wouldn't dive deep enough to exit the moon pool. The deck crew decided we needed to help the poor little thing out. One of the guys climbed down the access ladder inside the pool and tried to catch the turtle. All it did was swim away from him though and he didn't want to get in the water – in fact he couldn't get in the water because of the liabilities. When that didn't work, he climbed back out of the moon pool and we threw some ideas back and forth about rescuing the turtle.

That is when I learned about the Turtle Girls. We had a pool skimmer to clean trash out of the moon pool – just like what is used on swimming pools but with a longer handle. I thought that was the best idea, as did some of the other crew, but we were told that we were not allowed to handle the turtles at all. Only Turtle Girls were allowed to handle the Sea Turtles. We were not trained in the handling, so we might accidently cause harm to the immature Chelonian. Immature what?! Chelonians – you know taxonomically the family Cheloniidae – Marine Turtles. Ha-ha! Scientific names – sorry, I just got tired of saying "turtle" all the time and wanted to break it up a little. Anyway, we were not supposed to touch it.

We couldn't leave it in the moon pool either. When the bell comes up out of the water, it might snag the turtle and cause harm to it. We had to get it out of the moon pool and there weren't any Turtle Girls on board yet – it was a little early in the season. We – the deck crew – talked amongst ourselves and decided the best thing to do would be to catch it and lift it out with the pool skimmer. We would do it quickly and hopefully no-one of consequence would be watching. After rescuing it from the pool, we would rush it over to the Port side of the ship and lower it to the water surface with the pool skimmer. That seemed like the best plan.

It was decided that I would do the actual handling of the turtle since I at least had a degree in Biology. I wouldn't mind explaining myself if we got caught and reprimanded for it either. I mean really, what would they do? Kick me off the ship for touching a Sea Turtle? Not likely. If all went well, our diving support deck crew would be the only people who knew about it. We wouldn't tell the supervisor, superintendent or anybody.

Two of us scooped the little animal out of the pool with the skimmer. It took three of us to get it on deck – those things are heavier than you would think – especially when they are in a net on the end of a fifteen-foot pole. When we got it to the deck, I grabbed it by the sides of its shell and carried it over to the side of the deck. We were pretty sneaky about it and I don't think anybody else saw us do it. One of the guys grabbed a five-gallon bucket on a rope. He suggested we put the turtle in that and lower it to the water – that way it wouldn't slip off the skimmer and hit the water hard. We all thought that was a great idea and that is exactly what we did.

When the Sea Turtle reached the water, it swam away. It looked a little worn out, but I think they always look like that. Anyway, we had freed it from the moon pool and we felt good about ourselves. I think April O'Neil and the Teenage Mutant Ninja Turtles would be happy with us. We thought we were turtle heroes for the rest of the day.

*   *   *

After I was a full-blown LST we were still getting lots of new guys – or at least new to Global and SAT. We were constantly breaking in new crew members and training them how we did things on this rig. I have always had issues with people who are full of themselves or think they are better than others. When I meet people like that, I am not the nicest person in the world to them. I am not vicious or condescending, but I can be fairly sarcastic towards them. One of the things that always irks me a little is tenders or breakout divers that have a Mark V tattoo. Especially by this time in the history of diving – how many of these new guys have ever dived a Mark V? I mean, I'm okay with a dive helmet tattoo, but why not get one of a hat that you have actually used?

Anyway, it is the day after crew change and I am having dinner in the dining room. For the most part, the different crews on the Boa eat in their own groups – four to a table. I'm having my dinner with Gulf Breeze. There is an open seat at our table. One of the new dive crew sits down in the empty seat. He is wearing a white t-shirt and has several tattoos on his arms. One of them is a Mark V with two dolphins on either side of the helmet. Yeah, yeah, it is the USN Diver's insignia. I look at him and ask him where he is from. He tells us he lives in Oklahoma. He has come from the US navy.

After a little bit, I start giving him shit about having a Mark V tattooed on his arm. I am probably being a bit of an ass, but I tell him I don't think a guy should sport a tattoo of a Mark V if he has never dived one. You know, diving a Mark V is way different than diving the newer "lightweight" gear. I tell him if he wants a tattoo of a dive helmet, why not get one of a hat he has actually used. He doesn't say much. Later, I feel a little ashamed of the way I have berated him. I don't ease up on him much though, we are getting so many new people out and many of them only work one hitch never to return. When I find out that he has been in the US Navy dive program, I give him a hard time about that too. I tell him how the commercial dive industry is very different from the Navy diving program.

I have worked with quite a few navy divers; some are good and some are not. I will hold my opinion of him until I get to know him better. I watch him on deck. He works on the deck just as hard as any other hand. He is courteous and he doesn't think he is better than anyone else – not even the greenest tenders. I decide that he will be an asset to our crew. I will help him any way I can. We end up working quite a bit together. After I get to know him, I feel bad about the shit I gave him for his tattoo. He goes into SAT shortly after that. We go on to work together on the Boa Deep C, the Crossmar Fourteen, and the Superior Performance.

* * *

While we were working on the Boa Deep C, we weathered quite a few storms. For me, none of them were as big as Hurricane Rita. Even though the Boa handled storms very well due to its size, it still rolled a little with the waves. Any kind of ship motion really affects crane operations. There were four hydraulic cranes on the Boa Deep C; a large one, a mid-size, and two smaller cranes. The large crane was located just aft of the moon pool on the Starboard side. The mid-size crane was located on the Starboard Aft corner of the deck. The other two smaller cranes were located just forward of the moon pool, but aft of the accommodation decks and bridge; one Starboard and the other on the Port side. They were operated by both the Canadians and the Norwegians.

The cranes were all equipped with Active Heave Compensation – which means the cables were let out and reeled in automatically with the wave action. This was a great feature to have when working with divers. It helped keep the loads in the water from moving up and down so much. That feature helped on deck some too, but didn't help with hanging loads swinging all over the place when working with them topside. The captain tried to keep the crane work to a minimum when the seas were rough. Sometimes, however, we had no choice; like when supplies came out on a supply boat. If the seas were really rough, the captain would make the supply boats wait, but if they weren't too bad, he would allow crane work. A good crane operator could work through mildly rough seas – especially if the deck crew was experienced and good at their job.

The guys on the deck crew of the Boa Deep C with us were from Nova Scotia and Labrador. They were very used to working in rough seas and seas that were much rougher than anything the Gulf of Mexico could throw at them. Most of the crane operators were used to working in rough seas also. We rarely had any issues. In fact, I can only think of one instance where things got out of control. Supplies had come out – including several eight-tubers of gas that we used for the SAT system and the divers. An "eight-tuber" is a rack of high-pressure tubes; like giant, extra-long propane tanks. The rack is thirty-seven feet long by eight feet wide and four feet high. Inside the frame are eight tubes, twenty inches in diameter and thirty-three feet long. The tubes are stacked four across and two high. We had six of those racks stored on a deck just forward of the moon pool and one level up from the main deck. We had the racks stacked three wide and two high. They fit together just like Conex boxes so we didn't have to worry about them sliding around. We usually only swapped them out when the racks were empty and we tried to only do one or two at a time. Once-in-a-while we would have to swap out three or four.

We had one eight-tube rack of pure Oxygen, a couple of pure Helium and the rest filled with different Heliox mixtures that we were using for system storage and diver breathing. The gas mixes varied with the different storage depths and diving depths. The LSTs on board were responsible for mixing and testing the gases we utilized. I started learning how to mix the gas shortly after I got on board the Boa. I really enjoyed the math and the actual mixing of the gases. For me, that was a really fun part of the job – figuring out what gas mixes were needed and then making those mixtures. Off on a tangent again, sorry.

Anyway, back to cranes, waves, rolling boats, and swinging loads. The two smaller cranes located midship were used mostly for putting the large Oceaneering ROVs in the drink and pulling them back out again. When we needed the eight-tubers transferred to and from the upper deck, though, we utilized one of the smaller cranes – usually the one on the Port side. The large crane near the moon pool was the crane used most often to offload supplies from the supply boats when they came out. Changing out eight-tubers was quite an involved process. We, meaning the LSTs, would have to prep the empty racks of eight-tubers for transfer by making sure they were, in fact, empty. We planned for this as we used the gas during normal operations. Then we would have to make sure all our gas lines were disconnected and removed from each rack to be off-loaded. We would also make sure none of our regulators were left on the gas valves. We would have to make sure the bridge had the proper serial numbers of the racks leaving the ship for their records. Finally, we would rig up a four-point sling to the rack and hook that into the crane. Normally we didn't have any help from the Boa's deck crew for this operation – other than the crane operator. We would utilize our own deck guys.

    The crane would lift the racks and set them on the aft deck, positioning them for transfer to the supply boat. The supply boats weren't big enough to have both the empties and the full racks on their back deck at the same time. We would have to shuffle the racks around on our ship instead. The full eight-tube racks would have to come off the supply boat before the empties could be loaded on it. Plus, we had to have the empties removed from our storage area before the full racks could be stacked back in place. The supply boats didn't like to hang around long. They preferred to get all the supplies unloaded and the garbage, empty storage containers, and empty gas racks loaded back on as quickly as possible so they could head back to the beach. Time is money and they didn't want to waste time hanging around us while we were shuffling gas racks. We moved the racks as fast as we safely could.

Most often the full racks would be loaded on the back deck of the Boa by the large crane and the empties would be moved straight from where we kept them to the supply boat by that same large crane. Later, we would move the full gas racks into position on the upper deck most often utilizing the smaller crane on the port side. That was the easiest and fastest way for us – usually. Not so much if the seas were rough.

If the crane operators thought the ship was rolling too much to safely move the eight-tubers around, we wouldn't do it. One time when the seas were a little choppy – not so rough as to keep the experienced crane operators from wanting to move the gas racks into place – we needed to move two full eight-tubers from the aft deck to the upper deck. The empties had been removed and loaded onto the supply boat the day before. The seas had been rough enough that the crane operators didn't want to move the eight-tubers off the aft deck. This day the seas had calmed enough that everybody was comfortable moving them around.

The SAT diving was going on as normal. It was in the morning, my friend Portland, was on shift as an LST. SoCal was supervising. I was on deck to help move the gas racks around. I would be positioning the eight-tubers up on the deck in their normal location. At that moment, our deck crew were on the main deck tying handling lines onto the corners of the racks. A couple of the Boa's deck crew were helping. The crane operator was one of the Norwegians, and not the most experienced on board. I don't think he had much experience operating a crane in anything other than calm seas.

At that time – towards the end of our stay on the Boa Deep C – we had a second Dive Control Conex for surface supplied diving located just forward of our SAT control Conex. There were two eight-tubers to move. The first one was rigged up and lifted into place. It was swinging around quite a bit, but the deck crew kept it under control. After I got the first one locked in place, the second rack was rigged up and lifted. As it was being raised and was about ten feet above the main deck and being swung over the moon pool, the ship rolled a little more than it had before. The gas-rack swung to the Starboard side of the ship. Then it swung like a pendulum back to the Port side. A more experienced crane operator would have set the rack down on the deck as soon as possible.

This crane operator didn't do that. At first, he raised the load a little more. It banged into the second deck handrailing near me. I jumped back and out of the way. At this point the crane operator started lowering the load. Too slowly though, and it was really swinging around now. It swung way to the Starboard, barely missing the railing around the moon pool. Most of the deck crew couldn't hold on to the handling lines anymore. Eight-tubers weigh about forty-thousand pounds making them very hard to control once they start swinging – especially for a couple deck hands hanging onto three-eighths-inch poly lines tied to the corners of the eight-tube racks. When this rack started swinging out of control all the deck hands ran for safety. The last thing anybody wanted was to get squished between that rack and anything else on deck.

By the time the rack started swinging back to the Port side only two deck hands were holding onto lines and really had no control of the rack at all. The rack smashed into the Surface Supplied Dive Control Conex barely missing SAT Dive Control. The eight-tuber crumpled up the forward end of the Surface Dive Control box – door and all – like it was made of aluminum foil. My friends were in SAT Control watching what was going on. I was on the upper deck and had a clear view into SAT control. SoCal was supervising – sitting at the dive control station in the front of the Conex and saw that rack swing towards his end of the Conex - his eyes about popped out of his head. Everything was happening so fast, I couldn't do anything about it besides stand back, watch, and hope nobody got smashed into. My friends had to stay in SAT Control, because Portland had to take care of the divers in the system and SoCal had to take care of the divers in the Bell. They were stuck inside the little metal box and I was hoping they weren't about to get squished like grapes.

After destroying the Surface Supplied Control Conex, the eight-tuber swung back to the Starboard side. The crane operator was trying to set it on the deck. As soon as the eight-tuber was clear of the moonpool the crane operator dropped it on the deck. It must have hit something going down, because there was a loud bang – like a cannon blast - and a huge release of compressed gas. All I saw was a huge jet-stream and cloud of what looked like steam where one of our tenders had been. Before I could think of anything, I saw our tender erupting out of the rapidly expanding ball of gas – a look of terror on his face. He got away from the explosion without any injury. I was happy for that. It all happened so fast I didn't have time to think anything about it until after it happened. I can only imagine what was going through the tender's mind when that rack dropped onto the deck and exploded with a blast of gas.

After the dust settled, we got a good look at the damage. Nobody got hurt, we were lucky in that respect. When the crane operator dropped the eight-tuber, it hit the railing around the moon pool and busted off one of the valves. We lost a whole tube of gas. The guard-rail on the Starboard side of the moon pool was all bent up. The Canadian deck crew assessed all the damage caused by the swinging rack of gas. Reports were made and filed. It was decided that we – the LSTs – should transfer the remaining gas in the damaged eight-tuber into the available space we had in our other gas storage units.

The crane operator who had been transferring the gas racks was replaced by a more experienced operator. Then the damaged rack was lifted up to the deck where the other racks were stored so we could transfer the gas. It took us about a day – both shifts - to transfer the gas from the damaged rack into our other racks. When that task was completed, the damaged rack was red-tagged and loaded back on a supply boat a couple days later. Our superintendent had contacted the gas supply company, explained the situation to them, and got another rack sent out to us right away. Even though there was some damage done to the ship and to Global's Dive Control Conex, the incident wasn't as bad as it could have been, because nobody got hurt. The crane operator chalked it up to a "learning experience."

* * *

After the first year-and-a-half on the Boa, I cut my working down to only six or seven months a year. That's still more hours of work than your normal forty-hour-per-week job. I got more time off than your normal job too. How does that work, you ask? Well, when we work offshore, we are working twelve hours a day, seven days a week. No time off. My chunks of off-time were four weeks at a time. It was nice to have a schedule with time off like that. It allowed me to travel with my wife all over the place. I did a lot of motorcycle riding during my time off too. I rode my bike all over the U.S.

For the most part, everybody on the Boa Deep C got along with each other very well. We all meshed and worked well together. Even our crew (Global Diving and Salvage) and Oceaneering's crew got along with each other very well. That is not always the case with competing dive companies. Perhaps it was because we were doing the diving and they were doing the ROV work; I don't know. All I do know is that it was great working on a job with such a positive atmosphere. Because we meshed so well, we were very efficient.

The Boa and associated crews were contracted to deconstruct all of Noble Energy's damaged oil rigs. It was forecast that would take two to three years. It did not. We finished up with the last of their rigs in March of two-thousand-and-seven. Noble Energy and the company they had contracted to complete the job, Wild Well Control, were very happy with the performance of everyone on the Boa Deep C. I was glad the client was happy with our work, but I was sad we finished the work so early. Since the job was finished, the contractor needed to find more work or remove all the equipment and gear off the ship. Everybody was hoping the contractor would find more work.

In April, Wild Well was hired by Chevron to deconstruct some of their damaged oil rigs. They have very strict safety policy requirements and it is pretty hard to get hired by them. Global Diving and Salvage and the whole set-up on the Boa had an impeccable safety record. Chevron liked that a lot. Chevron also really liked the quality and the efficiency of the work we did for Noble Energy. The Boa set-up was quite expensive, but I guess Chevron figured we were worth the high cost. We were told that Chevron had so many oil rigs to deconstruct that it looked like we might be working for them for the next five to seven years. That sounded like wishful thinking to me, but you never know.

I don't know how many oil rigs we were contracted to do for Chevron. I heard through the grapevine that the oil companies would contract a company to take down a few rigs and then renew the contract on an annual or bi-annual schedule. I suppose that was done so they could try to get the price down for the following contract. It was always a battle between the client and the contractor over money. The client wanted more for less and the contractor wanted the same – just from the opposite side. Anyway, in July of two-thousand-and-eight we finished the contract that our employer had made with Chevron.

Just as we were finishing up the last oil rig of that contract for Chevron, their vice president of the Gulf of Mexico operations visited the Boa Deep C. She held a meeting with all of us on the ship. She told us what a great job we had done. She went on about how efficient we were; how we had less accidents than any other contractor in the Gulf of Mexico; how we had saved Chevron so much money; how great we were to work with. Hollywood and I were sitting next to each other and were talking about how it sounded like we would be working for Chevron for several more years if they were this happy with us and the setup on the Boa Deep C.

After the V.P. of Chevron was done thanking everybody for their wonderful job, she went on to say "Unfortunately we won't be hiring this package anymore. It is just too expensive. We want the main contractor and the dive company to set up on a less expensive vessel and keep working for us."

Both Hollywood and I about fell out of our chairs – actually off the sofa. The meeting was being held in one of the rec rooms on the Boa and the seating was more relaxed. Needless to say, we were all stunned. It was hard for us to imagine that she could go on and on about how great the setup was, how efficient we were, and all that, just to finish up by saying we were too expensive. Everybody started wondering what would be next. The Gulf guys all figured they would continue doing the same sort of work for Global on a different rig. The northwest and west coast guys figured we would go back to doing the dam work and other infrastructure work that we had done before this hurricane work brought us back down to the Gulf of Mexico.

It was really sad to be leaving the Boa Deep C. I think Oceaneering got to stay on board – one of the Boa Deep C's main attributes was that it had ROVs on it. It didn't need to have a dive company on board to do most of the types of work it was designed and built to do. We had just been lucky to be on that nice of a boat for a while. I wasn't sure I would be returning to work in the Gulf of Mexico regularly if I wouldn't be working on something comparable to the Boa. I would just have to wait and see what my future held. The regular work and the good pay were quite a draw for me though. If the conditions weren't horrible, I would probably keep working in the GoM.

* * *

Shortly after we were told by Chevron that they wouldn't be contracting the Boa Deep C with us on it anymore, Global had a meeting for all their employees working on the Boa Deep C. In that meeting we were told that we would demobilize all our equipment from the Boa and put it on another vessel. I think Global was working on at least two other vessels in the Gulf of Mexico at this time. It took us a little under a week to get all our equipment off the Boa. Within a week we started setting it up on a barge owned by Crossmar. It was the Crossmar Seven and the only thing it had in common with the Boa Deep C was that it was floating in the Gulf of Mexico.

I didn't do a whole lot of the setup. I was on my four weeks off when the equipment removed from the Boa was put on the Crossmar. After my time off, I returned to help with running some of the gas lines. I did a lot of system testing after everything was put in place. Mostly I helped our SAT Tech from Gulf Breeze, Florida. After the system was set up on that vessel, which was a barge, not a ship, we went right back to work. Since it was a barge, it got anchored at the job site rather than using dynamic positioning.

The Crossmar Seven was not as convenient nor as comfortable as the Boa Deep C on many levels. It took a lot longer to get to the new job site because we were being pulled by tugs. When we got to the job site, the anchors had to be set. They were using a four-point anchor system – an anchor in each corner – but sometimes they set six or even eight anchors. Also, we couldn't work in water as deep as we could on the Boa. The worst thing, though, was dealing with the weather. *Now,* if a storm came blowing in or the seas got too rough, the barge couldn't just sail away. It would take several hours, maybe even a whole day, to pull up anchors and be towed out of the area by the tugs. After the storm passed, they would move us back in and reset the anchors; again, taking several hours to a day to complete.

I didn't really like life on the Crossmar. Sure, it was better than being on an old dive boat, or a supply boat with a dive station set up on it. The accommodations were much better than either of those scenarios, but it was horrible in comparison to the Boa Deep C. I had been spoiled. Not really, I mean, I knew I didn't like the normal living situations offshore. By this time, however, I had become used to the regular work schedule of this oil rig work. I figured as long as I could work a regular schedule like this I would, regardless of the living situations. Well, not really. If it got worse than the Crossmar, I would probably quit working in the Gulf again. If not for the Boa, I would not have kept working in the Gulf for so long as I had.

My accommodations on the Crossmar weren't horrible, really. I was in a berth with two sets of bunkbeds and a bathroom (shower, sink, and head) that was shared with the berth next to me. Since I was an LST, I only shared my room with the LST on the opposite shift. That meant that while I was off shift, I was the only one in my cabin, except when we didn't have any divers pressed in the system. Then we both would be in the cabin at the same time. The deck crew had four guys in each cabin – two from each shift. At least I had it better than they did.

There wasn't a steward crew that cleaned our rooms. We were responsible for that. I am a pretty clean guy, so that didn't bother me much. Most often the LST on the opposite shift was Portland. He was very clean also, so we had zero issues with cleanliness. The biggest change for me was that I had to change my own sheets. They still had a crew that did the laundry for us, so at least I didn't have to do that. To get our personal laundry done, we just left the dirty stuff in a laundry bag outside our cabin door. The laundry guys would collect it, then deliver it back to our cabin after it had been washed; usually the next day. They would even fold it for us; kind of.

The food. Now that was the biggest change; or the most impactful anyway. No more five-star chefs from Europe. Boo Hoo. I don't think the cooks on board were even chefs at all. They were more like line cooks. Now, don't get me wrong, some of them were very good. Others, though, were just like what I had experienced back in the eighties; offshore cooks that used a deep frier more than any other means of cooking. Fridays were horrible for me. I called it "Fried Fish Friday" and I rarely ate the prepared food on that day. I am not a big fish-eater in the first place. Battered fish swimming in tepid to cool vegetable oil is not very appetizing to me. I usually had salads or peanut butter and honey sandwiches on Fridays. The other days were hit and miss.

If I remember correctly, Tuesdays were usually Grilled Steak days. I love a good grilled steak, but if anybody could ruin one, it would be an offshore cook. The saddest part is that people in the south burn their beef when they grill it. I like my steaks rare; very rare – but it needs to be a good cut of good beef. I am slightly spoiled in that regard; living in Montana. We have good beef – range fed and raised Black Angus finished off with corn. Yumm. I don't know where they get the beef for offshore, but I am sure it is the cheapest they can find; probably comes from some overcrowded cattle factory like what they have in central Washington. Lord knows what they feed those animals and how many shots they get – hormones, antibodies, and all that kind of stuff. The cooks took those steaks and cooked them in the ovens first, then threw them on the grill, so they weren't really grilled anyway. You were lucky if you didn't get one that was cooked well done.

They did the same thing with the Swordfish and the Tuna steaks. I know they got good cuts of Tuna and Swordfish, because we helped transfer groceries when supplies came out. I saw the frozen Tuna and Swordfish. It could have been really good if they didn't overcook it. Sometimes the cooks' helpers would get the grill going and they would drown the charcoal in lighter fluid to get it to light easier. The problem with that was, that everything cooked on the grill tasted like it had been dipped in butane before being served.

The vegetables were mostly boiled, and boiled some more. I didn't have a great sense of smell – due to a past head injury from a motorcycle accident – so not a great sense of taste either. If I closed my eyes, I usually couldn't tell what type of vegetable I was eating; Carrots, Cauliflower, Broccoli, Green Beans; all were mushy and shapeless after going through the galley on the Crossmar. Fresh vegetables were usually pretty good, but they didn't last long. Same with the fruit. It was good the first couple days after it arrived, but after that not so much.

We had all the milk we wanted. I liked chocolate milk and there was usually plenty of Hershey's Chocolate Syrup, so I could have chocolate milk whenever I wanted it. Pop too - you know - Coke for you southerners. I liked Mountain Dew and drank that stuff by the case. That wasn't a problem on the Boa. When we moved to the Crossmar, however, there was no Mountain Dew. Their caterer didn't carry Pepsi products.

Mountain Dew is the only pop I liked. I used to drink Root Beer when I was a kid, but I've been drinking Mountain Dew since nineteen-seventy-one or two and nothing else. I don't like colas or any of the other stuff. For me it's Mountain Dew, Chocolate Milk, or Water. I don't even drink coffee; never have – not even when I was in the navy. I'm not Mormon or anything, just never got into the coffee habit.

Enough of us working on the Crossmar Seven must have said something about the lack of Mountain Dew, because after a couple hitches, we started getting cases of it on board. That was a huge relief for me because I had been bringing cases of Mountain Dew onboard myself. I couldn't carry enough for a normal hitch though – I normally drank about a case a day – that worked out to twenty-eight cases per hitch. I only felt comfortable carrying about five cases onto the crew boat with me. We were utilizing Crew Boats for the crew changes now, rather than helicopters like on the Boa Deep C, so there weren't really any weight or space limits on our baggage. Sometimes some of my fellow crew members would bring cases of the Dew for me when they came on board. I appreciated their support.

There was a lot of canned food on the Crossmar. They ordered Spam, Deviled Ham, Vienna Sausages, and other stuff like that by the case. If you liked any of that, you never had to worry about going hungry. I liked a Deviled Ham sandwich once-in-a-while. I love Spam, too, but not day after day when you are stuck offshore. Cookies. Lots and lots of cookies; chips too. The best, like Fig Newtons, Chips Ahoy, or the Nutter Butter Peanut Butter Cookies always disappeared with in the first couple days. I think some people would take whole bags to their rooms leaving the rest of us to do without. That bothered me a little, but I didn't really need the empty calories anyway.

It was easy to get up on the helideck on the Crossmar. That was a good place to exercise by walking or jogging around its perimeter. Occasionally, I would see one or two other guys up there, but not always. I tried to walk a couple miles every day on the Crossmar. I had a weird loop where I would walk around the top two decks and the helideck going up or down a staircase – called a ladder when it's on the outside of a boat or barge – whenever I encountered one. Since I was an LST I did a lot more sitting than I had when I was diving or tending. I figured I needed to keep some form of physical activity up so I wouldn't get fatter than I already was.

This SAT work was good for the paycheck. It was interesting too, but it was a little boring. For the topside crew, especially the LSTs, it was extremely repetitive. The most exciting thing for me was figuring out what breathing mixes we would be using. I only had to do that at the beginning of the jobs or if we changed the storage depth of the divers significantly enough that the breathing requirements would change. Usually at the beginning of the job, someone else had already figured out what gases we would be using, so I would just be verifying that the mixes were correct for the depth of diver storage and dive excursions. Excursions are what the actual dives were called and there is a certain allowable range of excursion depth for each storage depth. It was a lot of math, which I enjoyed doing. I missed the inshore diving though. One of the things I enjoyed most about inland dive work was that it was always different from one job to the other. Things would change sooner than later for me and many of the rest of us working with Global.

* * *

The first Christmas hitch I did on the Crossmar Seven, I wanted to cheer up the divers in the habitat. There would be six of them in the system on Christmas Eve and Christmas Day – four working and two decompressing. With the regular schedule I was working, I knew I would be offshore over the holidays. That made it easy for me to plan a little Christmas surprise for the SAT divers. I could buy all the supplies I would need before heading to the barge.

I went to Shopko and Target to buy six cheap felt stockings – a dollar apiece. I gathered up treats; Chocolate Santas, Maple Sugar Santas, Chocolate Christmas Bells, Snowmen, and Elves. I got Christmas-coloured M&Ms, Reeses Mini Peanut Butter Cups, and Hershey's Kisses. I also got six Matchbox cars and six different decks of card games – Old Maid, Crazy Eights, et al. I got six little books of crossword and sudoku puzzles. I got little Christmas character finger puppets. I also gathered up some Swag from Global and the other companies we were working with on the Crossmar. By the time I was done, the little stockings were filled to almost bursting.

I didn't let anybody on board know that I had these Christmas surprises with me. If people know about it, it's not a surprise! It was about two weeks until Christmas Day from when I first got on board. Portland shared my cabin, and was there when I wasn't, so I couldn't leave the stockings out. I had to keep them hidden in my locker and hope he didn't accidently open it up. We never kept our lockers locked – we trusted each other.

I was anxious for Christmas to arrive. I knew the guys would really appreciate the treats. Most of them were married and a at least three of them had children. It was hard for them to be offshore during the holidays. I wanted to help them have as merry a Christmas as possible offshore. The cooks always made a huge Holiday feast, so they would have good food. We were lucky on this hitch to have a cook who enjoyed baking. She made all sorts of Christmas goodies.

On Christmas Day, when I came on shift, I had the Betty make up a couple nice trays of Christmas cookies and treats from the galley. We pressed in the treats followed by the stockings – four in the main lock and two in the HRC. The stockings were all different colours, but they were stuffed with the same things. It didn't matter which diver got which stocking. When they opened up the medlock and found the stockings, they asked how to tell whose was whose. I told them it didn't make any difference; they were all the same.

They asked where the stockings came from. Of course, I said Santa Claus dropped them by for the divers. They all got a laugh out of that. They thanked me for sending the stockings in. They thanked me and the Betty for the plates of baked goodies. I passed their gratitude onto the cook.

One of the divers in SAT at the time was Duck Fart. When he got out of the chamber, a couple weeks later, he thanked me for the stocking full of Christmas gifts. He told me that had made his Christmas, because growing up, the stockings were always his favorite part of Christmas morning. That made me feel good and let me know that little effort on my part was well worth it.

* * *

We had to go through regular training and get recertified for many things every year or two; things like CPR, OSHA Ten, HUET, and others. I had been through the HUET (Helicopter Underwater Escape Training) class twice so far; at two different training centers in Louisiana. I was due again and it was to be done at a third and new training center. All the increase in offshore work due to the hurricanes had caused a huge influx of money to the training centers as well. This new training center Global was using had spent a lot of money on new buildings and new training equipment. The equipment was much better than what we had been trained on in the past.

This time I flew into New Orleans. I met a couple other Global guys at the airport. There was a limousine waiting to give us a ride to the hotel. Global put us up in a pretty nice hotel on Canal Street just a few blocks from Bourbon Street. It was not really a safe place to put a bunch of divers who like to drink a little. The hotel was fancy compared to what I usually stayed in, but Global had been putting us up here since NOLA had been opening back up. We were only a few blocks from Harrah's too. We were to meet a van out front of the hotel at seven in the morning. It would take us to the training center where we would go through the HUET class.

I had dinner at Mother's. I had been there with Gulf Breeze and Hollywood several times before. – it had been recommended by one of the Global crew. It was very good and not very expensive. I didn't want to get drunk or anything. They had dark beer, so I had a couple of those. After dinner, the beers, and a little chatter with a couple of the Global guys, I went back to the hotel and went to bed.

This new training center offered classes in all the certifications needed to work offshore – not the main jobs, but the stuff like CPR, OSHA, Water Safety, etc. I ended up taking quite a few classes from them over the next couple years. There were a lot of people there from lots of different companies. About six of us were there from Global out of thirty or so total students.

The HUET class was half classroom and half in a swimming pool. The classroom stuff was typical safety class stuff about helicopter etiquette and rules. They also explained how the in-water training would go and what we were to do. They wanted the experience to be as real as possible. In the pool session, we changed out of our street clothes and into swimming suits. They had us put coveralls on over our swimsuits so the clothing would be more realistic. They led us to the pool room. There was an elongated box with windows and doors in it that was a mock-up of a helicopter body. It was on a track system that went into the swimming pool. It had six standard helicopter seats with four-point seatbelts in it. Pretty cool. There were four assistants who would be in the pool in SCUBA gear to make sure we didn't drown.

Six of us climbed into the fake helicopter. We sat in the seats and buckled in just like we would in a real helicopter. The teachers explained the scenario. The helicopter body would slide down the track and flip upside down into the pool. The two people in the front seats would open their doors, undo their belts, then escape the pod. The four in the back would have to push out one window, undo our belts and escape through the window one at a time. The person facing the front on the right would be responsible for removing the window and be the first one out. We would do this several times so everybody would get to sit in each seat. Okay, no problem – sounds like fun to me.

I was sitting on the left; facing forward. The instructors closed the doors and tapped on the shell. That meant we were ready to go. The shell lurched forward and hit the water. The back flipped up and we turned upside down into the water. It was like a carnival ride. Water flowed into the shell and filled it up – with us strapped into the seats and hanging upside down. It was time for the guy sitting to my right to push open the window. He was struggling, so the person facing him gave him a hand pushing out the window. Then the guy couldn't get his belt undone. The two people facing back escaped through the open window. I was watching this guy trying to get his belt undone. When I could see he wasn't going to get it, I unbuckled it for him. I guided him towards the window, because he was obviously becoming disoriented. He went out the window, kicking me in the head as he escaped. I unbuckled and swam out the open window. Two SCUBA divers were by the opening and followed me to the surface.

When we all got out of the water, the SCUBA divers asked if I was okay. I told them I was. They said they hadn't seen anyone stay under as long as I had without becoming flustered and dis-oriented. I told them I was fine, and very comfortable under the water. I also told them I hadn't stayed under so long by choice, it was because the person next to me was having troubles with the window and their buckle. That particular student didn't want to get back in the water at all; he quit the class. I, and the rest of us, went back in the water five more times and passed the class.

I went to two more classes at the same place on Friday and Saturday. At that point, I had all the documentation needed to join the crew on the barge offshore. I went out with the other Global personnel for dinner and drinks Saturday night. Two of the guys went to Harrah's after dinner. The other four of us ended up barhopping on Bourbon Street. Hollywood and I were drinking Irish Car Bombs. I love those. I probably drank more than I should have, but we didn't get out of hand.

Sunday morning a van picked us up outside the hotel. I was there, bright-eyed, bushy-tailed, and ready to go. Everybody else was ready to go too. A couple of the guys were pretty blurry-eyed and obviously hungover. That was okay, though, because we had an almost two-hour van ride to Fourchon where we would get on a helicopter that would take us out to the barge.

* * *

When we are utilizing SAT, the system needs to be kept clean. The warm, moist environment is a perfect breeding ground for bacteria and fungus. Because of that, the systems need to be routinely cleaned. It was Global's policy to do that every ninety days. In order to clean the system, it needed to be brought to the surface – depressurized. Divers were in the system, so we would have to decompress them out on the appropriate schedule. Global management tried to schedule the cleanings during crew changes in order to disrupt the work as little as possible. Our SAT Techs would utilize this time to calibrate, replace, or repair – as needed – any equipment on the system requiring maintenance.

One hitch, when Oklahoma was in SAT, the system had to be surfaced for its ninety-day cleaning. On our crews, the divers were required to help with the cleaning of the inside of the system. The deck plates had to be pulled up so the bilge could be cleaned. The mattresses are pulled out, cleaned, and aired out. All the walls are scrubbed down. The bathroom area is given an in-depth cleaning. Once all that was done, they were not required to work on the outside of the system. Hopefully, all the outside work would be completed about the same time as the inside anyway. This time, however, there were some other repairs to be made; some on the bell itself.

Oklahoma was not one to sit around while other crew members were working. He always volunteered to help with the outside cleaning and repairs. Our SAT tech at the time was Gulf Breeze. He preferred help from experienced workers over green tenders, so he was happy to have Oklahoma's help. Oklahoma wasn't afraid to jump right in and do the dirtiest work either. He would crawl under the chambers to grab trash, dead fish, dead birds, bugs, or whatever.

This time the bell required more extensive work than usual. Some of the tubing on the top of the bell needed replacing. Other gages had to be removed for inspection and service. The umbilical had to be removed so Gulf Breeze could test the end connections. Some of the zincs needed replacing as well. Oklahoma jumped right up there to help. One of the bolts he needed to remove was stuck, so Gulf Breeze gave him some penetrating oil to put on the threads. Next, he was handed an impact wrench to remove the stubborn bolt. This impact wrench had a side handle on it to help steady it when removing bolts. While Oklahoma was using it, his hand slipped off the side handle and the handle smacked his wrist – fracturing it, but he didn't know that at the time.

He might have said ouch or damn, when it happened, but I didn't hear him. I did see the wrench spin and smack his wrist. He didn't say anything or complain about it to anybody. Both Gulf Breeze and I asked him if he was okay. Of course, he said he was fine – "nothing to see here!" He kept on working and removed the stubborn bolt. He got all the equipment removed and replaced that Gulf Breeze wanted taken care of. After that, he climbed down off the bell and went to lunch.

A little later, several of us noticed him guarding his wrist and forearm when he was doing other tasks. We suggested that he go into the medic and have it looked at. He didn't want to lose any work time, so he stated that he didn't need to. It took several of us a fair bit of deliberating to convince him to have his arm checked out by the on-board medic.

When he came back out on deck, his wrist was wrapped up. The medic told him that it appeared to be fractured and he should get into the beach, get it x-rayed and go from there. Oklahoma was sent to the beach on a helicopter. We were told later that he did have a hairline fracture or small fracture of his wrist or forearm. He was off work for a little bit, but when he came back, he was right back to his old, happy self; working as hard as ever with no complaining.

* * *

In two-thousand-and-eight Barack Obama was elected president of the United States of America. He took office the following January. Remember what I said about Democrats being good for infrastructure work and Republicans being good for Oil Field work? Well, the Obama administration stopped as much of the oil field work as they could. The ten-year moratorium on the removal of all the damaged oil rigs in the Gulf waters was taken away. Now there was no target time for the oil companies to deconstruct the damaged rigs *and* they lost their government funding for that work.

What that meant for us was that all the work we thought we were going to have for the next five or six years was now gone. The rigs still needed to be taken down; it's just now it was on the oil companies' nickel without any government aid. So, of course, the urgency to remove the rigs went away. During the aftermath of the hurricanes, Global had set up four SAT systems and had them working as much as they could. I had worked on the refurbishing of a couple of the systems. Now the work that had been planned for two of the systems went away.

All of a sudden, Global had way more employees than they had work for. To make matters worse, I think their contract with Crossmar ran out in early two-thousand-and-nine. I don't remember for sure when Global moved off of the Crossmar Seven, but my last hitch on that barge ended the second week of April two-thousand-and-nine. There was still some work though and Global was doing their best to work as much as they could, keeping as many of their employees working as possible.

Towards the end of May I was sent to the Rem Clough. That was a ship more like the Boa Deep C. Some of our guys thought it was nicer than the Boa, and others didn't. It seemed smaller to me. I didn't think it was quite as nice as the Boa. I only did a partial hitch as an LST on that ship. In fact, I was brought out to replace an LST who had been taken off the job for a little while, so only did a couple weeks on that ship. When Global had been hired to put their system on the Rem Clough, I had wanted to get on it, but they already had their full crew to run that system. Besides, I was working on the Crossmar Seven.

Everybody that is not an LST thinks the LST job is super easy. It looks like it compared to other jobs on a SAT system. I mean the LST sits down for most of the job, just looking at gages and analyzers. Sure, the LST has to log the readings once an hour and answer the radio when the divers in the system call. Oh, they have to check the gas in the storage systems once-in-awhile too, but really, don't they just sit around for most of their job? When you enter SAT control the LST is often seen reading a book, working on crossword puzzles, or lately, playing on their laptop computers. It appears they spend way more time doing that kind of stuff than actually working. Of course, that is not really true. The LST must closely monitor all the pressures and gas percentages on the whole system at all times as well as take care of all the needs of the divers in the system.

The LST position was another job that needed lots of new people after Hurricanes Ivan, Katrina, and Rita hit. Of course, this meant that people became LSTs with less training and experience than they used to need for the job. People would take the position, not realizing the importance of the job, then end up not taking it as seriously as they should have. I think it is because of this that I was sent to the Rem Clough. I replaced a newly certified LST that had allowed the habitat system pressure to slide up seventy-some feet while he was on watch.

I wasn't on board and certainly not at that LST station when it happened, so I don't know any of the actual details. I only know what everybody told me about it after I got on board. I didn't know a lot of the people working on this system either, many of them were not regular Global hands. What I was told, was that the storage depth of the system was one hundred-seventy feet. When the LST went to log his hourly readings, the system "was suddenly under one hundred feet." How that had happened nobody knew. The LST swore up and down that he had been watching the gages like he was supposed to be. According to him there must be a leak in the system somewhere. One was never found from what I was told.

My personal opinion is that the LST was playing on his computer and not paying attention to the gages. Every time a hatch is opened or the toilets are flushed in the system, the pressure drops a little. Even if the system is leak-free, with those actions the system depressurizes slowly. The LST is supposed to add gas to make up for those losses and that has to be done several times an hour. Like I said I wasn't there, so I don't know what really happened, but a seventy-some foot difference between calculated required storage depth and actual system depth is huge.

One of the divers in the SAT system on the Rem Clough when this happened was Illinois. He is a good friend of mine and he told me what he experienced. He told me there wasn't any rapid depressurization – especially one that would have resulted in a seventy-foot loss in less than an hour. He did say that he could feel the depressurization in his ears and had mentioned something about it to the LST, who told him that everything was fine. Obviously, it wasn't. Even Illinois doesn't know how long the system was not at its proper storage depth. He and his bell partner were on their break and sleeping. Anyway, because of this, that LST was sent home for a while and I was sent out to finish his hitch.

While I was on board, we – the other LST (Sante Fe) and the SAT Techs – tested the system and searched for any leaks. We checked all the valves and O-rings and other seals. We didn't find anything wrong. I never read any incident reports and certainly didn't write any on that incident, so I don't know what the final determination was. As I said before, I think it was due to LST inattentiveness. I'm just glad that nobody got injured or suffered any form of Hyperbaric Trauma from it. I think that was the last time that Illinois went into SAT, but you'd have to ask him to be sure.

At the end of that short little hitch, I went home for my time off. I spent a fair share of the summer working with Gulf Breeze, Portland, Santa Fe, and a couple other guys refurbishing one of Global's SAT systems in a shop on the West Bank of New Orleans. When I went back offshore in September, the SAT system I was assigned to was set up on a different barge – no longer the Crossmar Seven, we were now on the Superior Performance.

* * *

The Superior Performance was another Barge – like the Crossmar Seven, but smaller. The accommodations were smaller, but again I shared my cabin with the Night Shift LST. Our bathroom was shared with the cabin next to us which had tenders in it – again two on each shift. The Galley was smaller and that was okay because the full complement of people on board was less than what had been on the Crossmar Seven. Our SAT system was the same size so it had to be set up a little more compactly than it had been. We also had a Surface Supplied Dive Control Conex on board because the customer had some shallow projects for us to do in the future. This set-up was closer to the set-ups that had caused me to leave the gulf back in the eighties. It seemed that with each new move, the living conditions were getting worse and worse. Where would it end, I wondered. How long would I remain working in the Gulf? How bad would the conditions have to be before I refused to work on the barges anymore? I wasn't sure, but the conditions were no-where near as nice as they had been on the Boa. The regular work schedule and regular pay was still nice though.

Almost all the crew that was assigned to this SAT system when it was on the Crossmar remained with it when it was transferred to the Superior Performance. I was on Day Shift as usual. The Night Shift LST was my friend Portland. The dive superintendent was the same also – he was the same superintendent who had yelled at me on my first hitch as a Betty on the Boa Deep C several years earlier. By now we were friends and got along well with each other. Gulf Breeze was the SAT Tech on Days. Some people thought he was a little hard to get along with, but I got along with him quite well. He was one of the best SAT Techs I ever worked with. He had worked for CAL-DIVE decades ago and was very experienced. He had very little patience for tenders new to the industry, which was understandable. We had seen tenders who didn't know the difference between a Crescent wrench and a pipe wrench, or couldn't tell a hammer from a screwdriver. I kid you not. New guys had to prove themselves to Gulf Breeze before he would give them the time of day. If they valued their lives, they wouldn't dare touch any of his tools without his express permission. Most of the dive support crew had come with us as well. We did get new guys regularly though. Most of the divers were the same too. Sometimes we would get different divers, but not often. Crews that knew each other and worked well with each other kept spirits up and usually the work went smoother. Once-in-a-while there would be personality clashes, but not often.

    The Performance did have a larger capacity crane on it than what was on the Crossmar Seven. I think the crane was rated at Eight Hundred Metric Tons – It was HUGE! The rigging we were using was gigantic also. The shackles we were using were over six feet long and four feet wide. The shackle pin alone weighed over a hundred pounds. We took a picture of Portland standing inside one of the shackles – he was a smaller guy and could stand on the inside of the crown and not hit his head on the pin. We all got a good laugh out of that.

The large capacity crane and rigging allowed the damaged rigs to be deconstructed with less demolition by the divers. Optimally, the divers would cut off the Topside decks as one unit that would be hauled away by a barge. Then they would cut the jacket legs down by the pilings so the whole Jacket assembly could be removed as a unit and hauled away. After that, the divers would kill the well if required, and take care of the piling stubs as designated by the customer. The actual demolition of the rigs would take place at a salvage yard on the beach. That was much more cost effective than having a dive crew do all the demolition and deconstruction underwater.

*   *   *

We didn't get helicopter rides out to the Superior Performance. It was much less expensive for the contractor to handle crew changes with a Crew Boat. Most often the crew changes were coordinated with supply runs, and handled by a Supply Boat that had a dining area large enough to handle the crew change. Typically, there was enough seating for forty or fifty people. There was usually a big screen T.V. with a VHS player - or more often these days, a DVD player - in the dining area also. All our personal gear was stowed on the back deck in a large basket. If we were lucky, we would have an enclosed box for it – that happened less than half the time though. Water often splashed over the back deck and it rained a lot of the times too. Because of that it was nice to have an enclosed box for our gear.

Boarding and deboarding the boat was a lot different than getting on a helicopter too. At the beach, we used a gangway to get on and off the boat. All our personal gear had to be hand carried onboard. Transfers between the crew boat and the barge were made with the use of a Billy Pugh. A Billy Pugh. Ha! What memories! I hadn't been on a Billy Pugh since my first time working in the Gulf for American Oilfield Divers back in eighty-six and eighty-seven. The Katrina Babies had never had to use Billy Pughs and most didn't like them - they had been spoiled by the helicopter crew changes.

What is a Billy Pugh you ask? Well, it is kind of like a Man Basket – but not really. It is more of a Cargo Net for people and small baggage. The original ones consisted of two disks; a large one about six feet in diameter with yellow padding around the edge on the bottom and another smaller disk about two feet in diameter, also padded around the edge on the top. The two disks were connected by rope webbing that was about seven feet high – like what is on tall ships to climb the masts. You know - what the pirates are always climbing up and down on in the movies. There is an eye on the top disk where a crane wire can be shackled in. There is no vertical support between the two disks. If the crane wire was completely slack the top disk would rest on the bottom disk.

When transferring personnel with the Billy Pugh, the crane operator from the barge would hang the Billy Pugh over the back deck of the supply boat and set the bottom disk on the deck. The rolling and heaving of the boat in the seas required that the crane operator keep enough slack in the wire that the Billy Pugh wouldn't jump up off the deck, but not so much slack that the upper disk would hit the bottom disk or a crew member trying to climb on to the Billy Pugh. Loading onto a Billy Pugh was a matter of timing with only seconds to spare. Normally four crew members would ride it at one time, sometimes only two. It had to be balanced since it wasn't a rigid basket. As soon as it was fully loaded, the crane operator would come up on the load and swing it out away from the supply boat over the seawater and onto the barge. At that point the personnel would step off and the luggage would be removed. Crew members going back to the beach would then climb onto the Billy Pugh and transfer to the supply boat.

In bad weather or strong seas, it could be quite an adventure getting on and off. The supply boat would be bobbing up and down – the higher the seas, the more movement on the back deck. That gave the crane operators less time to safely come up and down on the Billy Pugh. That meant that we – the crew members – had less time to climb on. This is when your timing really comes into play. All four of us getting on the Billy Pugh would have to synchronize our actions. We would put one foot on the bottom disk, grab onto the rope web, and push off the deck with our other foot as the crane came up on the load. We would be swooped off the deck and swung out over the seawater – hanging on for dear life. The crane operator would then gently (hopefully) swing us around to the landing spot on the barge. Since the crane doing the lifting was on the barge, we weren't bothered by the seas during off-loading. Of course, the crew members going back to the beach had it easy climbing onto the Billy Pugh. When they were off-loading onto the crew boat, though, they would need to let go and clear themselves quickly.

We always wore life jackets when making those transfers. We weren't secured to the Billy Pugh by any means other than our death grip on the rope web. The transfers could be pretty hairy – especially if it was dark, windy, rainy and in rough seas. Those were most common in the late fall and winter, sometimes into spring. On nice sunny days with calm seas, though, the transfers were not scary. Some people were always scared using the Billy Pugh, no matter the conditions. Others – like me – loved using it, especially in inclement weather. It was another one of those offshore experiences that made me feel like a real Salty Dog! Arrgghh! Ask a Pirate what their favorite letter is and the response will be "Ye'd think it be R, but me first love is the C!" Haha. Sorry, I couldn't resist. Smirks.

Newer Billy Pughs have a seven-foot post in between the two disks now. Those are much safer than the older ones because the rig is in its full upright position no matter how much slack is in the crane wire. Loading can be much more relaxed with this new type. If the seas are rough, the crane operator still needs to come up quickly so the load doesn't bounce on the deck – that would be bad for the passengers. Some companies even use real man baskets – fully enclosed and rigid cages. I have never used one offshore and I am not sure I would want to be trapped in a cage while being transferred ship to ship – or ship to barge - over the open sea. If the crane wire parted you might not be able to get out in time. I imagine in the future the crew transfers might be made in fully encapsulated, buoyant pods – like offshore lifeboats – all in the name of safety. Big Smile.

* * *

Things were changing a little in the dive industry again. Or maybe not. It seems that "the more things change, the more they stay the same." What I noticed was that a lot of the people who had gotten into the dive industry during the Katrina surge were leaving the industry. Why? Well, several reasons I could see. There was less work for one, the tender pay declined a little for another. Companies weren't offering to pay for dive school or buy hats for the crew who stayed on for two years either. The helicopter rides offshore went away too. Most companies went back to the crew boats for crew turn-overs. Basically, there was less money and less comfort than what a lot of the new kids were used to. So, they left.

Dive schools were still pumping out hundreds of new wannabe divers every few months. Most of them had heard all the stories of high pay, exciting jobs, and lots of travel. Many of them had friends or acquaintances who had done pretty well for a few years right after the Katrina and Rita mess. They all wanted a piece of the pie, no matter how imaginary it was. Of course, that also brought in older guys who really had no business trying to start a career in diving. Honestly, I don't know what some of these people think. Maybe it's just me turning into a grumpy old man, I don't know.

We had a new tender show up on the barge. He was in his mid-forties and had graduated dive school just a couple months previously. Coming out to a SAT barge, he was to work as the SAT Betty. Naturally, he thought that job was beneath him. He told everybody how much experience he had in life and in other jobs. According to him it only made sense that he be put in a position of more responsibility and authority. I told him that, like everybody else, he had to start at the bottom and work his way up. I also told him he was too old to try to start a career in diving. He couldn't keep up with the younger crew members. If he couldn't keep up on deck, how was he going to keep up in the water?

I tried to tell him how important the Betty was, but he didn't see it that way. So many people just don't realize how important the Betty's job is. That always irked me. The Betty is directly responsible for the well-being and good moods of the divers in SAT. They prepare the food, take care of all the laundry – bedding, dive wear, and surface clothing, and all the diver's gear. If the Betty is not doing a good job, it affects the attitudes and well-being of the divers. After a few days, the divers can tell who their Betty is just by the way their food is presented and their laundry is done. They can tell if their Betty really hates the work. Sometimes divers like to agitate the Betty who is not doing a good job or has a bad attitude about the job.

On this project we had two teams of two divers in SAT at any one time. The working depth was around three-hundred feet. That meant when we swapped out a dive team, there would be six divers in the habitat; four in the main lock working, and two in the HRC decompressing. At this depth it took about four days to decompress. Often, when a Betty is having issues with the job. It is the team in the HRC who gets the worst of it. On top of that, four days of decompression in a little chamber can get extremely boring.

So, here we are on a barge in the middle of the Gulf of Mexico. There are four divers in the main chamber working a twelve-on-twelve-off work schedule. Two other divers are in the HRC decompressing from three hundred feet. I am the LST and my Betty is a guy who is as green as green can be, but because of his age thinks he is above the job. He also doesn't have a great sense of humor. I don't know if that's in his character or if it was brought on because his new job hasn't met his expectations. The two divers decompressing are my friends, Hollywood and Duck Fart. They have been working together for a long time and have been Bell partners for quite a while. They make a great team. They are both practical jokers too – like many divers.

After the second day of decompression, they'd had about enough of the aged Betty's attitude. They regularly had issues with their food. Their laundry had gotten lost more than a couple times. I tried to keep the peace. There is only so much I could do though. I don't know whose idea it was, but when the Betty went to get dirty laundry out of the HRC med-lock, he found a couple turds rolled up in a t-shirt. Of course, he came screaming to me that he was being mistreated by the divers. Oh, no! That's the first time that has ever happened! Eyes rolling to the top of my head.

He told me that he'd had enough of this job. He didn't feel appreciated and now he felt disrespected on top of it. Didn't anybody here realize that he deserved more respect and a more important job. Oh. My. Gawd! Not this again. Anyway, I told him I would talk to the divers about the incident. I also told him that if he did a good job as a Betty, he would move to the position of a regular deckhand when a crew member with less experience came out. He was not happy with that and told me he wanted to quit. He demanded that either he be moved off the Betty job right now or he wanted to go home. I told him, I could easily send him home and get a replacement for him. I also told him if he wanted a day or two to calm down and think about what he really wanted, that might be for the best.

I called Hollywood and Duck Fart on the radio to see what their deal was. After I explained what I had been told, they burst out laughing. I told them poop was for the toilet and not to be sent out the med-lock. I asked them if they didn't realize what a sanitation hazard it was to send human waste through the same lock that their food went through. They were laughing uncontrollably. Finally, Duck Fart explained to me that it wasn't poop they had sent out. Rather it was a couple of warm, half-melted, ooey-gooey, chocolatey Babe Ruth candy bars they had wrapped in the t-shirt. Then they burst out laughing again. Very funny guys.

I knew, but asked them anyway, why they had done that. Didn't they realize this guy was having a tough enough time being the Betty. They told me they were tired of not being taken care of properly. They told me they had sent notes out trying to explain the issues in hopes of getting them resolved. After days of no improvement, they had decided to harass this guy a little. They were hoping he might wake up and take his job more seriously. I asked if their notes were rude or demeaning in any way. I was assured that the notes were respectful. I believed them because I knew them well. We had worked together for years on many different projects with several different companies.

I called the Betty into the dive shack. I told him the poop wasn't poop, but Baby Ruth candy bars instead. I asked him if he had received notes from the divers and if so, could I see them. I tried to tell him that the divers were just blowing off steam and trying to have a laugh. They didn't have many ways to release any frustration while locked inside the habitat. Maybe he could try to be a little more understanding of their situation. He told me he had thrown all the notes away, but they had not been disrespectful. He also told me that the other deck crew had discovered the poop was really just candy bars, but he didn't appreciate that kind of humor. Okay, then. Maybe we can put this behind us and just do our jobs. He assured me he would try.

This guy had more issues than just being a Betty. He didn't get along well with the rest of the dive crew. He was always trying to boss them around even though he was never the deck foreman. He didn't do well with the offshore lifestyle either. After a couple more hitches, I never saw him again; not even on inland jobs. Maybe he realized he wasn't cut out for the dive industry.

* * *

One of the hitches I worked was over the Easter weekend. I was working a schedule of four weeks on, four weeks off - more or less - so I could plan for it. I knew life inside the habitat during SAT wasn't much fun for the guys. Most of them were friends of mine that I worked with on other dive jobs. I always tried to find ways to make life inside more enjoyable, or at least break up the monotony. Before I went offshore, I went Easter shopping. I started out with plastic bags decorated for Easter that I could fill with treats. I bought chocolate eggs, Cadbury Crème Eggs, and plastic eggs that I could put treats in. I bought six small chocolate Easter bunnies. I bought Easter colored M&Ms, jellybeans, Rice Krispie treats, and of course Peeps – both bunnies and chicks in bright colors.

I kept all this stuff packed away so nobody would see it. I didn't want anyone to ruin my surprise. Easter was just a week after I got on the barge, so it wasn't difficult to keep my secret. I worked the day shift – starting at noon – so I came on shift right at the noon meal. That would be a perfect time to send the Easter bags down to the divers. I had the bags prepared before I went on shift, so I could press them in right away.

Every bag contained an Easter bunny, a couple Cadbury Crème Eggs, a bag of Easter-colored M&Ms, Rice Krispie treats, and four of the plastic eggs – two filled with chocolate eggs and jellybeans; the other two had a Peep-each in them. You know, one Peep bunny and one Peep chick. I sent them down as soon as I got on shift. I didn't tell anyone who they were from. After pressing the bags into the med-lock, I went up to the LST station and relieved the night shift LST.

Shortly thereafter the divers asked who had sent the Easter bags in. I told them I didn't know what they were talking about, but maybe it was the Easter Bunny. Haha! They all got a good laugh and thanked me for the treats. I told them I hoped they enjoyed them and would have as happy an Easter as possible.

They were enjoying the chocolates. A couple of the guys really loved the Cadbury Crème Eggs. The Rice Krispie treats were a favorite of theirs. None of them said anything about the Peeps, and I didn't ask. I thought that was a little strange, though, because Peeps are my son's favorite Easter treat and I knew several of the divers like Peeps too.

We had the divers stored at three-hundred-and-fifty feet. That meant it took just over four full days to decompress the team in the HRC. They had started their decompression on the Saturday evening before Easter Sunday and finally reached the surface on Thursday morning. While I was giving them their neuros, they were laughing and talking about the Easter treats. Then they showed me two sparkly, hard little clumps of stickiness about the size of a peanut M&M. "What are these?" they asked me. I looked at them, responded that I had no idea and asked where they found them. They told me they were inside the plastic eggs I had sent. What!? I didn't send anything like that.

I told them I had sent Peeps. No Peeps had survived the compression. I hadn't even thought about them being squished by the pressure. Peeps are made of puffed-up marshmallow coated in sugar; mostly air. The sugar coating on top of the skin of the Peeps must have sealed the Peeps and not let any gas inside. When they were pressurized, all the air was compressed and the Peeps were mushed into hard little sparkly blobs. We all got a good laugh out of that. One of them asked if I had any Peeps that didn't get sent down. I had a few and gave them to him. He smiled and thanked me for them. They were his favorite Easter treat.

I was usually pretty good about not pressing items into SAT that would get squished by the pressure. Bags of chips must be opened so the chips don't arrive as a flat bag of crumbs. All containers – ketchup, mustard, etcetera – are sent down open so gas can get in and they won't implode. Boiled eggs are sent in already peeled; and so on. I had not even considered that Peeps would suffer the effects of compression. We all know now, though, that Peeps won't survive the trip. The guys still enjoyed the Easter treats even without the Peeps.

* * *

Dam It - Not Again!

The summer of two-thousand-ten Global was awarded a job at Cheesman Dam on the South Platte River just west of Castle Rock, Colorado. This job had been going on for about a month before I went on it. It was going to be a long enough job that Global was going to rotate crews in and out just like an off-shore job. I was not involved in the set-up nor was I on the first four-week hitch. I was with the second wave of crew going in. It was all up and running by the time I got there in August.

It was a SAT job because the working depth was two-hundred-and-twenty feet. There was a lot of work to do so it would be much less expensive to put the divers in SAT rather than dive them surface supplied. The interesting thing about diving SAT in the mountains is that with the increase in elevation, the atmospheric pressure lessens – that's why I always had to use Altitude Adjustment Tables for decompression when working in Montana and Idaho. I was used to this and familiar with the way the analyzers read the gas percentages differently. All the guys whose dive careers had developed at Sea Level never even thought about the differences in Atmospheric Pressure at different altitudes. The Cheesman pond surface elevation is six-thousand-eight-hundred-and-forty-two feet above sea level. Also decompressing SAT divers is completely different than decompressing Surface Supplied Divers. I could get into all the technical stuff with you, but you would probably be bored to tears and quit reading. Maybe you'd throw the book in the garbage because there's too much science and math involved and it makes you crazy. Or, if you're like me, you'd really get into it – for those of you like that, you can go elsewhere for that info – or talk to me. I love that stuff.

Anyway. the lack of familiarity of working at higher altitudes caused some issues. The cause of all the main issues stemmed from the fact that a SAT system is a closed system. All the living spaces, gas storage bottles, and gas lines are under pressure that is *NOT* altered by the altitude. All the analyzers, however, are not part of that closed system. The gas from the system is vented through a tube or hose to the analyzing equipment which is open to the outside atmosphere – less pressure. Gas expands at a lower pressure so analyzers calibrated for sea level will not read the correct gas percentages at higher altitudes.

The sad thing is, most of the analyzers used can't be calibrated to read the correct percentages – at least back then. You have to use a conversion table. Another sad thing is that – at the time we were doing the job – none of the manufacturers had any conversion tables for their analyzers. The need for them just wasn't there. I mean who dives SAT in lakes and rivers anyway? Everybody knows SAT is only done in the oceans. That's not true though. Oceaneering did a SAT job in Lake Shasta years ago – in the late nineties. Blanchard. Kalispel, and I think the Greek all worked on that job. I wanted to, but by the time I had heard about it they were all crewed up. I wasn't a real LST then either. I am sure there were other SAT jobs at higher altitudes, I just haven't heard of them – they weren't very common.

Back to the analyzers reading gas percentages at higher altitudes. There was a formula for figuring the conversion. You had to look for it though, the analyzer manufacturers didn't supply that formula with their analyzers. During the set-up of the job, a couple guys – the Greek and one of the LSTs who had trained me - mentioned something about the difference in atmospheric pressure affecting the analyzers, but they were assured by the superintendents and a couple other LSTs that the effect would be negligible. They were told there was nothing to be concerned about. Think about it; we're talking about a difference of only three pounds per square inch – how much could that affect the readings? You are aware that even at sea level atmospheric pressure changes with the weather – you know, high-pressure systems and low-pressure systems – we don't need any conversions for those changes in the atmospheric pressures. Or do we?

Well, let me get a little technical here for just a minute. A very strong high-pressure system can add about half a pound per square inch to the atmospheric pressure at sea level. Conversely, a very strong Low-Pressure system can lower atmospheric pressure at sea level by one-and-a-third pounds per square inch. That sounds like a fair amount, but those are extremes. Normal weather systems usually cause changes in pressure about half that or less. This means at sea level the analyzers don't really need any conversions during changing weather patterns. Well, that's a good thing – what a pain it would be if we had to use conversion tables every time a storm blew in.

A difference of three pounds per square inch, however, makes a substantial difference in how the analyzer reads the gas percentages. The easiest way to envision what is going on is this: imagine a balloon filled with air. The analyzer is designed to read the percentage of a gas in that balloon and it is calibrated to read that same volume of air all the time. Say the balloon's volume is set at one cubic inch and the analyzer effectively counts the number of gas molecules in that cubic inch. Now, let's bring that cubic inch balloon up the mountain. That balloon expands – let's say it doubles in size to two cubic inches. We haven't added any molecules of gas; the gas just expanded – same number of molecules in twice the space. The analyzer is calibrated to read only one cubic inch. What does that mean? It means that the gas analyzer reads a one cubic inch sample and at the top of the mountain there are only half the number of molecules in that cubic inch, so the analyzer displays a lower percentage of gas than what is really there. If it used to show ten percent Oxygen at sea level, it now shows five percent Oxygen at the top of the mountain. The balloon still has the same ten percent in it though. See the issue now?

How this plays into the SAT diving operations is that at two-hundred feet, we ran the divers on an eleven percent oxygen/eighty-nine percent Helium mixture. At the Cheesman reservoir the analyzers read that mix as eight-point-five percent. That didn't cause a problem for the divers when they were working, because they were breathing gas that came pre-mixed at eleven percent – no issues. The issue was the atmosphere of the chamber where all the divers were living. At eleven percent oxygen – what the divers should be breathing – the analyzers showed eight-and-a-half percent. So, the LSTs brought the oxygen up to what they thought was eleven percent but was actually fourteen-point-three percent. The highest percentage gas they should have been breathing at that depth is thirteen percent. The divers were spending the majority of the time in the living chambers breathing *way* too much oxygen. I don't want to get into too much of the formulas and math and stuff – probably already have (sorry) – but what that meant is that the divers were breathing an amount of oxygen equal to breathing more than a hundred percent on the surface. Effectively too much oxygen was being absorbed into their bodies and they were suffering from Oxygen Toxicity.

The divers had been living in this situation for four weeks by the time I got to the job site. The LSTs had shown me all around the job site and showed me the gases we were using – a normal turn-over. One of the LSTs showed me how the analyzers read about seventy-seven percent when analyzing a k-bottle of pure Oxygen – it should have read one-hundred percent. He thought it was really funny how a bottle of pure Oxygen changed to seventy-seven percent when it was brought up to an altitude of seven-thousand feet. I couldn't get it through his head that the bottle still contained pure Oxygen – there was no way it could magically change to seventy-seven percent.

One of the other LSTs – just an assistant LST really, still in training – told me how the divers all had sore throats and some of them were not feeling well. She said one or two of them were having problems focusing when they were reading their books and magazines. She had been sending the divers throat lozenges for their sore throats. She suggested they eat saltines to settle their stomachs. I absorbed all this information and thought about it a little bit. I talked to a couple other LSTs (not on the job) and asked them if they knew anything about how the analyzers worked at different altitudes. None of them had any ideas.

When I came out to be the Day Shift LST, the Greek had already spent two weeks on the job as one of the SAT diving supervisors. I talked to him about the analyzers not reading correctly at this altitude and he said he had brought that up with the superintendents. They had all – there were three of them – told him that the difference was negligible and nothing to worry about. None of us had much experience with SAT diving at altitudes and most of us only ever worked at sea level. I contacted the company that made the analyzers and explained to them what we were doing and what my concerns were. They informed me that their analyzers were designed to work at sea level. If we were going to be using them at higher altitudes there was a formula that we needed to use to come up with the actual percentage being used.

I made a bunch of calculations and decided we were poisoning the divers with Oxygen. I talked to all the divers; asking them how they felt and ran through all the symptoms of Oxygen Toxicity with them. The conversation that assured me I was right, was when I was talking to one of the divers who happened to be from Australia. He was a great diver and a very calm individual. No-one ever saw him get angry or agitated. I'm sure he must have sometimes – were all human after all – but he never yelled or got excited or anything like that when he was on the job. Anyway, one of the other divers had told me that they noticed the Australian appeared to be agitated all the time and had been snippy with a couple of the guys. When I talked to the Australian, I ran through the symptoms with him and suggested he might be irritable. That's when he snapped at me: "I'm not irritable! Who says I'm irritable?! Who-ever it is doesn't know fuckin' irritable!"

At that point I knew there was a problem. I gathered up all my calculations, the information from the company that made the analyzers, my altitude tables I used for surface supplied diving, and took them to the superintendent working my hitch. He had only worked at sea level and said none of that stuff really made any sense to him. I called Issaquah, who was the main superintendent of the whole job, and talked to him about my concerns. He said he had talked to one of the salesmen at the company who made the analyzers and was assured they would work fine at any altitude. I told him they still worked fine – the readings just needed to be adjusted with a formula. He wasn't buying it. He asked me to send him all my information and tables.

By this time, I had made up tables for the divers' decompression that showed the actual gas percentages and the calculated differences that the analyzers would show at each depth. We also had to decompress them to a surface pressure of less than sea level. I sent all those tables to Issaquah also. He still wasn't sure about it. I was adamant. I told him that we were making the divers ill and it wasn't healthy for them. He didn't want to take the responsibility for changing the gas percentages we were using. I told him I would take the responsibility. He sent me a form declaring that I was taking responsibility for the change in gas percentages and wanted me to sign it before we changed the gas percentages being used. I probably shouldn't have, but I did sign it. Then I made copies of my decompression schedule that had both the actual and adjusted gas percentage numbers on them and gave each LST a copy. I talked to all the LSTs so they would understand what we were doing and why. I also went over it with all the dive supervisors and superintendents.

A few days after I had adjusted the atmosphere in the living chambers all the divers said they were feeling much better. The best development was that the Australian was no longer irritable. I was happy that the divers all felt better and I think they were too. For the rest of the job, the company used the decompression tables and gas percentages that I had calculated to be the proper ones needed for that job. My Christmas bonus from Global was a little bit bigger that year. It made me feel good to know they appreciated and valued the work I did for them.

* * *

Another issue we had on the Cheesman job was keeping cooks for the divers. Since we weren't on a Dive Boat, a ship, or a barge, like in the Gulf of Mexico, the company had to hire a cook to feed the divers. Global had put together a really nice galley in a Conex box that was set on the Flexi-Float barge the SAT System was on. They also wanted to hire locals when they could, to help keep a good relationship with the people who lived in the area. The main problem was that we were running twelve-hour shifts, seven days a week. Most people aren't used to working like that. Even though the local hires were told what the hours and conditions would be, they didn't realize how grueling it would be working those hours. Several women were hired – one after the other – and for one reason or another they only lasted two or three weeks, maybe four or five. I don't think any of them actually did a full seven days of work in a row. One of them got the brown-bottle flu every Saturday and Sunday morning. That was a real pain for us, because it meant that one of our deck crew would have to step in and do the cooking. Some of them were good cooks, but they were needed on the deck.

One of our deckhands from Pensacola, Florida - who had worked on the Boa Deep C and the Crossmar – volunteered to hire on as the night cook for the duration of the job. He was a great cook and everybody liked having him on the job. It was the day-shift cook that we couldn't keep. Well, about the third Saturday I was there, our day cook got the Brown Bottle Flu again and didn't show up. Everybody was complaining about it. I suggested to the superintendent that my wife might be interested in working as the cook. He thought that was a grand idea. I called her that Saturday afternoon and explained to her what we needed. She thought about it a little bit and told me she was game to give it a shot. Then she asked when she was needed. I told her we needed her for the day-shift starting tomorrow – Sunday at noon. She would have to get on a plane that evening – in less than four hours – could she, would she, do it? She said she would. Yay!

I was working the day shift and couldn't pick her up from the airport. Global sent one of the other guys to retrieve her. They brought her out to the barge after they had helped her drop off her bags at the trailer camp we were staying at. They put her in my room instead of giving her a room to herself. That was nice for us. It was very rare that a married couple got to work together on the same job and on the same shift. I was really happy that she came out to work on this job with us.

She didn't have much of a chance to settle in when she first showed up – she was needed on the barge to prepare the mid-day meal as soon as she arrived. Talk about trial by fire! Temeculah was working on the deck and he had stepped in several times to prepare the meals for the divers when the local girl hadn't shown up for her shift. He was working the day shift and showed my wife around the galley and the barge. All the guys treated her very well. When Pensacola showed up, he talked with my wife about the menus, ordering food and supplies, and how that all worked. They worked very well together.

The divers in SAT really liked my wife's cooking. Most of them were acquainted with her from before and appreciated having their meals prepared by someone they knew. She had previously worked in restaurants and also owned and ran the Wolf Creek Internet Café, so she was used to cooking and preparing meals on a commercial level. She wasn't used to the long hours and no days off for several weeks though. She handled it well and never missed a shift. The company was very happy with her work. Did she like it? I think she did. I do know the experience gave her a whole new appreciation for the hours I worked. Finally, she realized that we actually worked when we went out of town rather than just partied all the time, like many spouses think we do when we are out on a job. It is not all fun and games when we are working, although we *do* try to make it that way! Haha!

* * *

There wasn't much going on in January and February of two-thousand-eleven. The weather in the Gulf of Mexico was kind of bad, so none of Global's SAT systems were doing anything there. I let all the other companies I worked with in the Pacific Northwest know I was available for work – mainly that was Harbor Offshore. I did a couple little jobs for them in February, March, and April.

In late May, Global sent me down to the Bay of Campeche on a boat called the Ocean Carrier. Global was sending a large crew down to the Bay of Campeche to work on some oilrig salvage project there with Mammoet. The Ocean Carrier was going to support a Mexican dive team down there as well as one of Global's surface supplied dive teams. I was sent down a couple weeks early with one of our SAT Techs (our Hydraulics Specialist from Houston), and a Superintendent from Mississippi that I had worked with only a couple of times.

The Ocean Carrier itself was a pretty nice boat. It was small. The accommodations were cozy and clean. The galley and dining area were tiny, but the cook was excellent. It was nice for me and Hydraulics because he and I were the only work crew on board other than the steward crew which consisted of just a few hands. We had our own cabins with our own heads too. It was very clean also.

I worked okay with this particular Superintendent but didn't think much of the way he ran things. His philosophy was more of a "Hands off – don't fix it if it ain't broke" type of deal. Unfortunately, that meant he wasn't a fan of preventative maintenance either. Mine and Hydraulics philosophy was more along the lines of keep everything in good shape, well maintained, and test run on a regular basis. This Superintendent had been on the Ocean Carrier for quite a while with a different crew – I think he had been on a job in Trinidad with it, but don't remember exactly.

Anyway, none of the Standby equipment had been serviced or tested in gawd knows how long. We were told by the Global office to make sure everything was ready to go within a couple weeks of us getting on board. There was a crane on this boat and unfortunately it was having issues and in need of repair. I think it was some Filipino machine and had to have parts specially made in the Philippine Islands.

Hydraulics and I set about servicing and changing the oil in all the dive equipment. We checked all the gaskets and O-rings. We started all the engines and compressors. We pressurized all the lines, hoses, and pressure vessels. In the process of doing that we found leaks, broken valves, dry-rotted hoses, and dry-rotted ropes on pull starts. We found leaky fuel tanks – they were bone dry when we got on board. How can you have equipment on board ready to go if there isn't even any fuel in the tanks? What a mess. Hydraulics and I ended up working fourteen to sixteen hours per day.

We got into it several times with the Superintendent too. At first, we had to go through him to get parts and supplies, but after communicating with the office about the situation, Hydraulics took care of all the parts ordering. The office had a hard time accepting that the equipment on the Ocean Carrier needed so much attention. According to them, this superintendent had been great, he never complained about faulty equipment, his system never cost the company much in repair – they thought he was doing a fantastic job.

The office guys never saw the equipment on his jobs though. All they saw were his reports and expense sheets. The bean counters loved him. At first the office thought Hydraulics and

I were exaggerating the situation, but after we sent them some photos and detailed explanations of the state of the equipment, they understood our plight. I didn't see that superintendent come back from his four-week break while I was on the Ocean Carrier. I don't know what the situation was between him and Global after that, but I was happy not to be working under him any longer.

Hydraulics and I had all the equipment pretty much ready to go by the time the dive teams arrived on board. There were still a couple little things to finish up that we were waiting on parts for. When the parts came, a couple of the Global guys gave us a hand finishing everything up. After that we went back to dive support.

We were doing Surface Supplied Diving from then on. I was running the decompression for the Global guys. The Mexican team took care of themselves. We offered any help they wanted, but they were only speaking Spanish and didn't really want to mix with us much. I spoke with them a little in my broken Spanish/Portuguese mix and got along with them just fine. They just had their way of doing things and it wasn't the same as ours. They had a female diver on their team also. She seemed to do as well as the male divers and worked better and harder on deck than a couple of them. I thought that was great.

A lot of the Global guys came down to work on the Mammoet barge. They had a day and night shift going on over there. We only had a day shift going on the Ocean Carrier. I did get to see a lot of those guys though. We even got to spend a little time on the beach in Ciudad del Carmen. We ate at a couple restaurants there and went to a couple bars. That was a lot of fun. The Coeur D'Alene Kid was there as Superintendent. Divers included the Australian, Duck Fart, the Mouth, and Kalispel. I think the Greek and Illinois were down there as supervisors. Lots of Global's regulars were there. It was a lot of fun.

It was a salvage job though and those can be quite dangerous. Our dive crews were helping Mammoet salvage a ship that had caught on fire and turtled. I think it was a large lifeboat or rescue boat. It was drifting towards a working oilrig near the Bay of Campeche. I do remember thinking it was a little ironic that we were "saving" a rescue ship in the Mexican oilfields.

I remember one incident where the Mouth was working on the top of the wreck. The water wasn't deep enough for dive gear where he was doing some rigging. He was splashing around in the knee-deep water, getting soaked in his topside gear. Waves were crashing over the wreck and causing a lot of problems for the rigging crew. Often, the waves were coming up over their waists. At least, that's what it looked like from my vantage point.

The upside-down ship was drifting closer and closer to the oilrig. Pemex, the owner of the oilrig, wanted Mammoet to salvage the ship before it smashed into the rig it was drifting towards. It was not far from the oilrig by the time the salvage crew started working on it. The management crew from Pemex was worried that Mammoet wouldn't get it salvaged in time. They were pressuring the salvage crew to work quickly.

The sun was shining bright and there were minimal clouds high in the atmosphere. It was hot. The water was warm – probably around eighty-four degrees Fahrenheit. There were about six crew members working on the bottom of the boat sticking out of the water. They all had their PPE on – hardhats, gloves, boots, life jackets, and stuff – but other than that, they were wearing minimal clothing; just t-shirts and jeans.

A crane was swinging rigging and equipment from the salvage barge over to the crew working on the wreck. The seas weren't real rough, but there was a little chop, causing all things floating to bob up and down. Hydraulics and I were working on a project on the Ocean Carrier. We could see what the Mouth and the other crew were doing on the overturned ship, but we weren't watching them work. We had our own things going on. We could hear them yelling at each other and we could hear their communications with the salvage barge over our radio. Every once-in-a-while I would look over to see how things were going. It didn't look like they were going well.

Waves kept washing over the upturned hull, knocking the crew around. Most of the waves seemed to hit the guys just above the knees, maybe a little higher. The Mouth isn't small, but he is not real big either – maybe five-nine or ten and a hundred-n-eighty pounds. The waves seemed to knock him around a little more than some of the others. He was smiling and laughing every time I looked over at what was going on, so I figured he was having a good time.

All of a sudden, I heard a lot of frantic yelling. Hydraulics and I looked up and saw the Mouth sitting down on the hull and yelling; water coming up to his chest. The rest of the crew had surrounded him, some were holding on to him. I didn't see it happen, but the Mouth had put himself in a bad position – a pinch point - and ended up getting one of his legs broken. It took quite a bit of time for the barge crew to get a Stokes Litter swung over to the wreck. Waves kept washing over everyone. No one was having any fun at that point. Finally, the Stokes Litter made it to the group and they got the Mouth loaded into it. He was swung over to the barge and lifted to the deck.

I couldn't see what was going on over at the barge, but I could hear the chatter on the radio. A crew boat had been ordered to take the mouth and a couple other crew members to the beach. An ambulance would meet them at the dock and take him to a hospital. I don't know what all happened and what the Mouth went through – you'd have to ask him about it to get the real story. All I do know is that he was out of commission for a while, but not as long as you might think. It wasn't long before he was back at it; working on dive jobs again. He is one tough bugger. My hitch was up shortly after that incident and I went home.

Overall, it was a fun job and interesting experience, but not nearly as good a job as the one I had been on in Cozumel years earlier. That project finished up shortly after my hitch was done, so I didn't go back down to see the completion of the job. That was okay. I went to work on another small job on a dam in eastern Washington for Harbor Offshore when I got home.

* * *

In July, the Engineer from Global Diving and Salvage informed me they had a job coming up at Canyon Ferry Dam on the Missouri River just outside of Helena. He wanted to know if I would like to be part of it. I told him I would gladly be on the crew since the job site was only twenty minutes from my front door. The job was to take only a week and it would be supervised by Illinois. He asked if I had a problem with that. I let him know, of course, I did not have any issues with that. Illinois was a good friend, an excellent diver, and a great supervisor. Besides, if he was the supervisor, he was responsible for the job and I wouldn't be.

I saw the little barge and the equipment they were sending out to do the job. I thought it was a little on the light side. I didn't think the crane was big enough, and I thought the barge was on the small side. We could work with it, but the job would take longer than they wanted. That was just my own personal opinion though. The Engineer was the superintendent of the job. He had overseen the bidding of the job and was certain the equipment he was sending would be adequate. Yeah, yeah, sometimes engineers just don't get how things work in the real world. I knew this Engineer from several jobs. I liked him and we got along fine, although he was the same Engineer who ran the Canyon Ferry job in two-thousand-and-four and wasn't very communicative with me then. I learned later that he had graduated from the same Dive School I went to - Highline Community College – run by Maurice P. Talbot.

The scope of this job was to remove the Head Gate Guides from the Spill Gates, bore out the old guide bolts, and fill in the holes with grout. The Gate Guides would be replaced at a later date. I thought it would be more cost effective to remove the rusted nuts and bolts, then replace them with new nuts and bolts all at the same time, but the Bureau of Land Management – the owners and operators of that dam – informed us that the Head Gates weren't scheduled to be used for ten years. They were in no hurry to re-install the gate guides. Okay, your dam, your nickel.

The dive crew was a very good group of guys and we all worked well together. As I said, Illinois was supervising, the Australian, Kalispel, and two other Global regulars, one from Seattle and the other from the mid-west, would be the divers. I would be the Standby Diver and dive when the other divers ran out of time – that happened several times. We also had a designated tender – a new hire at Global.

As stated earlier, the job was to take only a week. We had to knock the mild steel nuts off the stainless-steel bolts and remove the gate guides. That is why we were there in the first place: the company that installed the gate guides fifteen years, or so, ago had cut corners and installed mild steel nuts on the stainless bolts. They had pulled a fast one on the Bureau of Land Management to make a buck. It was a non-union dive company from southern California that did it. You get what you pay for, I suppose. After we removed the nuts, we were to core-drill the bolts out of the concrete and fill the resulting hole with grout. We were to work ten to twelve hours-a-day, six days a week. The job should only take a week, but no more than two weeks at the outside. At the end of two weeks, we were only half-way done.

One issue we had, was we left the barge anchored at the worksite. That was a common thing to do when working on dams, but the barge we were using was really small and we were anchored out away from the dam itself. I told Illinois I didn't think that was a good idea, because it can get really windy on Canyon Ferry Lake sometimes and the waves can get really big. Nobody on the crew took me seriously. None of them lived here, though, and weren't familiar with the weather we could get. Anyway, one morning as I approached the dam, I saw our little barge half sunk, the Port-a-Potty we had on board was in the drink and all the crew besides me was in boats working on getting everything back together on the barge. I met one of them at the boat launch where we had a staging area set up. I was informed that Seattle, who was camped in his trailer on a spot overlooking the dam, had called Illinois about two-thirty in the morning. Seattle told Illinois that it was very windy and he looked out at the barge and saw that it was being beat up pretty good by the wind and waves. Illinois had called all our crew – except me – to get to the site so they could save the barge and equipment. They had been working in nasty weather conditions, to save the barge for about four hours before I got there. All of them were wet and tired. We got everything put back to normal, but that wasted a day of work. Also, all the other crew members were worn out. I was upset that Illinois hadn't called me to help. He told me that he hadn't wanted to bother me in the middle of the night and had enough help with the rest of the crew. Sure, whatever you say. All in all, the worst of it was that the crew had to work all night in in-clement weather and our Port-a-Potty was dumped in the lake. Of course, Illinois had informed the office and let them know that we got everything taken care of.

At the end of the second week, the Engineer joined us at the job site to see what the issues were. He got me away from everybody else on the beach and asked me why I thought the job was taking so long. I told him the truth. I told him the crane was too small for the job and our barge was also too small. We had to pull the gate guide pieces out of the water and put them on a separate float that was tied to our work barge. The crane wasn't strong enough to pull the steel out of the water – it would only raise the guide pieces just to the surface. We had to sink the little float enough so we could slide it under the steel at the surface then refloat the barge with the piece on it. All that moving around took twice as long, at least, as it would have taken if we had a crane that could lift just a ton more than the crane we had.

The compressor Global had supplied was having issues as well. I found out at the start of the job, Global had sent the compressor out knowing it needed some work and figured we would just fix it on site. The problem with that is we were in central Montana and there are no dive equipment parts suppliers anywhere close by. Parts came from Seattle, southern California, Texas, or Louisiana. That ended up wasting some of our time also. He wasn't happy to hear that.

He saw how we were working, though, and was happy with our performance. At least he knew he had a good crew working on the job. He wanted us to finish as quickly as we could with the equipment we had. He wasn't going to give us anything different. He saw that we were making decent forward progress and just decided that it would be most cost effective to continue on the same way we had been working. Whether that was true or not, I do not know.

It ended up taking us a month to complete all the tasks. For the most part, we had really good weather and it was an enjoyable job. For the duration of the project, besides the wet and windy night, the weather was nice and the work went very well. The customer was very happy with our work at the end of the job. That is always what we want.

Every Sunday we all got together and had a Bar-B-Que. One of the days that the Engineer had come over to check our progress, we all met at my house. The Engineer bought all the fixings for our Bar-B-Que - beef, bison, beer, and all – and we had a great time. It was a warm, sunny, late-August afternoon. The food was good and the company was great. That is what I remember from that little job.

* * *

There are Old Divers and Bold Divers
but No Old Bold Divers

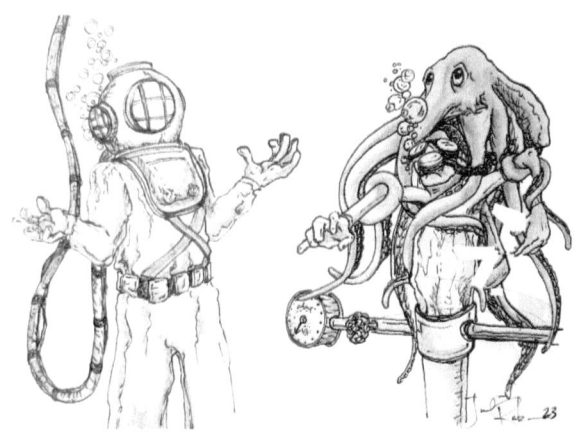

In the fall of two-thousand-eleven, and over the winter, I mostly worked in the Seattle shop for Global. They were refurbishing one of the SAT systems and making it into a real modular system that could easily be shipped anywhere in the world. Global had earned an excellent reputation in the Gulf of Mexico for getting the work done quickly and keeping and exceptional safety record. They were bidding on work all around the globe. They were also pursuing work with large maritime salvage companies like Titan and Mammoet.

I also worked a little with Harbor Offshore – I was mostly supervising, but also did some tending, diving, and standby diving. I didn't really care what position on the crew I held, I just liked going out on some of the smaller jobs. I also wanted Harbor Offshore to do well in the Pacific Northwest because my friend, Blanchard, was running the office in Spokane for them. Boston ran a lot of jobs for him and I always enjoyed working with him.

In the spring I was sent back down to the Superior Performance by Global. I was back to being an LST for them and also a Surface Supplied Supervisor. I was also working on getting my IMCA (International Marine Contractors Association) certification for SAT Supervising. I already had my ADCI (Association of Diving Contractors International) certification for that, but to work overseas, IMCA certs were required.

Anyway, I was back to being an LST – mostly – in the GoM. I wasn't super excited to be back on the Performance, but this was the best offer of work I had at the moment. At least I was working with the same bunch of guys and we all enjoyed working with each other.

Everything was going along as usual – nothing out of the ordinary – when one of the divers in SAT asked to talk to the Superintendent. I got a hold of the Superintendent and informed him that one of the divers needed to talk to him. I don't know what the whole issue was, but the diver needed to get out of SAT. We couldn't just shut the job down or remove one of the dive teams from SAT just because one diver had an issue and needed to be de-SATted. What the Superintendent had decided to do was to send two divers into SAT – one to ride out with the diver that needed to get out, and the other to stay in and take his place on his dive team. SAT dive teams were made up of a pair of divers.

On a SAT crew there are always topside guys that are anxious to get into SAT. There was a common path to become a SAT diver and that usually included being a Surface Standby Diver on the SAT support crew. That person was usually the next in line to become a SAT diver. Global didn't really follow that protocol. Most of their surface support crew members were divers and rotated the assigned positions. The next SAT diver could be anyone of them.

Anyway, the SAT diver needed to decompress out of the system and two other crew members needed to be sent in – one to replace the diver and another to accompany him during his decompression. The Superintendent asked me if I would like to go into SAT and take the diver's place on that dive team. I thought about it a little. I had never done SAT before. I wasn't really interested in it. I didn't really like the idea of being locked in a twenty-foot by eight-foot tube with three other people for several weeks. I thought about my future dive career. Becoming a SAT diver was not a goal of mine.

Besides, I had just turned fifty – that was a little old to be breaking into SAT diving. It was not likely that I would do much more of it. I was more interested in being an LST or Supervisor, which I was already doing. There were a couple people on our support crew that were young and had a prosperous dive career to look forward to. I thanked the Superintendent for the opportunity, but told him that I thought it would be better to put in a couple of the younger guys. I gave him the names of a couple I thought would be good choices. Of course, he had his own preferences for who he thought would be good. His choices and mine happened to be the same.

We pressed in the two younger crew members. They were both excited and happy about being put into SAT. The one who replaced the diver on the dive team ended up going into SAT several more times. He was a good worker and a good diver. This job was a nice boost for his dive career. I was happy for him that he was moving up the ladder.

* * *

While we were on the Superior Performance, we did more than just SAT diving. If the work was less than eighty feet – I actually don't know what Global's cut-off for depth was at the time – we would do Sur-D-O_2 diving. You remember: Sur-D-O_2 is Surface Decompression using Oxygen. We did some very shallow SAT diving also. I remember one SAT run we did where the divers were stored at seventy feet. I also remember there was a concern that the SAT divers might accidentally reach the surface when they were outside the bell. We had a couple issues keeping the system sealed as well. The shallower storage depth made for less pressure in the system. That made it harder to get the hatches to seal. Such a shallow SAT sounds kind of silly from a Commercial Diver's point of view, but it makes sense financially for the company, if there is a lot of diving to be done between sixty and a-hundred-and-fifty feet. Remember SAT divers can stay in the water all day - but usually work in four-hour blocks. Surface divers are limited by the decompression tables, even when utilizing the Sur-D-O_2 tables.

Anyway, one job we were doing involved a lot of rigging and some burning on a rig that was shallow enough for us to do with Sur-D-O_2 rather than SAT. We had decompressed the SAT system – divers and all – for its three-month cleaning. It would take the SAT Tech and some tenders a few days to clean the system and make minor repairs. All the O-rings would get serviced and replaced. The deck plates would get pulled up so the bilges could be cleaned – that was usually a very nasty job. The mattresses would be sterilized. All the bulkheads would be washed down with a sanitizing agent that killed most bacteria, fungi, and things like that. It was quite an involved process, but needed to be done to keep the divers healthy. A clean system is a healthy system. It cost money to keep the SAT divers on board for the several days the system was being cleaned, so the client scheduled work on a shallower project that could be done utilizing surface diving. It was not cost-effective to send the dive teams to the beach just to bring them back a few days later. SAT divers can still dive surface-supplied – the pay is just a little less. Waa, waa, waa. The other diver/tenders on board were happy to have a chance to do some diving for a change.

We had two SAT teams – four divers - and a couple surface divers that we could use, but we needed another diver. I volunteered to go into rotation. I dove almost every day on this little project, but not always at the same time of day. I was working the day shift – noon to midnight – as an LST and for the most part my dive would take place sometime during my normal shift. Once-in-a-while my dive took place when I wasn't on shift. On those days, which only happened once or twice, I got paid extra for my dive and decompression time. It was really fun for me to get back in the water. I did some burning – rigging holes mostly - and did some of the rigging.

Sur-D-O_2 decompression is more involved than regular deco because we use both air and nitrox on the water stops. The time-keeping is vitally important also. Usually, the supervisor would run the dives including the decompression, but since I was on board as an LST (I was a certified SAT supervisor also), I ran the deco when I wasn't diving or in the chamber. It gave me something to do besides helping the SAT Tech clean the SAT System and it gave the supervisor a little break. I was offshore getting paid to work a twelve-hour shift, so I had to do something even though we weren't running SAT at the time. Since I was an LST it only made sense for me to run the decompression for the other divers during my shift when I wasn't diving. It was a nice change to do something besides watching gages as an LST when we had the system pressurized.

Being in dive rotation, you dive under different supervisors. Offshore there are usually at least two dive supervisors – one on the day shift and another on the night shift. On this job, our dive superintendent would help with the dive supervising – such as relieving the supervisor for meals or head breaks and things like that. Our superintendent on this job was the diving supervisor that I had given a piece of my mind when I first got on the Boa Deep C. We were friends now and respected each other's experience and abilities. Of course, he had a year or two more experience in the industry than I did. He didn't have a good idea what kind of a diver I was though, as I had never dived for him before.

Anyway, I was up to dive at dinner time and the superintendent had relieved the supervisor for chow. I was fine with that; didn't think anything of it actually. I went over what my tasks would be and got dressed in. I was going to be doing some rigging. Rigging with very large shackles. The shackle pins were about three feet long, eight inches in diameter, and weighed around a hundred pounds. The pins were tied to the body of the shackle, leaving the shackle open, making it easier for us to set up the rigging. The more the topside crew could do for the diver the better. We also had a line tying the pinhead to the crown so the diver wouldn't accidentally drop the pin. We were currently rigging at a depth of eighty feet or so and the bottom was close to three-hundred feet. No one wanted to be responsible for having to make a dive to the bottom just to retrieve a dropped pin – even if it could be found in the muddy bottom.

The normal process was to set the shackle on the jacket leg, cut the poly rope securing the shackle pin to the shackle, stuff the pin through the lugs, screw the nut on the end of the pin, then place the safety pin. We were using "safety shackles" on this job. Safety shackles have a pin that goes all the way through both lugs and is secured with a nut rather than screwing the pin into one of the lugs. It is easier for divers to set that type of shackle; especially when the seas are rough and the rigging is moving all over the place.

I had two knives with me – part of my typical dive rig – both were Big Chief foldable knives. Not many of the younger guys had ever seen those knives before, but when I first started diving in the Gulf of Mexico, that was the knife to have. Most of the new guys these days use Spydercos. Those were too expensive for me to use as a dive knife. The Big Chiefs didn't hold an edge very well, though – I wasn't diligent about sharpening them either - which caused me a little issue on this dive.

I jumped in the water, went down to the rigging site and called for the rigging. When it got to me, I guided it into position and placed the shackle. I turned the shackle so the lug went through the rigging hole. That would hold everything in place while I freed the pin and put it in the shackle. That way I didn't have to fight to keep the shackle in position. I went to cut the poly rope and my knife was just too dull to cut it. My second knife was quite dull also. Trying to cut the poly with the dull knives was just too slow. I decided to untie the knots – not a big deal.

As I was working the knot loose, the superintendent came over the radio and asked me what I was doing. I explained that I was untying the poly to free the pin so I could place it in position. He asked if I had a knife and I informed him that I had two. He asked why I didn't just cut the poly. I told him both my knives were dull and I thought it would be quicker to untie the knot. He told me to stop and use my knife to cut it. He thought it would be quicker to cut than untie the rope. I agreed with him that if my knives were sharper, that would be so. He told me again to cut the rope rather than untie it. I didn't want to, but he made such a big deal out of it that I got one of my knives out again and started sawing on the poly; to no avail.

The superintendent huffed and puffed a little and told me I needed to sharpen my knives. I agreed with him. After about five minutes of hacking away and not getting anywhere, he relented and told me I could complete the task however I thought best. "Finally," I thought, now I could get back in my groove and do my thing. I realized that he was used to micro-managing divers, but I would rather he just let me do my thing. It wasn't like I was a newbie or anything. He didn't know what my dive experience was though.

I completed all the tasks on my list for that dive, even though some time was wasted with the dull knives. I would have finished quicker if I had ignored the superintendent and just untied the ropes, but I didn't want to cause any undue stress for him. I had more dive experience than the other supervisors and they just let me do my thing. It didn't matter on this dive, but sometimes the diver can see the conditions better and know how to complete the task better than the supervisor can.

On another dive, I was following a diver that was cutting a jacket leg loose. The process on this task was for a diver or two to go down and cut rigging holes. After the rigging holes were burned, the rigging would be set and the crane would take a slight strain on the load. The next diver would go down to cut the piece free from the rest of the wreck on the bottom. When it was time for my dive, the rigging had been set and most of the legs and crosspieces had been cut. Three divers had been sent down just to cut the four legs and a couple diagonals. I figured two divers should have been able to cut it free.

The diver I was following said there was quite a bit of burning left to do before the piece could be raised. I had been watching what he was doing on his dive. We had a camera and light mounted on the Superlite so the supervisor could see everything the diver could see. I liked to know what the diver before me was doing so I knew what to expect when I got to the work site.

I had seen most of the areas they had been working on and it appeared to me that not much more cutting needed to be done. Certainly not as much cutting as he had alluded to. It appeared to me that he had cut as much or more than what was needed to remove the section we were removing. I would see what the situation really was when I got down there.

I splashed and dived down to where the burning gear was. I looked at all the places that were left to cut. There wasn't much steel left. I scouted out the far leg – it was fifty or sixty feet away from the burning rig. I looked at the cut there and determined no more steel needed to be burned away. I looked at all four legs, the bottom two were completely cut through. From what I saw, the piece was ready for the crane to come up on it.

I asked the supervisor to come up on the burning gear and get it out of my way. He told me I needed to finish the cutting first. I told him I thought it was ready to go and again asked him to pull the burning rig up. He complied and had the deck crew bring the Broco torch up to the surface. He told me the divers on deck thought I would have to do more burning before the piece would come up. I told him to trust me and have the crane come up on the load. I was out of the way, behind a horizontal where I could keep an eye on the rigged piece.

Nothing was happening. I told the supervisor to come up on the load more. He said the crane operator wanted to know if I was sure the piece was cut. I replied I was sure. I asked what kind of a load strain he had on the crane. The supervisor told me and it was about three-quarters of what the calculated weight of the piece was. I asked the supervisor to ask the crane operator to come up on the load until he had about one-and-a-quarter what the weight of the piece was calculated to be. The crane operator agreed to do that.

I saw the piece start to move. Suddenly, I heard a small pop and the piece jumped about six inches. The supervisor asked if everything was okay. I told him it was. I told him it appeared to me that the piece was free to the surface. The crane operator informed the supervisor that he had only pulled ten percent above the calculated weight of the piece when he saw the wire jump and the crane load went down to ninety-five percent of the calculated weight. The supervisor informed the crane operator that the piece was free and clear to the surface. After the piece was on the deck, I left the work site and headed to the surface. I didn't need to make any in-water deco stops and only had to do about a half-hour in the chamber on oxygen. That was one of the easiest dives I made on that project.

* * *

I think most of the SAT divers enjoyed being out of the system and still getting to dive. I am sure most of them are like me, and liked the actual diving part of the job. It is an incredible workplace under the water – especially when the visibility is good and the water is warm. There is a lot of sea life living around the oil rigs. It is usually like diving in a gigantic aquarium. That might scare some people, like my sister, but most of us divers really enjoyed it. It is hard to describe the beauty and the attraction if you haven't actually experienced it. Watching it on T.V. or in the movies – even in an IMAX theater - is just not the same. You don't have the weightlessness. You don't feel the aquatic atmosphere. You just aren't immersed in the whole situation like you are when you actually make a dive. It's like riding motorcycles – if you haven't actually experienced it, you just can't know what it is really like. What do they say? "If I have to explain it to you, you wouldn't understand."

Most often I dove during the daylight hours. Even though I had a light on my helmet, I didn't use it. We were quite a way offshore, so the visibility was very good. Usually there was plenty of ambient light filtering down so I could see everything really well. The rig had been out here quite a while so there were lots of fish around. Lionfish – an invasive species in the Gulf of Mexico, most likely introduced by people who had salt water aquariums dumping the fish in the Gulf rather than flushing them down the toilet because they didn't want them anymore – were all over the rig. They spent the night down at the bottom, but came up to shallower water during the day to munch on baby fish from other species. I saw lots of them, and although they weren't as big as the Lionfish I had seen in the Philippines, they were not small. Lionfish used to be one of my favorite fishes in the ocean. They were beautiful even though they were toxic. After I learned how bad they were taking over the waters of the Caribbean, I didn't like them so much anymore.

The Lionfish were causing a huge problem in the Gulf of Mexico from Florida – where they were most likely first introduced to the waters around Miami and had really taken over - all the way to Texas. They have spread even further since I last worked in the Gulf. Several organizations – including NOAA - are tracking their invasion of the American waters and beyond. There is a great site from one of the groups that really explains the issue: https://lionfish.gcfi.org/. Another website I found was https://www.invasivespeciesinfo.gov/aquatic/. It's unbelievable what a problem Lionfish have become in the Caribbean Sea and surrounding waters.

I went on the dot-gov website and filled out surveys of theirs adding to the data pool they were building. At one point I was contacted by them and asked if I could collect some of the fish and send them to their headquarters. I told them I was working offshore and really didn't have any way of doing that. Then they asked if I could at least trap them, weigh them, measure them, then destroy them. I explained to them that I was working a construction job in the Gulf and couldn't really justify taking the time to do that while I was working. I couldn't ask the other divers to do that either. I am sure the company we were working for would be pretty upset if we spent time catching Lionfish while we were supposed to be working on deconstructing damaged oil rigs.

Lionfish weren't the only fish there, of course – they had to eat something! Seriously though, it was like diving on a miniature reef. There were Corals, Encrusting Sponges, Tube Sponges, Anemones, Tubeworms, Hydroids, Spiny Oysters, and Barnacles of course – not to mention all the types of algae - all attached to the oil rig itself. Those life forms attracted other life forms like Shrimp, Crabs, and Urchins that climbed all over the oil rig. Towards the bottom of the rig, you might find Spiny Lobsters or even Slipper Lobsters. All this life attracted fish. The longer the rig had been in the water, the more life there was to be found on and around it.

Common fish, were the Lionfish, Trigger Fish, Angel Fish, Butterfly Fish – I could go on and on with this. All these smaller fish attracted larger fish like Barracuda, Amberjack, Grouper, Sheepshead, Mackerel, and all the other types of game fish you could imagine in the Gulf. This, of course, attracted fisherman – both sport and commercial. The larger fish also attracted even larger species like Sharks, Dolphins, and Porpoises. You might even see a Turtle or a Ray if you were lucky. It was so colorful. Like I said, it was just like diving in an aquarium. It was very easy to get distracted from your task at hand if you let yourself. All the sea life around the rigs is one of the reasons I enjoyed in-water decompression. I never got bored looking at all the life under the waves. It was a far cry from diving the barren waters encountered on inland diving.

One of the most memorable dives I did on that job was very early in the morning. I was diving relatively shallow – less than eighty feet – so had a couple hours in the water. We were quite a way offshore too, where the visibility was quite good. This oil rig had been here since the late sixties. There was quite a bit of life on and around it. The work we were doing made for a lot of biological debris in the water which attracted even more fish to the area. I went in before the sun came up. It was dark out and really dark in the water – nothing new for me. The sea life was not very active. All the creatures that were active during the day were hiding from the terrors of the night. Even though I had a light on my helmet there wasn't much active life to see. That was probably a good thing. I was there to work, not watch crabs fuck - as my dive instructor, Maurice Talbot, would have said.

After I had been in the water about half-an-hour, I noticed the water was getting lighter and lighter blue. The sun was coming up over the horizon. From my perspective it was like being in a theatre where the lights had been off but were slowly coming on. I noticed the fish and other sea life come out from where-ever it was that they spent the night. It was a grand display and very beautiful. It started with the crabs and shrimp becoming more active. Then the smaller fish appeared, swimming in and out of the verticals and horizontal beams. The awakening of the smaller fish brought in the larger fish. It was an incredible presentation. I stopped working for a few minutes just to take in this awe-inspiring display put on by Mother Nature. As I was enjoying the spectacle, I was reminded of why I had gone into diving in the first place. The underwater realm is so beautiful and so much like a whole other world. I hadn't realized how much I missed this part of diving.

*   *   *

In May, Issaquah - from Global - informed me that a job was coming up in Saudi Arabia and asked if I would like to be one of the supervisors on it. I told him that I would love to do that – we would be diving in the Persian Gulf. Awesome. He said they would get all the paperwork completed for me to go on that job. He told me I would need to make sure my passport and inoculations were up to date and I had the ones needed to work in the mid-East. He informed me I would get a little more than my regular four-week break in between working on the Performance and being sent to Arabia.

Then I was called on Tuesday, July tenth, and told I was needed to do a hitch as supervisor on a dam project they had going in Kentucky – on the Ohio River; the Olmsted Dam Project. I wasn't sure how long Global had been involved in the Olmsted project, but I had heard about it at least a year earlier. They were having a few issues keeping it crewed up properly. Several supervisors had been sent there to work on it but for one reason or another didn't want to be a dive supervisor on this project. Looking back, I think it was just growing pains on a long project. It ended up being a very enjoyable and lucrative job for me, but not just yet.

I was flown to Paducah, Kentucky on Wednesday the eleventh of July. Thursday morning, I rode with a couple other crew members to the job site. I had to go through the job site orientation before being allowed to actually go to work. Right off the bat I had to give a urine sample and do a breathalyzer test. This job was an Army Corps of Engineers job and had a zero-tolerance policy to drug and alcohol use. That's why I had been called in. The supervisor who was scheduled to do this hitch had come on site Monday morning and failed his breathalyzer test. He was just getting back to Olmsted from his time off and apparently had too much to drink the Sunday before. Unfortunately, his breath registered a little sign of alcohol, but since the ACoE had a zero-tolerance policy, they wouldn't let him on the job. They demanded he be replaced for this hitch. There was another Global dive supervisor on site that took his place on Monday, but then the ACoE said he didn't meet their requirements for a dive supervisor. That's where I came in. I have been an approved ACoE supervisor since the early nineties. I was supposed to have my four weeks off before heading to Saudi Arabia, but that was not to be.

I passed my urinalysis and my breathalyzer tests. Then I had to go through about an hour-long orientation and introduction to the job site. They went over all the typical safety stuff, required PPE, site etiquette, and all. After that I was sent down to the dock area where all the tugboats and crew boats were moored and where the crews met to be taken out to the different parts of the job sites on the river itself. I was headed off to Dive Barge One.

At this point in the job, DB-One was just monitoring the placement of a concrete form for the second section of a toe piece located towards the Kentucky side of the river. I liked to know what conditions the divers in my crew would be working in, so I made the first dive of the day. I did the survey of the area where the form would be positioned and made sure it was cleared of debris and ready to go. On this side of the river, the current wasn't too strong. Visibility was about ten to fifteen feet which was pretty nice for this type of work. The conditions weren't bad. Knowing what it was like down there would let me know what kind of divers I was working with by how they felt about the working conditions. The next diver in monitored the setting of the concrete form. A second diver checked that everything was in place and ready for the concrete.

The next task was the concrete pour. We would have a diver swimming around the top of the form, monitoring the overflow pipes and vents in the frame used to tell how much concrete was in the form and if it was filling up as it was designed to. The concrete form had very large tremie pipes on it with some sort of electrical monitoring system that was supposed to indicate the progress of the concrete pour. The diver was a back-up just in case the remote system didn't work. There is too much engineering and technical stuff for me to get into here to explain the actual construction of the dam. I just want to tell you about the diving side of it without all the technical reasons behind what we were doing.

The river level was low this time of year so the diving wasn't too deep – less than twenty feet for this task. The concrete pour was scheduled to take just a few hours, but depending on how things went could take quite a bit longer. At this depth, I could keep the diver in all day if I wanted. I had a team of six divers though and they all wanted to dive. Also, working underwater – especially construction work – really wears a diver out. I have found that three-and-a-half to four hours is where you get the best work out of a diver. After that the diver's energy and progress really goes downhill – especially when working in a current of any sort. It's bad enough having to work against the stiffness of the dive suit and the bulkiness and weight of the dive gear underwater. Any current usually just makes it worse. Anyway, I typically kept my divers in the water somewhere between three and four hours. If the dive was particularly strenuous, I would pull the diver earlier. Also, if the diver felt he, or she, was getting tired and wanted to come out of the water, I would let them. I was not a slave driver!

The Monday after I arrived was the designated day for the concrete pour. Our task was to keep an eye on the overflow tubes on the top of the form and let the engineers in charge of the pour know how it was going. The piece being poured was the downstream piece that another concrete shell would butt up against on the upstream side. The shell was pre-formed on the beach and would be floated out and placed in position after a majority of the toe pieces were placed. Just upstream of the toe piece was a prepared landing area for the shell. That area was an engineered footing area that had been excavated and prepped. I-beam pilings and round pilings had been pounded into the river bottom and the area needed to be kept clean in readiness for the placement of the shell. An important part of the readiness was that no concrete overpour would be left in the shell area.

I explain all this because as the pour for the toe piece was completed, many, many yards of overpour spilled into that footing area. It would have to be removed. The sooner it was removed the better. It would be much easier to remove before the concrete fully cured. In my opinion that should be the next task for the dive team even though it wasn't the next scheduled task. I informed the ACoE Dive Safety Officer of the overspill. In reality, I didn't need to do that, but this particular DSO thought he was in charge of the whole job.

The actual job of the DSO is just to observe the dive ops and make daily reports of how the dive procedures were followed. I informed the Day Foreman of the project. I also informed the overall superintendent of the whole job – he was the most important one to inform because he is the one who made all the actual decisions on what was to be done. I told him that if we didn't get right on this overspill removal and put it off until it was "more convenient" it would take quite a bit longer.

The DSO wanted us to put the overspill removal off until the divers had a break in our scheduled tasks. The Day Foreman agreed with me that the overspill should be removed as soon as possible in order to save time in the long run. The overall Job Superintendent wanted us to keep to the schedule – the dive team had a couple other tasks scheduled to take place right after the pouring of the toe piece. I explained to him, and he knew as well, that the concrete would get harder and harder as it cured. I told him if we could start clearing it right away, we would end up saving some time, because the concrete would break up relatively easily and we could probably get it all removed within a day. If we waited, it might take up to a week to remove it.

As we were talking, I had a diver down working on removing the overspill. I figured I might as well get as much of the concrete removed as possible while the management was deciding what to do. In the middle of all this, I got a phone call. I didn't recognize the number so I didn't answer it. I was running a dive, talking with the Day Foreman, talking with the job superintendent, trying to ignore the DSO, and the last thing I needed at this moment was to take some random phone call. The phone rang again – same number – I declined the call. A minute or two later my phone rang again from the same number. I decided to answer it in hopes of getting the caller to stop ringing me during this stressful moment.

"Sam here," I answered.

"How's everything going?" the caller asked.

"Fine," I answered, "a little hectic right now, but everything is going well."

"This is an Army Corps of Engineers job you are working on here and you need to get along well with the DSOs on the job," the caller stated.

That agitated me, I was busy trying to do my job and some kook on the phone was telling me I needed to be nice to the DSOs. "I know all about working for the Army Corps of Engineers!" I snapped. "I've worked on Corps jobs for years. I've supervised many jobs for them, I know the protocols. Now if you'll excuse me, I'm going to get back to work," I said shortly as I hung up the phone. Both the Day Foreman and the Job Superintendent asked me who that was on the phone and I told them I didn't know, but it didn't seem very important. We got back to the task at hand and the Job Superintendent decided that we should go ahead and clear all the overpour. So that is what we did.

My dive team and I finished out our shift at a little after sixteen hundred hours. Swing shift came on board and I went over with that supervisor how things were going and where we were at. He would have his team keep on removing the overspill and hopefully they would get it all done by the end of their shift. My crew and I went back to the beach. I went to have a little chat with the Job Superintendent - as was the protocol at the end of the day shift – to go over the days progress and let him know where we stood so he could explain everything to his swing shift counterpart.

At seventeen hundred hours, while I was talking to the Job Superintendent, I got a phone call from the same unknown number that had called earlier in the day. "Sam here," I answered.

"Don't hang up! This is so-and-so and I just wanted to know how you were fitting in." It was the Engineer from Global who oversaw the Canyon Ferry jobs and had sent me here to Olmsted Dam.

"Oh, Shit!" I thought to myself, "I'm fired now." I grimaced, "Hey Engineer! How are you doing?" I asked. He said he was doing fine, then I apologized for jumping on him earlier in the day. I explained how I didn't recognize the number and he had caught me at a hectic moment. He told me that was no problem and he understood. He apologized for the unrecognizable number and let me know that he had lost his phone so was currently using a "burner." He then went on to say that he had received a call from the DSO on my shift. It seems the DSO didn't feel I was giving him the respect he deserved – he was, after all, in charge of the whole job. I laughed. I couldn't help myself. DSOs aren't really "in charge" of anything; let alone a major dam building project like Olmsted.

The Engineer said I was correct, but this particular DSO was the head of the DSOs in that region of the United States. He was the guy who had the last word on whether or not any tenders, divers, or supervisors were actually ACoE certified to work on this project. He had asked for my certs and then asked to see them again. He had scrutinized my certifications looking for some reason to disqualify me from the project. The Engineer asked if I would please treat him a little more like a manager than just a DSO. I told the Engineer I would do my best. I could schmooze this DSO a little, but I wasn't about to let him push me around. The Engineer was happy with that and wished me well. He wanted to talk to me a little more in depth when I was off the job site. I told him I'd give him a call when I got back to my hotel room.

Later that evening I called the Engineer. He told me that DSO was upset because I wasn't waiting for him to arrive on our dive barge before I put my first diver in the water. I explained to the engineer that our work day started at oh-seven-hundred. We were on the dive barge by seven-thirty and usually ready to dive within fifteen minutes of that. I always called the DSO on the radio when we were headed out to the dive barge as was the protocol. He knew we would be ready to dive by eight at the latest. He never showed up until after nine-thirty or ten though – every day. I knew that according to ACoE regulations, I didn't have to have a DSO on board to dive. The DSO was just the eyes of the ACoE and if he didn't want to be present when we were diving, that was his choice.

This particular DSO just thought he was special enough that diving operations would be shut down if he wasn't present. I knew that wasn't so. The Engineer knew that wasn't so. He told me he would have a talk with the upper management of both the ACoE and the construction company doing the job. He told me that by no means was I to postpone or stop the dive ops just because the DSO wasn't on the dive barge. The silly thing was that the DSO showed up to our morning supervisor's meeting every day at oh-six-thirty, so really had no excuse to not be on the dive barge along with me and my dive crew. He just preferred to go back to his office, check e-mails, drink coffee, and do gawd knows what. He could do all that on our dive barge if he wanted.

I was only filling in on this Olmsted job and didn't think I would be there long. I was scheduled to be in Saudi Arabia in less than a month anyway. I didn't make any waves for anybody and I bit my tongue several times when talking with that DSO. He hung out at the back of my dive shack almost the whole day every day. I ignored him as best I could and only spoke to him when absolutely necessary.

The funny thing was that the second day after my talk with the Engineer, that DSO started showing up on the dive barge by eight in the morning – every day. I always said good morning to him and snickered to myself. He may have been pissed at me, but he could not get rid of me, and he realized he had to do his job. He could not stop or slow our progress even if he wanted to.

* * *

On the twenty-first of July, I was relieved by another dive supervisor and sent home. I was told that I needed to get home and packed up for the job in Saudi Arabia. I would be flying there the following weekend. Busy, busy, busy. My wife was glad I was coming home for a week, but I wasn't sure she was too happy about me heading off to the Persian Gulf. The restrictions for entering Saudi Arabia were almost unbelievable.

I got a new phone before going to Arabia and didn't take my laptop. It is forbidden to bring any form of "Pornography" into Saudi Arabia. To them, any photo of any female showing any skin besides her face is considered porn. That means any pictures one may have of their girlfriend or wife in shorts, a t-shirt or tank top, a swimsuit, or even capri pants is considered porn and you can be thrown in jail for that. Any items pertaining to any religion other than muslim is expressly forbidden and can result in jail time also. That means any book, picture, jewelry, whatever that even remotely appears to be religious is outlawed. My wife didn't want me to get into trouble so we decided it was easiest to leave my computer and old phone at home. I went over there with a blank phone other than my contact list.

I was flown over in first class on United Arab Emirates because I was a "supervisor" on the job. I thought that was a little silly, I mean it was a huge expense for the company, but I wasn't about to complain. First class on UAE is pretty fantastic. It was probably the most comfortable flight I had ever been on. I was also appointed a guide to take me through the airport when I had to make my transfer in Dubai for the final leg of my trip. I was expected to wait for my flight in the first-class lounge also, which I wasn't real comfortable with. Drinks were free and I had a guide to make sure I made my next flight, so it wasn't all bad! Haha!

From the airport, I was taken to my hotel room in the "European Village." The European Village is a hotel complex with a couple hotels, several little houses, a couple restaurants, post office, and small market, and a very nice large swimming pool with ample room for people to lay out and sun tan. The place is surrounded by a pretty thick, ten-foot high, concrete and brick wall topped with coiled razor-wire. There was a massive steel gate that blocked the single-lane entrance. A guard in a fortified shack let people in and out of the complex, *if* they had the proper papers to enter or leave. I have the impression that the guards were armed, but I don't actually remember seeing any weapons.

The compound was actually very nice inside. Several of our crew were at the complex when I arrived. The Coeur D' Alene Kid was there – he was the Dive Superintendent and pretty much in charge of the dive operations. Hollywood was there as one of the divers. Several guys I had worked with on the Crossmar Seven and some from the Superior Performance were also here. They were from California, Texas, Washington, and several other states. We all had our own rooms and all the meals were charged to Saudi-Aramco – the company we were working for. We got special privileges in town and around the city because we were working for Saudi Aramco. We were stared at all the time when we spent any time in town outside of the compound. It was somewhat unnerving.

One of the most irritating things I encountered here on the beach was the islamic call to prayer. That call blared out from megaphones mounted on high posts all over the city. They moaned for about fifteen minutes every four hours all day every day. Yep, starting at four in the morning, I was wakened by that noise. Then again at eight – just about breakfast time, then again at noon. Yet again at four in the afternoon, then at eight in the evening and lastly at midnight. Just to start all over again at four in the morning. It was like being in some Dystopian movie – hot sandy landscape, sand-colored buildings all over, living compound protected by a high concrete wall topped off with coiled razor wire, large steel gate guarding access to said compound, loudspeakers on telephone poles blaring the state's propaganda – it was a pretty weird situation from my point of view.

Hollywood and I went out on the town a couple times. We wanted to experience the culture as much as we could. We had a very nice steak dinner at a fine restaurant. The food and the service were excellent. While we were there, the call to prayer came over the loudspeakers outside. Suddenly, about half the patrons in the restaurant left their tables and went to an open area to the side of the restaurant near the restrooms. These people then laid out small carpets that had been rolled up and stacked against one of the walls. Then they kneeled on the carpets – all facing the same direction and started bowing down touching their foreheads to the floor. Some of them were moaning – I am sure that was their form of praying, but I didn't understand Arabic, so it sounded like muffled moaning to me. That lasted ten or fifteen minutes, after which they rolled and stacked the little carpets and returned to their tables. They went back to their conversations and meals just like nothing had happened. That also was very strange to me.

After a few days on the beach, we headed out to the Semi-Submersible Drilling Rig. We loaded up on a crew boat and rode that to the rig. When we got within about five-hundred feet of the drilling rig, the captain of the crew boat radioed the captain of the drilling rig to let him know who we were and what our purpose was. They had to do that because there were pirates and terrorists in the Persian Gulf that would attack the offshore rigs. Because of that, the rigs had armed guards on board that were ordered to fire upon any vessel that approached the rig without communicating its purpose. I ended up spending about nine weeks on that rig and twice, that I remember, little boats approached the rig and had to be warned off. It seemed a little like a big game of Cat and Mouse to me, but still a little unnerving.

Global had a crew on board for two weeks before I arrived. I was coming out to dive for a couple weeks and also assistant supervise under one of Global's older SAT Supervisors. I had worked as an LST under this same supervisor on many jobs going all the way back to the Boa Deep C. He had been in the dive industry since the early seventies and was trying to retire, but he wouldn't say no to Global when they asked him to supervise. He rarely worked more than four weeks at a time though – that's why I was called in. I thought that was awesome, because I wanted to dive in as many of the world's oceans as I could.

This job was to kill one of Saudi Aramco's oil wells that had been struck by a ship and bent over. It was a lone well – not right next to an oil rig – that had pipework rising up about seventy feet from the sea bottom. The bottom was about one-hundred-forty feet, if I remember correctly, and we had to dig down about ten or twenty feet to get to the spot where we could hot-tap and kill the well. We would also remove all the damaged pipework.

I dove a few times which was incredible. The sea life in the area was amazing. The main deck we were working off of was about forty feet above the surface of the water so the diver rode a stage to and from the bottom. A crossover line had been established from a weight below the stage to the worksite at the well. We were doing Sur-D-O_2 dives (Surface Decompression using Oxygen – remember?). The stage stopped about five or six feet off the bottom. On my first dive I jumped off the stage when it stopped near the bottom and landed on a very large ray – I think it was a butterfly ray because it was the same color as the bottom sediment. I am sure that I startled it when I landed on it because it immediately lifted off the bottom and flew away. I know it startled me when it swam off from under me. I located the crossover line and followed it to the work site. The visibility was excellent and I could see all kinds of sea life around; sea snakes, puffer fish, and rays, that I noticed right off the bat. My task was to chip concrete away from the well pipe. My depth was one-hundred-forty-seven feet so my bottom time was limited to forty-five minutes. It took three minutes from my last in-water deco stop to get me down to fifty feet in the Deck Decompression Chamber (DDC) where I finished my decompression on oxygen. There's a little more to the deco than that, but you don't want to read all that technical stuff here.

My main reason for being out there the first couple weeks was to work under the supervisor and get a feel for the job. I didn't really have to dive, but the supervisor let me because he knew that I enjoyed it and knew that I liked to get a feel for the underwater conditions so I would know what my divers were dealing with. That supervisor left a couple weeks later and I took over as the day shift supervisor working under the Coeur D' Lane Kid. We had a really good and highly experienced crew.

Many of the divers had more dive experience than the Kid did, but they preferred diving to superintending and even supervising. I guess they didn't really want the responsibility. I understood – the diving was much more enjoyable than dealing with all the paperwork. I didn't know it at the time, but I would only make a few more dives for the rest of my dive career.

* * *

Desiccation

I am starting this chapter by continuing with the dive job in the Persian Gulf for a couple reasons. First, because we are working in the Persian Gulf off the coast of Saudi Arabia in the summer and it is really, I mean *really*, hot during the day. We recorded temperatures on the deck of the drilling rig in the shade of one-hundred-thirty-seven degrees Fahrenheit! It was hot! Yes, that was an extreme and not what we normally worked in but I just had to let you know how hot it could get in the shade there. The average temperatures that day shift had to work in were one-hundred-fifteen to one-hundred-twenty-five degrees Fahrenheit. Still plenty warm. I had to make sure my deck crew kept hydrated and took breaks in the air-conditioned parts of the rig every twenty minutes or so. Heat stroke and heat exhaustion were major concerns and we did have a couple crew members suffer from both.

Secondly, this is the point in my career where I didn't really dive anymore. From here on out I was almost always supervising. I could still be a productive diver, but there were many younger guys who were more fit and had more energy for that physical work. Also, that is just where my career was heading. I think I was more valuable as an LST or a Dive Supervisor. I had no interest in becoming a superintendent, but I did enjoy being a supervisor.

As I said before, there was a lot of sea life in the Persian Gulf here. The divers wore a camera on the top of their dive helmet and I could see what they saw in the water. Since I was not actually doing the work, I could look around the video monitor and see all the fish and other life while the divers were concentrating on the task at hand. A few of the divers were wary of sharks – we were in warm water, so there were quite a few in the area – and would keep looking around for them as they were working. A couple other divers seemed to be bothered by a few of the sea snakes that lived around this well. We didn't really have any issues from any of the sea life though.

Once, when one of the younger divers was doing his thirty-foot in-water deco stop, a thirty to forty-foot Whale Shark swam slowly by the diver's stage. The diver was nervous about that big a fish being so close to him. I don't think he really believed me when I told him whale sharks ate small things like plankton, so he had nothing to worry about.

The oilfield we were working around had lots of Hydrogen Sulfide (H_2S). It is a very hazardous gas, exposure can lead to death, so we had to take part in safety drills on a weekly basis. We also had to shave our beards so the gas masks could make an airtight seal around our face. The alarm for the drill would go off and we would have to stop what we were doing and don our masks – they were positioned all over the rig. Then all the non-essential personnel (if we were diving – that meant everyone except the diver in the water, the dive supervisor, standby diver, and one tender) would have to climb several flights of stairs to the muster site. More than once, one of our crew members had to get first aid treatment for Heat Stroke due to the extreme conditions.

One day while we were out on the rig, the sky started to get a yellowish-reddish glow. We looked to the west and saw a huge dusky red cloud rolling towards us. All the regular drill crew told us we needed to shut down operations, put covers over all the openings in our equipment, and get everyone inside. We weren't really sure what they were talking about. They said we needed to cover up our equipment and close up anything that we didn't want sand all over and in. Then they started running all over and closing everything up and covering up their equipment. We did the same thing. Shortly after we completed that task and got inside it got really dark and windy.

It was quiet inside the drill rig, but we could hear how nasty it was outside. The storm had pretty strong winds and it sort of sounded like it might be hailing outside. We asked the drill crew what it was and they told us it was an Haboob.

"What's an Haboob?" We asked.

"A sandstorm," they answered.

A Sandstorm!?! We were several miles offshore. How could this be a sandstorm? Well, when the winds are strong enough, they lift sand from the desert several hundred feet into the air. Extreme sandstorms can raise sand and dust up to four or five miles into the air and be sixty miles wide. They can travel thousands of miles. Typical windspeeds are around twenty to twenty-five miles per hour. These storms can blot out the sun for several days. They also shut down air traffic and cause real problems for automotive traffic – not to mention health hazards for people caught in them. The only thing I could relate this experience to, was what happened in the Pacific

Northwest when Mount Saint Helens blew its top in nineteen-eighty. We had no idea how long this storm would last. When we looked out the portholes all we saw was red. It was like the apocalypse.

It lasted for several hours, more than a whole shift – twelve hours – and then it was quiet outside. My shift – day shift – was on duty when the storm arrived and we were back on duty after it left. We went back out on deck after the winds had blown by. It was calm and clear outside now. Everything was covered in orangish-red sand; well, it wasn't really sand, it was lighter than that, but it was heavier than dust – kind of like dry silt I suppose. There were little piles of it everywhere. We had to clean it up before we started any of our equipment and got back to the diving. It took us several hours to do that. We really had to make sure the air intakes of all our equipment were super clean and dust or silt free. We didn't want that stuff getting into any of the engines and we certainly didn't want to be breathing any of that silt or dust.

This job lasted into September. It was originally supposed to be just a four-to-six-week job. It stretched out longer than originally planned. I was told it would only be four more weeks after I arrived. I ended up spending just over nine weeks there. It was an interesting job and the whole experience was really eye-opening for me. It was the first time I had worked in a muslim-controlled environment. All I really want to say here is that they do things very differently than we do.

* * *

Global had been contracted by Trident over the summer to help with the salvage of the Costa Concordia. The first dive crew of Global's would be sent over in mid-September. If you remember, the Costa Concordia was the gigantic Italian cruise liner that had hit an island - Isola del Giglio – off the coast of Italy in January two-thousand-twelve and sank. Well, it didn't completely sink. It hit some submerged rocks and rolled over on its side. The ship was so big that even though it was resting on a slope at a little over fifty feet deep, still more than fifty feet of ship was protruding out of the water. It was resting on a fairly steep slope, precariously held in place by the rocks it had hit. The lower part of the hull was over a hundred feet below the surface.

The area the Concordia sank in was an underwater preservation area popular with tourist SCUBA divers. It was home to some of the largest mussels in the world. The salvage operation would have to be done in such a way as to do as little damage to the area as possible. There would be many stages in the salvage process. First was removal of the giant mussels immediately threatened. This was done by a European dive team before the salvage operations started. The mussels were moved to another part of the nature reserve out of harm's way.

When Global announced that they had been hired by Titan to help with the salvage, everybody and their brother wanted to get on the job – even me. It would be awesome to get on a job like that, and it would be another sea for me to dive in that I hadn't yet been in. I let all the superintendents know that I really wanted to be involved in that project. Of course, I was busy doing other things when they sent their first crew over. Global didn't have a regular rotation schedule for that job yet. It was forecast to take about a year. Some of Global's crew wanted to be on the whole project, others wanted to swap out every four weeks. Global management had determined a four-week rotation would be too expensive, and decided people would go over for a two-month hitch at the minimum. That was still okay with me.

The first supervisor to go over was the same guy who had started the job in Saudi Arabia. After two months, he was more than ready to go home. I had my time off and had also gone through some supervisor training paid for by Global. Towards the end of my class in November, I was asked by the Global management if I would be interested in going over to Italy to work on the Costa Concordia Salvage. They wanted me to go over as a supervisor for the first month, then spend the second month training one of their younger divers to be a supervisor. I told them I would gladly do that. I asked my wife if she was okay with me working in Europe for a couple months even though it was over Christmas. She said she was, and seemed excited that I would be working on such a project – especially if I was supervising rather than diving. She had always been nervous about me working under the water and was much less anxious when I was supervising or working as an LST.

I flew over to Italy the first week of December. The Mouth flew over with me. He was going as a diver and assistant supervisor. We flew into Rome where we met a hired driver who took us to Porto Santo Stefano. From there, we would take a ferry to the island the Concordia had run into. We arrived at the ferry dock in the morning, after more than twenty-four hours of travel and waiting. We were tired, but didn't want to miss the ferry, so didn't dare take a nap. We had to buy our own ferry tickets that would be reimbursed by Titan. Nobody we talked to in Italy wanted to speak English – I'm sure many of them could. I think they just enjoyed torturing us with the lack of communication. I spoke a little Portuguese, which is similar to Italian, so I could communicate a little. I think I understood more of the Italian than the Italians understood of my Portuguese. It was entertaining to say the least. We were successful in getting to the island intact and with all our luggage at the scheduled time, that was good.

Titan had rented a whole hotel in the little town, Giglio Porto - on the island - that had a great view of the wreck. We had to check in with Titan there and fill out a ton of paperwork, get our ID cards, and get our assigned berth on the accommodations barge anchored close to the Concordia. We could rent a place on the island if we wanted to, but that would be on our own nickel and was strongly discouraged. Both the Mouth and I were happy with living on the barge. Most of the people working on the job were living on the barge. There were plenty of little boats that would take us to the beach on our time off. These same boats ferried us to the barges we would be working on too.

The accommodations barge was really nice. I had my own berth with its own head and shower – just like on the Boa Deep C. The roomy berth was almost exactly like those on the Boa. The only differences were that there was a two-tiered bunk bed rather than just a single bunk, and there were two wardrobes. The room could comfortably support two people without any form of hot-bunking or overcrowding. My berth was on the third level out of four. The large galley and dining area were located on the first level. They took up half the barge level. A very nice recreation room with a large screen television took up the other half of the first deck. Chefs rotated out every few weeks so they wouldn't get tired of being on the barge. They were all highly skilled and made a point of varying the menu a lot. Breakfast was the only meal that stayed the same and it was a comfortable mix of European and American style foods. Most of the other meals were more European.

This project ran twenty-four hours a day, seven days a week. There were dive crews from several countries working on this project at the same time. There were four dive barges crewed up the whole time. Two barges were crewed by Italians both shifts – the job was taking place in Italy, so they were sort of overseeing everything, although Titan had the last word on all the goings on. Another dive barge was crewed by British teams – both day and night shifts. The fourth barge had two dive teams on it for both shifts. Half of the barge was crewed by

Canadian teams day and night, while the other half was crewed by Global during the day and a Dutch dive crew at night. Day shift was eight in the morning to eight at night. Night shift was the opposite of that.

Global's crew, while I was there, was made up of many guys that I had worked with in the Gulf of Mexico, as well as many that I had worked with from other dive companies. SoCal had been on the crew before I got there, but left just before I arrived. The Mouth came out with me. Several guys that had been on the Cheesman Dam project were on this job – a couple of them from Alaska. Hollywood was on this job the same time I was. There were also a couple newer guys that I had never met before. We had one or two that were only tenders and didn't have enough experience to jump right into Sur-D-O_2 diving.

There were many other work crews besides just the dive crews. I think there were twenty-six work crews or something like that. People from all over the world worked on those crews, Norwegians, Scots, and many other Europeans. I don't remember any South Americans, but that doesn't mean there weren't any. We got along with them, although many of them didn't care for Americans as a rule – especially the Italians. The Dutch thought pretty highly of themselves. The dive system we were using was supplied by the Dutch company. At least everything was labeled in English. That was good for us. I got along very well with the Canadian and the British dive supervisors. It was great fun and quite educational talking with them about the way they did things. All in all, it was not that different from how we did things. Each country had their own dive tables and decompression schedules, but they all respected the USN tables we used. The Canadian tables were the most conservative – that is, the shortest dive times at depths, with the longest decompression as compared to the other tables used.

We were diving Sur-D-O_2 at depths from one-hundred feet to one-hundred-forty feet. While I was there, our main job was to position large polypropylene bags and fill them with concrete. It was a somewhat difficult task and had to be done quite precisely. More important than placing the bags as precisely as possible, was letting the engineers know exactly how they were positioned after being filled with concrete. One of my most important tasks as a supervisor (according to Titan) was making accurate diagrams of the concrete bag positions after they were placed and filled. We were working in the same area as the Canadian team and essentially doing the same task. The Canadian supervisor and I worked well together in coordinating our diver's work. While I was there, we had no issues with them and nobody had any issues with us.

Just like in the Persian Gulf, I made a couple dives on this site under the same supervisor before I took over. We had a downline established that took us to the bottom on the starboard side of the ship. That was the side towards the island. The downline hit the bottom at just about fifty feet. There was another line – a crossover line – that led from the downline, under the ship to the actual work site which was on the port side of the ship. The depth there was close to one-hundred-fifty-five feet. As we worked, piling concrete bags on top of each other, the work depth gradually became shallower.

On my first dive I splashed and followed the downline to the bottom. The water was fairly warm. It was very blue and the visibility was quite good - over a hundred feet. There wasn't much to see right off the bat. I didn't notice any fish swimming around. The bottom was silty sand and the ship loomed large over my head. The crossover line led under the middle of the ship between two very large rocks upon which the ship was resting. The space wasn't huge. It was plenty big to get through without any issues – in fact a diver in heavy gear would have been able to walk upright under it with plenty of room overhead. It was still kind of eerie going under the wreck though.

Thoughts going through my head were; there is a chance the ship could slide deeper and take me with it. Maybe the hull that was resting on the rocks could give way and the ship would sink lower squishing me between it and the bottom. It was even possible that the ship hull might split in half and who knows where the pieces might end up and what they might do to me while they were moving. Those kinds of thoughts always go through your head. The thing is, while you need to be aware of the dangers and possibly changing conditions, you also need to be practical and realistic. If you let your fears run out of control, you probably shouldn't be in the dive industry. You have to keep your head about you. I followed the crossover to the worksite. I was carrying a couple polypro bags with me to put into place.

From our worksite underwater, I could see in the distance, the work being done by one of the Italian teams building a platform that the ship would eventually rest on at a later stage of the salvage. There were already many concrete-filled bags in place forming a base that I would add to. The bags were pretty good size and it was sort of a pain to lay them out. It was like trying to make a king-sized bed underwater by yourself. There were ropes to be tied along the sides of the bag to keep it in place. Once the bags were filled with concrete and the concrete cured, there was no chance of slippage.

After getting the bags in place I connected a tremie hose to the bag inlet. This would guide concrete from the surface into the bag. When the bag was full, I informed topside and the concrete flow would stop. I took the tremie over to the second bag and got that one filled also. Positioning and filling those two bags took my whole dive time. I returned to the down line and followed it up to the surface, doing my in-water decompression as I approached the surface. Once on the surface I got out of all my dive gear – with topside's help – and climbed into the chamber to complete my decompression, breathing pure oxygen.

My turnover with the supervisor I was replacing took just a few days. He went over the equipment we were using, the dive systems, and the decompression set up. He introduced me to the other dive supervisors we were working with. He showed me all around the barges and showed me who I had to radio for permissions to do things and who to notify in case of emergencies. He showed me what the reports should look like and who I had to turn them in to. He seemed somewhat anxious to get off the job and I didn't really know why other than he was really ready to retire. I was happy to take over from him. I really enjoyed working with people from all over the world and the job was very interesting.

* * *

Isola del Giglio was an interesting place. It was a very popular tourist area, but more so in the spring, summer, and fall. It was the winter season here now, so not many tourists. The Italian government wanted to keep the tourism down to a minimum anyway during this salvage. They were hoping the salvage would be completed as soon as possible. The local business owners didn't seem to mind too much because of all the workers on the job. The bars and restaurants were always full. We were allowed to go to the beach when we weren't working which was nice because there were some interesting things to see on the island.

There was a castle on the top of the hill – Giglio Castello – overlooking the whole island. The castle was a little medieval-era walled village. It had a couple good restaurants and bars. There were several ways to get there. One was by road – you could hire a taxi or rent a scooter and drive up there. Of course, by the time I got there, the scooter rental place wouldn't rent any scooters to any Americans on the salvage crew because of some brouhaha involving several of Global's crew members before I got there. I was a little disappointed about that, but what can you do?

The other way to get there was hike up the hill. There was a road leading out of the port village heading up the hill. About half-way up the hill on the road, a trail led off more directly towards the castle. It was a shortcut to the top of the hill. It was a good trail, but had some pretty steep parts. It took about forty-five minutes to get to the castle by foot from the boat launch. It was good exercise and after I found out about it, I vowed to make the trek every day that the weather allowed. We did have a couple rainy days while I was working on that project. I got up to the castle five or six days a week on average though. There were usually three to five of us that would make the hike.

Giglio Castello was quite interesting. The walls surrounding the village date back to the twelfth century. There is also a church – the Church of Saint Peter – that dates to the twelfth century. However, it was renovated in the eighteenth century so has more of a Baroque style. Most of the buildings in the villages are made of stone. The doors are mostly wooden and all painted in very bright colors, though most seem to be red or green.

There is another little village – Giglio Campese - on the other side of the island that I never got to. It was too far to walk to in the time I had off. While I was there, I never got a whole day off. I could have taken a taxi, but that would have been expensive. The town was mostly shut down because it wasn't tourist season. As I said before, the Italian government sort of shut down the tourism on the island until after the salvage was complete anyway. There are a couple towers on the island that were built in the sixteenth or seventeenth centuries. I didn't visit those either though, because of the distance from Giglio Porto.

Hollywood rented a house, like an Air-B-n-B, on a little hill above Giglio Porto. It overlooked the village cemetery which was interesting. The cemetery was all walled in and had some very ornate tombs, small crypts, and one whole wall that was a columbarium. There was no grass, but lots of vases and urns for flowers and flowering bushes. It was pretty in a macabre sort of way. It looked very old, but not worn, with lots of marble and large iron decorations. There were also a couple angelic statues. When we were sitting on the patio having a beer or whatever, we could see into the cemetery. It seemed like there was always someone in there placing flowers or communing with the spirits.

I was on this job over Christmas and a bunch of us wanted to put up a Christmas tree on our dive barge. Italy celebrates Christmas so it was easy to get a tree. We all got together and found a small tree – five feet tall or so – and set it up on the dive barge just outside of Dive Control. It was in a covered area so we didn't have to worry about it getting rained on. I made a little angel out of paper coffee cups to top off the tree. Somebody found some lights somewhere, brought them out and put them on the tree. The tree was decorated with handmade decorations from all the crews working on the barge – Canadian, Dutch, and us. Somebody made a garland out of microwaved popcorn and dental floss. It was quite festive and we took photos of us next to the tree and e-mailed them to our families back home. I think all the families at home got a kick out of the photos, I know my wife did. We had a good time setting up the tree and decorating it.

Many of the workers on this job celebrated Christmas. The fact is, that many people all over the world celebrate the Christmas holiday season no matter what religion they are. There is a lot going on this time of year to celebrate – Hanukkah, Winter Solstice, Yule, Kwanzaa, the New Year, and I don't know what else – so the galley crew made a really fantastic holiday meal for Christmas day. They worked several days preparing special dishes for the feast day. There were all sorts of fancy dishes and the desserts were exquisite. I ate way more than I probably should have. I know I ate way more desserts than I needed and way more than my wife would have approved of. Haha! It was a very nice Christmas for having to spend it offshore and away from family.

Since we were working the day shift, we got to celebrate New Year's Eve. Hollywood and his houseguest prepared an excellent late evening meal for a few of us. The Mouth, another guy and I brought a fair bit of alcohol to help us ring in the New Year. We all enjoyed a great meal and good company. After the meal, we went out to the patio for drinks and good conversation. We shared some good stories of past dive jobs and other escapades and shared some good laughs. We could see most of the village from the patio. At midnight lots of fireworks were set off in the village. We had a great vantage point to see them all. We all raised a glass and wished each other a happy and prosperous new year. It was a great way to celebrate the arrival of the new year.

*　*　*

I was on the Costa Concordia job until mid-January. Overall, I really enjoyed my part in the salvage. All jobs have good points and bad points. I had some issues with one of the superintendents and some of the middle management at Global's home office over their personnel choices for the latter part of my hitch. The guy I was supposed to be training as a supervisor let the position really go to his head and he treated the crew members under him very badly. He also falsified some of the drawings he submitted. When I tried to get him to correct them, he wouldn't do it. When the Dutch crew informed the engineers on the job that what was underwater was not what was on the reports, this guy blamed the Canadian crew. Unfortunately, there were so many green divers on the Canadian crew that the Canadian supervisor couldn't refute what my trainee was saying. My problem was that I didn't kiss any ass, I always told it how it really was. My trainee, though, was a world class kiss ass. One of the Global superintendents had gone to school with this trainee and they were friends. So even though I had the support of my crew, I did not have the support of the Global management in charge of this job. I got sent home a little early along with the Mouth and a couple other guys.

I made a point of going to Global's main office in Seattle to have a talk with the management about the situation when I got back stateside. I told them that they were not running things the way they had in the past. I was told by them that Global was not the same company it had been in the past. The two main owners had basically retired the previous year and handed over the reins of the company to the younger guys. It's funny how people's attitudes change when they leave the field and move into the office. I was told by the new management that I would have to get used to how things were done now, or not work for them anymore. I told them that if this situation in Italy was indicative of how things were going to be in the future working for Global, I wouldn't be working for them anymore. That was fine I was told. As far as I knew I was not working for Global any longer. The Mouth had been put on "disciplinary leave" for three months because of what went on in Italy. I don't know how other people that didn't agree with the kiss ass were treated and I never tried to find out. I was just going to look for a new place to work. Northwest

Underwater Construction seemed to be getting a lot of work, maybe I would give them a call.

*   *   *

I was happy to have a little time off. I hadn't been able to spend as much time at home as I normally liked with all the work and training I was doing with Global Diving and Salvage. I did a couple little jobs with Harbor Offshore. I called Northwest Underwater Construction, but didn't really pursue anything there.

The first week of March I was contacted by the Global manager who was overseeing the work in the Gulf of Mexico – namely the work being done by the Superior Performance. They needed an LST and a Surface Supplied Mixed Gas Supervisor. They wanted to know if I might be available for that work. So much for not working with Global anymore. I told them I would be happy to do that work, or any work for them actually, as long as I wasn't expected to work with the kiss ass. I was told that would not be a problem.

At the end of March, I flew down to the Gulf of Mexico to do a hitch on the Performance. It was just like I never left. I got back on the regular rotation as an LST and did that through October. They didn't have enough supervisors or LSTs, so my hitches were more like six weeks on with two or three weeks off. Nothing really exciting or special happened during my time spent on the Performance that summer. It was nice not to have anything go wrong and nice to be working with people who I got along with very well. Everything goes so much smoother when everyone gets along well with each other.

One little incident we did have was with one of the younger guys who was new to deep air diving utilizing Sur-D-O_2. He was a smoker. I always tell all the divers that smoking is bad for divers in more ways than one. The worst thing smoking does is interfere with off-gassing during decompression. See, smoking damages the lungs reducing their capacity for gas transfer. Less oxygen goes in, less carbon dioxide goes out, the transfer of ALL the gasses is slowed down. What that means for a diver during decompression is that the body off gasses slower than normal. When the decompression schedules were developed by the United States Navy, none of the test subjects were smokers! They were all physically fit young men. I'm not saying this kid was not physically fit – he was in pretty good shape - maybe on the skinny side – but he smoked like a stack. In fact, the first thing he did after getting out of the chamber from his decompression was grab a cigarette and light up.

His dive was to one-hundred-sixty-five feet on air. I ran his decompression. I put him on fifty/fifty Nitrox at his seventy-foot water stop and kept him on that for all his in-water stops. After he completed his forty-foot stop he was brought up to the deck, stripped of his dive gear and suit, then stuffed into the chamber. The chamber operator blew him down to fifty feet and started his surface decompression. When his decompression was completed, he climbed out of the chamber, sat on a bench, and smoked a cigarette. After about seventeen minutes he told the chamber operator he wasn't feeling well. I was called. I went to the diver and observed him. He was pale and didn't look well. I asked him how he felt. He said he felt a little nauseous. I asked him if he was dizzy. He replied he was not.

I started to do a neurological exam on him. About half-way through, he said he was dizzy and fell into my lap. I immediately called for one of the guys on deck to give me a hand and we got him back into the chamber. I told the deck hand to stay in the chamber with this guy. We were going to run him on a Table Six – a treatment table for the bends. At about forty feet the diver said he was feeling much better. I had the chamber operator press him all the way down to sixty feet and start the table six treatment. While I was doing all of this, our superintendent called a hyperbaric doctor on the beach – the one everyone in the Gulf of Mexico has used for as long as any of us can remember. He told us we were doing the correct thing and after hearing all the symptoms, told us to finish out the table six then call him back afterwards to let him know the diver's condition.

Five hours later the diver was back on the surface and had gone through another neurological exam. He said he was feeling fine and he didn't have any symptoms of any hyperbaric trauma. He was happy, we were happy, so the superintendent called the doctor back to let him know the condition of the diver. We were advised to keep an eye on him for the next twenty-four hours. Also, the doctor recommended that the diver not dive for two weeks, but left that final decision up to the superintendent. After all was settled and back to normal - more or less - the diver asked for a cigarette. Are you kidding me!?! He got one and lit up. I just shook my head. Of course, I had to tell him again that it was probably because of his smoking habit that he got bent in the first place and, in my humble opinion, if he wanted to be a diver, he should probably quit smoking. He smiled, looked at the ground, and continued to suck on his cancer stick. I shrugged my shoulders and went to the galley for a chocolate milk. What else could I do?

*　　*　　*

Sometime in the summer, I had been contacted by Northwest Underwater Construction about the big tunnelling job that was taking place in Seattle. They wanted to know if I would be available to work on their tunnelling crew when they were called in to do an intervention. I told them I would be more than happy to do that and they could just give me a call. I did tell them that I had a schedule with Global and, at the moment, they were top on the list. I also told them that if they had to do an intervention and I had enough notice I would probably be able to get someone to fill in for me in the GoM. They were happy with that.

My work on the Performance finished up at the end of October. After that I didn't go back down to the Gulf of Mexico for Global. I did a couple jobs in the northwest for Harbor Offshore before Christmas. Nothing much was going on dive wise over the winter. I was enjoying my time off with my wife. I got to spend a little more time with my kids too. We had a nice holiday season with lots of family time. That was a rare thing for me lately.

In the early spring of two-thousand-fourteen I did a couple jobs for Harbor Offshore. These jobs I went out as a tender/standby diver. Not much was going on. I called NUC to see if they had anything going on – they didn't. The TBM – Bertha, in Seattle – had run into a problem and the tunneling had been shut down for an undetermined amount of time. It turns out that it would be two years before that machine started working again.

In April Global sent me over to Aberdeen, Washington to work on a job inspecting large floating concrete blocks. These were pontoons for the refurbishment of the floating bridge that crossed the middle of Lake Washington from Seattle to Medina. The blocks were fabricated in Aberdeen then put in the ocean, inspected, and towed to Seattle. They would be floated through the Ballard locks into Lake Union, then through the ship canal and on into Lake Washington. We were looking for cracks and imperfections in the pontoons below the water line. There were several dive teams made up of a supervisor, two divers, and a tender. I was a supervisor on one of the boats and Hollywood was one of my divers. Since not much was going on, lots of divers wanted in on this job. There were at least five teams so quite a few guys did get on this job.

The first week of June Global sent me up to Valdez, Alaska for a small job there. We were inspecting an outfall for the city of Valdez and another line for Exxon-Mobile. I flew into Anchorage for that job and got to touch bases with the people out of that office that I had worked with on jobs in the GoM, Colorado, and Italy. It was fun to spend some time with those people on their home turf. I was up there about a week. Not much was going on up there either.

A couple years earlier, a friend of mine had started working for a new dive company based out of Houston, Texas – Ranger Offshore. In the spring of two-thousand-fourteen he contacted me to tell me they had won a bid for a job in Nigeria. They were looking for people to go on that job and he wanted to know if I might want to do that. I told him that I would. He said there was a lot of prep work to do for that job first. Also, I would need to make sure my passport was in order. Ranger would have to get me a temporary work visa and I would have to get quite a few inoculations. I was game for all of that and told him to let me know where and when he needed me to show up for appointments. He called me the second weekend of June and asked if I could head right down to Louisiana. I told him I could. My wife wasn't happy that I was leaving home right after getting back from Alaska, but it hadn't been a busy year yet and she knew I could use the work.

I drove down to Houston, arriving Sunday around noon. I met my friend at his office. He introduced me to everybody there, then asked if I could head over to New Iberia, Louisiana – where their Human Resources Dept was located – a shop and yard they had acquired from Tiburon Divers, Inc. I told him I would do whatever they needed me to do. I spent the afternoon driving and spent the night in New Iberia. In the morning I showed up at their office and signed in. Surprise, surprise, my friend Portland, was in the office doing the same thing I was doing. That made sense since my friend in the Houston office was also a friend of his. There was a whiteboard in the office that had a list of people being recruited for the Nigeria job – several of my friends were on that list. I looked at the names of the people applying and thought it would be fun to work with most of them in Africa.

When my name was called, I went in to the office of the guy in charge of hiring. He did a little interview and we talked about my dive career and experience. I showed him all my certifications and filled out all the paperwork to get hired on. The secretary made the necessary appointments for me to get a dive physical, MRI scan, drug screen, and all that stuff. When all that was done – a few days later – I went back in to sign the necessary documents, get issued the company PPE – hard hat, gloves, safety glasses, life jacket – and a couple t-shirts, stickers, and pocket notebooks. That was pretty nice. I also got my passport back with a work visa for Nigeria. Now I was just waiting for the call to go to Nigeria. I told them that I would probably be working for Global Diving and Salvage while I was waiting for the call to work in Nigeria. They were not happy about that and said they would see if they could find something for me to do. They would let me know. This was Friday and I told them I would be driving home, but my phone was always on.

Saturday evening - as I was driving through Amarillo, Texas – I got a call from the guy in New Iberia. He wanted to know if I was available to work for the next month or so. I told him I was. Then he asked if I could be at their Galveston shop Sunday morning to head offshore. My shift as a SAT Supervisor would start on Monday if I could make it. I told him I could make it and promptly turned around. I didn't get any sleep that night, but I did make it to their shop and was there when it opened. The shop manager was expecting me and got me all set up with a ride to the dock where I would meet the crew boat that would take me out to the Crossmar Fourteen. This was a regular crew change day for them, so it worked out well for me. I called my wife and she was happy that I would be working.

* * *

The crew boat ride out to the Crossmar Fourteen was several hours. It was stormy and the seas were a little rough. I was thinking this was turning out to be just like the jobs I had gone on in the mid-eighties at the start of my diving career when I had been working for American Oilfield Divers. The only difference now was that I was a supervisor rather than a tender. I wasn't sure how much better that would be. I had no idea what kind of vessel the Crossmar Fourteen would be. Oh Joy.

It was late, almost dark, when the crew boat reached the Crossmar Fourteen. I could still see it though and it was small. Really small; like less than half the size of the Superior Performance – which wasn't all that big anyway. This was looking more and more like a trip back in time. Well, I would try to make the best of it anyway. I could see the crane on the stern – not huge, but not too small either. I could see the SAT system – It looked old and in need of a fair bit of maintenance. The accommodations section of the barge didn't look all that big. I was hoping I would at least have my own berth.

We boarded the barge with the use of a Billy Pugh – no surprise there. A couple of the guys on the crew had never seen one before and had a little trouble getting on it. We all got on board the barge without any incidents though. I met the superintendent and he introduced me to one of the tenders who would show me all around the barge and get me signed in. The superintendent told the tender to grab my bags, but I told the tender I could carry my own luggage. Oh no, maybe

I really was in a time warp! I was keeping a positive attitude about it all though, and see how things went. Work was work, right? Maybe, maybe not. It would depend on the attitudes of everyone on the crew.

I did have my own berth. That was good. I did not have my own head though. Showers, sinks, and toilets were in a community space. Lovely. The dining area was small, but the crew was small, so it was adequate. There was a big screen television on one of the bulkheads. Yep, definitely a time warp. My shift wouldn't start until the next day at noon. I would be on the day shift. I made a point of going into the dive shack to meet the other shift anyway and get an idea of what Dive Control was like. It was like most of the others I had worked in – a Conex with the Dive Control and the LST station taking up about two-thirds of the box, and the rear third; a space for the Betty and surface diver.

I went back to my berth and unpacked. Then I went down to the dining area to scope that out. I had some chocolate milk. They had Coke products for pop – so no Mountain Dew. That was okay, though, because I had mostly quit drinking the Dew when I was in Saudi Arabia. They had Mountain Dew over there but it tasted so bad that I quit drinking it. By the time I had returned home from Arabia, it had been over three months without a Mountain Dew. I had decided that I might as well kick the habit. On board the Fourteen, they had the same snacks and food items as most of the other offshore rigs. There were all kinds of cookies, crackers, Spam, Vienna sausages, deviled ham, peanut butter, jelly, and honey. Well, I wouldn't starve anyway. I went back to my berth and lay down in my bunk. I had a few books and I read myself to sleep.

I got up around eight in the morning. I wasn't due on shift until noon – a quarter to noon actually – but thought I'd have some breakfast then go take a look around the SAT system and familiarize myself with it. Breakfast was as good as on any other barge I had been on lately, that was nice. I talked to some of the guys on the night shift about the barge, the SAT system, Ranger Offshore, and other things. They were all friendly for the most part. After that I went out to the Dive Station to see what I had got myself into.

I knocked on the Dive Shack door and was let in by the surface diver. I introduced myself to the three in there - night supervisor, LST, and surface diver. "Surface Diver" is what they called the deck foreman. He was also designated the next crew member to go into SAT if one of the SAT divers had to be taken out of the system for one reason or another. They all seemed like good people and seemed to know what they were doing. The inside of the dive shack was clean – that was a good sign. After a bit of small talk, I went back outside to look over the system. I found the SAT Tech and talked to him. He gave me a tour of the system with a narrative of his opinion of its present condition.

The system was old, not super old – like Global's SAT One – but it was just about ten years old. It had been built for one of the dive companies that had been contracted to work on the Ivan Main Pass project – yes, the same one that Global had been contracted for – back in two-thousand-five before Katrina and Rita had hit. This system had been used and abused by the look of it. It was in dire need of lots of maintenance. I had a hard time believing it had been approved to be on the job. The SAT tech informed me that he and the day shift SAT tech were constantly repairing things on this system. He didn't like the system at all, but he kept it going. My friend and SAT Tech, Gulf Breeze, would never have okayed a system in this condition to be used until after it had been refurbished.

At eleven thirty, a little meeting was held in the dining area. The captain of the barge and the superintendent of the dive job went over what had been done during the last shift and what was to be done during the next shift. We also signed the

JSAs (Job Safety Analysis documents) for the projected tasks of the day. I was in the dive shack at a quarter to twelve for the handover from the night shift supervisor. At noon I took over. The Dive Bell was down – about two-hundred-forty-five feet – and the second diver was out working on his task.

The main task was deconstruction of a fallen oilrig. The whole thing was on the bottom - two-hundred-sixty-five feet - and we were there to cut it up and bring up the pieces. The crane on board the barge was not a big one, so we had to cut the pieces rather small. There was no room on the barge to store them, but we had another empty barge tied off to us that the scrapped pieces were piled on. Most of the cutting was done by a wire saw set up by the diver. There was a little bit of burning with a Broco set-up, but not too much. There was also a lot of rigging for the diver to do. There were small pipes, hoses, cables, and other debris intertwined in all the bent and twisted steel of the rig's Jacket and pilings. At least the top package had been removed earlier, but even without it there was plenty of stuff for the diver to get fouled on. It was a real mess. The only saving grace was that the visibility was pretty good – at least seventy-five feet. It was very blue down there during the day and very black after the sun went down. The system had pretty good lights on the Dive Bell. That made it nice for the divers in the middle of the night.

The SAT system was a typical, for the time, four-man SAT system with an HRC (Hyperbaric Rescue Chamber) that was used for pressing divers in and decompressing divers out. The divers on the inside said it was nice enough. It was up to them to keep it clean. I talked to the SAT tech on my shift and he told me that the system had been gone through before it was set up on this barge several months previous. He agreed with the night shift SAT tech that the system was in serious need of maintenance and refurbishment. He told me he felt like Scotty, from Star Trek, trying to keep a ravaged Enterprise together and operable until they could get it into port for a proper overhaul. I asked him why it hadn't been overhauled before being set up on this barge. He told me Ranger didn't have the money and was hoping they would make enough from this job to refurbish the system properly. That seemed a little backwards to me, but all I could do was shake my head. I was hoping none of the issues would endanger the divers or surface support crew.

When the diver in the water had spent his time, I had him get back to the bell and prep for return to the surface. Everything went as it should and we got the bell back to the surface and locked on to the system without any issues. On this system the bell sat on top of the TL (Transfer Lock) to lock on. The dive crews swapped out and we got the next team into the bell and back down to the worksite. So far so good. The rest of my shift went well and the divers were pretty productive. The superintendent came in and went over the scope of the job with me and laid out a plan of how we would breakdown and remove the oil rig jacket. It was nice to have a plan laid out. At the end of my shift, I explained to the night shift supervisor what the superintendent had laid out for us.

When I got back on shift the next day, all was as it should be. The plans had been followed. The night shift had made good progress and left us in a good spot to continue on. After four days of this the job site had been cleared to the customers satisfaction. We were done here. So far so good. It was time to move on to the next work site. We were due for a grocery run and some of the crew were due to be changed out. The decision was made to take us into Fourchon (pronounced foo-Shawn, remember?) for all that. We left one dive team pressed in because they would continue their run. In fact, we would press them down to four-hundred-twenty feet for the next job. The other team we decompressed out in the HRC. It took us two days all said and done to get in to Fourchon and back out to the following work site. We got a new dive superintendent, a new night shift dive supervisor, a new dive team, and several new surface support guys including a new Betty. About half the barge crew changed out also – we got a new cook with that bunch. By the time we got the anchors set at the new work site, we had the SAT system pressed to the storage depth of four-hundred-twenty feet. The bottom was projected to be four-hundred-eighty to four-hundred-ninety feet.

* * *

It took almost eighteen hours to set the anchors. The tugs were having problems with a couple of them slipping. That was no good, because it was critical that we stayed in one place when the bell was down and divers were out working. While all that was going on, the superintendent went over the dive plan and deconstruction plan for this site. It would be about the same as the other site. The top deck package had already been taken away by some other crew. The jacket was laying on its side – like the other site – and we were to chop it up and rig the pieces so they could be brought up and set on another barge – just like at the previous site. Good deal.

The superintendent was in the dive shack when I sent the bell and the first dive team down to the work site. We lowered the clump weight with bell guide wires down to about four-hundred and forty feet. We would drop the bell down close to that and let the first diver go out and do a quick survey of the bottom. He would let us know if we should lower the clump weight and bell more and if we were in a good spot to work from.

It was a nice sunny day so lots of light penetrated the ocean well. Even so, at this depth it was fairly dark for the diver. The visibility was excellent – close to a hundred feet – but everything was a medium blue. The diver had us drop the bell down another ten feet to four-hundred-fifty feet. That would keep the clump weight high enough that it wouldn't get hung up on any debris if the barge did happen to move. We had a good view from the camera mounted on the diver's helmet. As the diver looked around at the work site, we could see it was a real mess. This diver did a quick survey and gave us a good assessment of what the work site looked like. From there the superintendent revised his work plan a little.

I had the first diver go back to the bell and the second diver go out and set up the saw on the first spot to cut. The first few pieces to cut were really easy because they weren't entangled in all the mess of cables, pipes, and other debris. This first bell run was very successful and had finished up just before the night shift supervisor came on shift. The superintendent was there for our turnover. He laid out the plan for the night shift supervisor. I went over what the divers on the first bell run had accomplished. It looked like everything was under control and all would go well.

The next day was basically the same. The only issue was that the night shift supervisor had the divers deviate from the superintendent's plan – as laid out to us – and left me with sort of a mess. He had the divers take the easy pieces which made it more challenging for the divers on my shift to set up the saw and remove pieces. That was okay, I could deal with it and the divers did as they were asked. We had another productive shift. At the end of my shift, I again went over with the night shift supervisor about what we had done and what he needed to do.

My next turnover was a repeat of the previous day. The night supervisor had not followed the schedule, but had done his own thing. This was somewhat of an issue because he was leaving more difficult work to my team. He was not taking the pieces from the top down. He was having his divers take the easy pieces away which was leaving the remaining pieces in precarious positions. He was creating unnecessary hazards and difficulties for my dive team to deal with. I asked him to kindly follow the plan in order to keep the divers as safe as possible. He ensured me that from here on out he would. He did not do that though.

Several days later after the same issue every day, the superintendent came up to me and asked me why the divers on my shift were not getting as much debris up as the night shift was. I showed him the drawings of our progress and pointed out that the night shift supervisor was not following the plan, thereby making progress harder for my dive team. I had one of the divers show him how he had to do extra rigging to support the piece he was going to cut because the previous team had cut out a piece that, while it was easier to remove at the time, left this piece in such a position that it couldn't safely be cut without a lot of extra rigging. The superintendent nodded and said he would have a talk with the night shift supervisor about this issue.

When I came on shift the following day, the night shift supervisor showed me that he had followed the plan and said I didn't need to cry about the job anymore. Whatever. I thanked him for following the plan and reminded him that it wasn't my plan, but the superintendents. I was just following orders and trying to get the job done quickly and safely. After that the night shift operator mostly followed the plan, but he still deviated from it enough to irritate me. I think he was doing it on purpose.

A few days after that I was back on shift as normal. All had been going fairly well and mostly as planned. The SAT techs had been doing their thing which included operating the winch that brought the bell up out of the water. The dive team had done their time and were back in the bell ready to come up to the surface and lock on to the system. The SAT tech came up on the bell like he always did at this stage of the operation. The seas were a little choppy, but not bad. The barge was rocking a little bit, but it had rocked back and forth worse than this before. There was also a light rain falling from the clouds, not really stormy, but definitely not a nice sunny day. The bell was slowly coming to the surface as it always did. The bell reached the surface and left the water. It was about fifteen feet above the surface of the water when I heard a loud *POP!* followed by lots of yelling. I saw the bell splash into the water and the divers started yelling and asking what was going on. The bell sunk like a rock, falling deeper and deeper into the sea. I told the divers I didn't know what had happened or what was happening and they needed to make sure all their valves were properly aligned for bell retrieval. They checked and assured me they were. I told them to hold tight and prepare for a jolt, if and when they hit the bottom.

Then the bell stopped at about two-hundred-seventy feet – around two-hundred feet from the bottom. I asked the divers how they were doing. They were shaken, but okay. The bell was intact and holding pressure. At least there was no immediate threat to life. That was quite a relief for me. I called the superintendent to let him know what had happened. He already knew there had been an issue and was on his way to the dive shack. He came in and I went over with him what had happened. I stayed in the dive shack to keep an eye on and comfort the divers as best I could. The superintendent went to have a talk with the SAT tech.

The Bell Umbilical Tension Wheel Driveshaft Knuckle had broken. Sounds technical, but basically it means that the knuckle from the drive motor to the winch that pulled the bell up broke. The tech had tried to stop the bell descent with the brakes on the clump weight winch and the bell winch. That is finally what did stop the bell's descent. Normally the clump weight would catch the bell and not let it descend, but this system was not in good enough shape for that. I didn't go into the normal procedure for raising the bell earlier because you don't really care or need to know the actual procedure. Here it is now though: usually the bell and the clump weight are raised together just for the prevention of this type of thing. Normally the clump weight system is strong enough to raise both the clump weight and bell – if needed in an emergency situation – like this one.

On this system, though, we couldn't raise the bell and clump weight together. The normal procedure on this system was to raise the bell fifty feet or so, stop it, then raise the clump weight fifty feet. This step system was the only way the machinery could handle the raising of our bell and weight. The idea was that if the bell winch failed the bell would only drop fifty feet before being stopped by the clump weight. What had happened was that the bell was on its last step of being raised and the clump weight was down about fifty feet below the surface. I don't know what actually caused the knuckle to break other than lack of refurbishment, but it broke and the bell fell. When the bell hit the clump weight, it hit with force enough to cause the release of the clump weight brakes and they both went screaming towards the bottom. The SAT tech did what he could to get them to stop at two-hundred-seventy feet.

Since the bell winch was effectively broken and the clump weight winch wasn't strong enough to raise them both back to the surface, the SAT tech had to come up with another plan. He devised a plan to use one of the deck winches. It took over two hours for him to get it all put together, even with the help of the surface support crew and the barge's deck crew. I wasn't on shift when the bell got back to the system, but I am sure the divers were greatly relieved to get back on the surface and into the system. The repairs to the system had not been completed by the time my next shift rolled around. Day shift was half over by the time the winch was back in working order. It wasn't perfect, but both SAT techs were certain it would hold until the end of this job. The divers weren't so sure.

My hitch lasted about another week or so. During that time, we didn't have any more issues with the equipment that would cause the job to shut down or anything like that. There were a couple issues with one of the spoiled Katrina Baby SAT divers. It's not worth going into though. Some other smaller issues kept occurring on the SAT system keeping both SAT techs busy, but the system held its depth and functioned like it was supposed to for the most part.

I swapped out on a crew boat along with the other crew members who had come on board when I did. I met a couple good guys on that job who I kept in touch with. Everybody that I worked with at Ranger Offshore were Gulf hands and I don't think most of them were too happy about having a diver from the Pacific Northwest on their crew – especially as a supervisor. Still too much of that Gulf Diver versus Inland Diver attitude with this company, and they still treated tenders badly. Ranger Offshore was hoping to get quite a bit of work in the future, though, so they would be depending on divers from the west coast, the Pacific Northwest, and other inland areas if they were to crew up the jobs they thought they might get.

I was supposed to be heading to Nigeria with them in mid-August anyway. That project was going to be crewed with a very mixed-up crew from what I had seen on the personnel boards in their New Iberia office. I was looking forward to that job. It was supposed to be some sort of dam job, so they would be wise to use the Inland divers who had dam experience. I went home to wait for the call to Nigeria. About the time I was expecting the call from Ranger, I got a call from Global Diving and Salvage. They had a supervisor's spot at the Olmsted Dam project in Kentucky that needed filling. They wanted to know if I would take it. I told them I was supposedly going to Africa with Ranger, but if that didn't pan out, I would happily go to

Olmsted. I asked them if they could give me a week to get word from Ranger. They told me that would be fine.

I called Ranger Offshore to see what the deal with the Africa job was and to let them know that I had other job offers. I was informed that my friend who worked for them in the Houston office was on vacation, so another guy had been put in temporary charge of the Africa job. They also let me know that it had been all crewed up and the crew was heading there this weekend – that was in two days. Lovely. I called my friend, who was on vacation but he didn't answer his phone. Well, I guess I wasn't going to Africa after all. Good thing I got all those shots.

I called Global back and informed them that I was available for work. They were happy and told me that I needed to be in Olmsted the first week of September. They would make all the reservations and e-mail me the plane tickets. I was informed that my friend, Seattle, would be the superintendent and I would be one of the swing shift supervisors. Okay, looks like I am back with Global for a while. I never worked for Ranger Offshore again. I heard they went out of business a couple years later, but didn't really keep track of what they were doing.

* * *

I am not a Mole, but I am in Tunnels

Towards the end of September two-thousand-fourteen, I was contacted by the guy who was the main force behind the Tunneling side of Northwest Underwater Construction, the Tunneler. He had a job in a tunnel coming up in New York City. A tunnel was being constructed utilizing a Tunnel Boring Machine (TBM) and the cutters on the Cutting Head needed replacing. There are two different types of crews used in tunneling projects. First there was the TBM Operating Crew who actually ran the TBM and got the tunnels dug and finished - consisting of miners and mechanics. Secondly there is the crew responsible for "Interventions." An Intervention is the process of stopping the TBM and changing out the teeth – or cutters – on the Cutting Head. The Intervention crew is made up of Compressed Air Workers (CAWs) and Chamber Operators. Not all Chamber Operators actually operated the chambers or ran the decompression though. There wouldn't be any actual diving involved. He wanted to know if I would be interested in something like that. I would be hired on as a

"Chamber Operator" to start. I told him I would be happy to be involved in a project like that.

The Cutting Head is the front section of the TBM that does the actual digging. On the Cutting Head are a bunch of Cutters – large, hard discs that cut through the ground chewing up the rock, mud, clay, or whatever, as the TBM moves forward. These Cutters wear out and have to be replaced every once-in-awhile. The length of the tunnel and what kind of ground is being bored through is what determines how many times the Cutters have to be replaced. There are different cutters for different types of earth, so an intervention may be required when the TBM enters a different type of strata also.

Both types of crews are made up of a team of workers including the foremen, operators, and laborers. The Operating Crew is responsible for the running of the TBM on a daily basis. After the machine has been digging for a while, the cutters become dull and need to be changed out. This is when the Intervention Crew is called in. When this happens. the tunneling is stopped. The forward movement of the machine must be stopped so the Intervention Crew can get access to the Cutting Head and change out the worn-out Cutters. This stops the progress of the tunnel building and consequently may cost the construction company a lot of money. Of course, this means that the construction company wants the Intervention Crew to work as fast as possible to keep the lack of forward progress to a minimum – Time is Money, you know.

Often the Cutting Head is under pressure – pressure caused by ground water – which results in the need for the Intervention Crew to be trained in Hyperbaric (high pressure) Work – like Divers. The Intervention Crew doesn't necessarily need to be divers, but often they *do* need to be trained to work in Hyperbaric environments. Where do you get workers trained like that? You get them from the dive industry. You hire Dive Supervisors, Divers, Life Support Technicians, and Dive Tenders.

They are already trained in Hyperbaric work. The problem is, they are usually more expensive than regular construction laborers.

When Tunneling first started happening in the Pacific Northwest there was battling between the Laborers and Divers unions. Laborers didn't have any personnel trained in Hyperbaric work and didn't know how to deal with the pressure chambers in the Cutting Heads of the TBMs. Neither did they have any idea of the precautions needed when working in Hyperbaric conditions. Back in the day – like when the Brooklyn Bridge was being built (eighteen-sixty-nine to eighteen-eighty-three) construction companies and workers didn't think anything about it. They knew they had to pressurize the working chambers – or Caissons - to keep the water out, but they didn't realize that might cause issues with the workers who were working under pressure. They weren't working under water – they were still dry – so why would they need to take any special precautions? They were still working and breathing in normal air, right? Right. Caisson's Disease – ever hear of that? That's what the workers were coming down with and they didn't realize it was the same condition Diver's referred to as the Bends. It took people a little bit of time to put two and two together and realize it was the pressure and not the medium that was causing the issue. These days we know better. Of course, some don't, but that's a whole other problem. The battle between the two unions went on for several years in the Pacific Northwest.

Anyway, the first tunnels I had heard about being constructed in the Pacific Northwest were the sewage tunnels being constructed under Portland, Oregon starting in two-thousand-and-six. Because that tunneling was done in variable ground conditions well below the water table, the City of Portland used what are known as Slurry Pressure Tunnel Boring Machines. It was the first use of this kind of machine in the United States. This meant the Cutting Head was under pressure and workers had to get pressurized to work on the Cutting Head. I don't know anything about how the construction companies did their hiring or who was sub-contracted to do what.

What I do know is that Global Diving and Salvage had their hands in it. At the time, I was kind of interested in getting into that work, but didn't know how, besides, I was working regularly in the Gulf of Mexico then. Portland did work a little on those tunneling projects for Global in the beginning. I talked to him a bit about it. Northwest Underwater Construction was trying to get that work at the same time too. In fact, I think Hollywood may have worked on those projects with NUC when they got them. I did tell him I was interested in getting into that work then. Like I said, though, I had been working pretty regularly in the GoM on the Boa Deep C and didn't want to give that cushy job up.

Northwest Underwater Construction more or less won the war for the tunneling contracts. They had people who had dedicated themselves to that work. They also didn't mind working with whichever union was supplying workers for the tunneling projects – be it the diver's union or the laborer's union. I think they even got the laborer's union to have a higher pay-rate for Compressed Air Workers (CAWs). That was good for the laborers, but bad for the divers – not that bad though – the pay was higher than tender pay.

By this time – twenty-fourteen - I'd had several issues with Global Diving and Salvage so was sort of looking for a new home. Most union divers keep their options open and are always on the lookout for a better company, better job, better situation or whatever – the grass is always greener, right? Ha!

When the Tunneler asked me if I was interested in going on a tunneling job, I told him I was. Luckily enough for me the tunneling job was taking place during one of my four-week breaks from the Olmsted project. I didn't have to leave a job or turn down any work to go on that tunneling job. Excellent!

In New York the unions must have worked out who had the rights for the high-pressure tunneling work because we had to join the Laborers Union and become Tunnel Diggers, or "Sandhogs," to work on that tunnel. There was no reciprocity between that union and our Divers union. NUC paid all those fees for us, that was nice because it wasn't cheap. We did have to go through the Sandhogs' initiation process and sign all the required documents though. It was a little disheartening that we had to do all this for a two or three-week job and it probably wouldn't benefit us in the future. It was okay though, because the hourly pay and overtime rate would make it worth it in the end.

When completed, the project would be a fresh-water supply pipe, or Syphon, that would move drinking water from Brooklyn over to Staten Island. A Slurry Pressure TBM was being used on this project - the same type used in Portland, Oregon years earlier. The outside diameter of this SPTBM was fourteen feet, I think, and the internal diameter of the pipe was about twelve-and-a-half feet. That's where we were working – inside that pipe; close to a mile from the opening on the Staten Island side and about one hundred feet under the surface of the New York City Harbor. There was fifty foot of muddy earth plus fifty foot of murky water above us. Inside the pipe it was dark and damp. There was a stream of water in the very bottom of the tunnel and you could hear water dripping and flowing all over the place. Everything inside the tunnel was covered in wet, grey mud called Slurry. Kind of freaky if you thought about it too much. I found out on this job that the Slurry used was Bentonite, the majority of which came from Montana around Billings. Interesting.

In order to do our work, the machine had to be stopped, meaning the project was effectively shut down. The project had already been shut down once by the Super Storm, Hurricane Sandy, in October two-thousand-twelve, causing a huge set back to this job. The TBM had to be refurbished after the storm, resulting in a huge extra expense for the construction company. Because of this - and other factors - they wanted to keep this shutdown to a minimum. That meant that we would be working around the clock, rotating the Compressed Air Workers through as fast as we could. The CAWs didn't wear dive gear – they were working in an air pocket, but they were still subjected to the pressure and had to be decompressed on a schedule.

There is a whole big process in prepping and sustaining the pressurized air pocket for the CAWs that I don't want to get into – too boring really – but they would be effectively working at one-hundred-fifteen feet below the surface. On TBMs the scale of pressure used is Bar. One Bar is equal to one Atmosphere which is equal to ten Meters; also equal to thirty-three feet; fourteen-point-seven Pounds per Square Inch (psi) in America, but only fourteen-point-five PSI in France – don't ask me why. To say the least, it could be a little confusing – not to mention that you had to differentiate between Bar Absolute and just plain old Bar. At one hundred Feet of Seawater (fsw) that would be three Bar - four Bar Absolute. Feet of Seawater, you ask? Yeah, Sea water is heavier than Fresh water and most of the dive gages are calibrated in Feet of Seawater, not Feet of Freshwater. I suppose that is why TBMs use Bar – it is the same scale no matter what medium you are measuring. At least we weren't using Inches of Mercury! Divers all learn about this stuff in Dive School, but most of them probably forget it the second they walk out of the classroom.

On top of the Bar, we were using a Canadian Decompression Table. It was more conservative than the USN tables. We weren't actually diving so weren't required by OSHA or any other regulatory committee to use the US Navy dive tables.

The Tunneler felt the Canadian tables were safer and I agreed with him. I wasn't hired on this job in any capacity of supervisor, LST, or actual Chamber Operator, even though that's what my job title was. On this project I was in charge of operating and monitoring the Armstrong Pump. The Armstrong Pump was a huge multi-cylinder air pump that kept the pressure up in the air pocket at the front of the Cutter Head. It moved a *huge* quantity of air. There is no way to make the air pocket in front of the Cutting Head air-tight, so the Armstrong pushes enough air to compensate for the air loss and still maintain the required pressure to keep the air pocket intact. That was a good thing actually, because it kept a constant flow of fresh air supplied to the Compressed Air Workers; negating the need for any type of dive mask or helmet.

Our crew – the Intervention Crew – consisted of the Tunneler who was the Superintendent and main Supervisor, two assistant Supervisors, several Chamber Operators – of which I was one – and a whole pile of CAWs. The idea was to rotate the CAWs through in such a way as to keep workers in the pressurized Cutting Head from the start of the Intervention all the way until all the Cutters had been replaced. Basically, it would be a twenty-four/seven non-stop operation. Sounds good to me.

NUC had flown us into New York, rented several vehicles for us to use on the job, and put us up in a hotel several miles from the worksite. On a typical shift, several of us would pile into one of the vehicles and head towards the job staging area. We'd stop at a restaurant and have breakfast on the way. After breakfast we would stop at a quickie-mart to grab a sandwich or two for lunch while we were in the tunnel. Once we were on site, we would have to get ready to enter the tunnel.

When we first arrived on the job, each of us was assigned a number and given two brass tags with that number stamped on both of them. We had to keep one on our body at all times and the other we would place on a board just before we entered the tunnel. We would remove that tag from the board after exiting the tunnel. That way the company knew who was in the tunnel in case there was some kind of emergency – like tunnel collapse or flooding – perish the thought.

After putting our tag on the tunnel board, we would get into a rickety construction elevator with several other guys and/or equipment just shy of maxing out the load limit of said elevator and take a seventy or eighty-foot ride down to the tunnel entrance. It may not have been that far down, but it seemed like several hundred feet to me. It was better than having to climb stairs in and out of the tunnel access though! After the elevator ride, we would load up on a train and take a mile-long trip through the dark, dank, musty tunnel to the TBM itself. Even though the tunnel was lined with pre-formed, interlocking concrete blocks, so much mud, water, and mist was all around that it seemed like a collapse was imminent. You really had to put those kinds of thoughts out of your head, or you wouldn't be able to work in these conditions. If you were at all claustrophobic, you wouldn't have stood a chance.

We sent the CAWs to work in pairs. They would press in, do their time – a little over an hour if I remember correctly – then move into the decompression chamber. Just as they were ready to move into the decompression chamber another team would press in to continue the work on the Cutter Head. The original team would climb into the decompression chamber built into the TBM and be decompressed according to the schedule we were running. After completing their decompression, they would ride the train back to the elevator, take it up to ground level, then hang around topside for about an hour, where we had another Deck Decompression Chamber on standby in case this team suffered any hyperbaric trauma. That would comprise their eight-hour day, after which they would drive back to the hotel where we were all staying.

The topside crew – supervisors and chamber operators were scheduled to work twelve-hour days, although we normally worked a little longer than that. I do remember a couple days that I worked over twenty hours in the day. That sounds like a lot and you might think that I would get tired, but the intensity of the job (and the gallons of Mountain Dew I drank) kept my blood flowing and I didn't feel worn out at the end of the day. The job lasted just fifteen days, but because of the hours I worked, I earned as much as I normally did in a month. That was a real nice boost to the Humphrey Christmas Fund!

As I said before, my job was to operate and monitor the Armstrong Pump. The Armstrong Pump was located towards the rear of the TBM at the bottom of the tunnel underneath the conveyor belt that carried the slurry and crushed earth out of the tunnel. It was an open conveyer system, so mud and water were constantly spilling off it and on to me. It was a very wet, cold, dirty job. Mike Rowe would love it! I wore rubber boots, a long raincoat with an attached hood – so water and mud wouldn't flow down my back - and gauntlet-type fuzzy-lined rubber gloves. I still got soaked and cold.

On one shift, about four days into the job, we were having a bit of a problem keeping the air pocket stable. Lots of water was leaking into the pocket and lots of air was leaking out. In order to try and stabilize the air space, we were pumping in quite a bit of Bentonite. Of course, lots of Bentonite and water going in meant that lots of Bentonite and water had to come out. That is what the conveyor belt was for. Remember, my work station is right under that conveyor system. Well, I don't know exactly what happened and I am not sure where the CAWs were at the time – my concern was the Armstrong Pump, not anything else – when there was a pretty loud Burp sound and a huge amount of water and Bentonite rained down on me. Rained? More like Poured down on me. I was covered, buried really, in a deluge of thick, slimy, slippery, grey mud. I got knocked off my feet and was basically swimming in this mud pit. Where are the lady mud wrestlers when you need them? I was soaked – head to foot – covered in Montana Mud.

Everybody asked if I was alright – I was. They offered to let me go back to the hotel – leave my shift early if I wanted, but I said no. I would rather stay and finish my shift. If I had left, they would be working a man short and we only had a couple hours left on our shift anyway by that time. I was warm enough, just soaked. A couple of the regular operating crew guys helped me clean off the pump and my workstation with a water hose. They also sprayed me down to rinse off all the mud. Everybody got a good laugh out of that episode after they realized I was okay. The regular operating crew told me now that I had been properly baptized, I was a real Sandhog. They even bought me a couple beers at the bar that night. Smiles all around!

Even with those hours, we managed to get some time off. Several evenings we went to a couple bars on Staten Island. There was some bar – the Drunken Monkey, supposedly owned by a mobster's wife known as "Big Ang" – that a couple of the guys wanted to visit. I had never heard of it, but they said it had been made famous by some television show. It was a dark, dive-type bar, with lots of artwork hanging on the walls featuring monkeys and figures of monkeys all over the place. We also went to the bar where the movie "Coyote Ugly" was filmed - *Hogs and Heifers* – in lower Manhattan. It was about half the size of what it looked like in the movie. It was pretty small. The bar was about fifteen feet long and there was room for only one pool table in the back. An old nineteen-thirties Harley Davidson motorcycle was hanging on the wall above the doors for the single stall bathrooms in the back corner. The barmaids did get up and dance on the bar though – that was entertaining to say the least. Both those places were fun.

We also got the majority of a Sunday off a day or two before we headed home. Hollywood was on that job with me and there was a Japanese restaurant in NYC that he and a couple others wanted to go to. We took the ferry over to Brooklyn, observing the Statue of Liberty as we sailed by. We walked by the Nine-Eleven memorial and walked on Wall Street too. We jumped on the subway and headed to Morimoto's in Manhattan. While we were waiting to be seated, who walked in but none other than celebrity chef Ming Tsai – you know from the PBS show *Simply Ming*? He was there with his wife and a couple others but he still took time to shake our hands and let us take photos with him. He was very gracious. Hollywood was really excited about meeting him. After that we went to a bar that had been around since the late seventeen-hundreds. All in all, it was quite an enjoyable day and evening.

That was my introduction to Hyperbaric Tunneling projects. It was completely different from the diving work I was used to. That was okay, because I was ready for a change. I really enjoyed it and looked forward to doing more tunneling projects in the future. The Tunneler was bidding jobs all over the world. I let him know that I would be available to work on any project he had going on. He told me he would let me know when the next one came along.

* * *

I didn't work on tunneling jobs exclusively or even consistently after that. There just aren't enough TBM Intervention jobs to keep a crew working steadily. However, I did work a few TBM jobs in between other dive work. I was working regularly at Olmsted Dam on the Ohio River for Global Diving and Salvage at this time. That was good for me because I had a schedule – usually four to six weeks on and about four weeks off in between. I had a good relationship with my opposite – the North Sea guy – and we would usually move our schedule around as needed to accommodate each other's work or vacation needs. Global was good about letting us work out our own schedule that was best for the both of us. That made it easy for me to accept any jobs I wanted that were offered me by the Tunneler.

Northwest Underwater Construction had acquired Ballard Diving and Salvage a few years earlier. They were in the process of combining assets and merging jobs, equipment, and personnel. After all the dust settled, I think they ended up calling themselves Ballard Marine Construction. That doesn't really make any difference to me, but I just wanted to let you know so you were familiar with who I was working with at the time.

I visited Ballard's yard in Washougal, Washington – where they kept most of their equipment. I went there to meet the office personnel and see what they had in their yard. I also wanted to check out the modular SAT systems they had. Those are a pretty nice and compact way to have a SAT system. Global's SAT systems were somewhat modular, but not anywhere near as clean and compact as the systems Ballard had. I was pretty impressed. It was this type of Modular SAT system that Ballard had set up to work on Bertha – the TBM utilized by Seattle for their SR-99 project.

The City of Seattle had a staging area set up at the south end of the tunnel project. The Tunneler had set up Ballard's SAT system there sometime during the first stages of getting Bertha ready to start tunneling. The tunnel would be dug from the south to the north. This project was announced by the City of Seattle in two-thousand-nine. The TBM for this project had been christened "Bertha" after Seattle's first female mayor – I thought the machine was called Bertha because she was so big. When I was in the navy, we called all the big machines Big Bertha – I don't really know where that came from. I thought we were doing the same thing here. This was, after all, the world's largest Earth Pressure Balance TBM ever built.

All the divers in the area were excited about this job and wanted to get on the project. The story was that there would have to be several interventions and it was going to be done in SAT. Many divers started calculating how much money they would be making on a Union SAT job – of course they were dreaming. The rumor was that the tunnel would be two-hundred-fifteen feet below the surface at its deepest depth, plus the machine was fifty-seven-and-a-half feet in diameter so the bottom of the TBM would be two-hundred-seventy-two or three feet deep. That meant a SAT pressure of a little more than nine bar or about one-hundred-thirty-six psi. That would require almost four days of decompression from SAT.

Divers started calculating what the average pay per day would be with overtime, double overtime, and depth. I think the numbers were something like two-thousand-three-hundred to two-thousand-seven-hundred dollars per day. They figured a normal intervention would be two to three weeks. You can see why so many of them were getting so excited about it. Another rumor was that there would end up being at least three, but as many as five, of these three-week interventions. Many of them figured they wouldn't have to do any other work for the next year or two. Ha! Ha! Ha! At least divers can dream big.

Ballard Marine Construction knew they had the tunnel support work in two-thousand-eleven. I don't know when they were actually awarded the support contract, but I do know that many divers in the Pacific Northwest were calling them about work vying for a position on the Bertha project. I had heard about it and, of course, calculated what the pay might be also. I knew I wouldn't be one of the divers – or CAWs, but I thought I might be an LST, Chamber Operator, or maybe even a Supervisor. I wasn't planning on it and, really, didn't think about it too much. I had other work to do and at that time in my career I was working consistently with Global Diving and Salvage.

Of course, the Bertha tunneling project didn't turn out at all like the dive community had figured it would. Ha! In fact it didn't even turn out the way STP (Seattle Tunnel Partners) - the construction group awarded the project - thought it would. The project didn't start on time. The TBM broke down stalling the tunneling for two years. There were other legal battles interfering with progress also. I think there was only one real intervention and that didn't happen until the summer of two-thousand-sixteen.

* * *

After the tunnel job in New York City, my next tunneling job was in North Dakota. The Tunneler contacted me in the early spring of twenty-fifteen to ask if I was available. He gave me the dates of the job and it fell on my time off from the Olmsted Dam project so I told him I would be more than happy to go on it. He said he would get me a plane ticket to some small town in North Dakota where we would all meet. From there we would drive a rental car north to the job site. I looked at the map and figured it would take me less time to drive from Helena to the work site than it would messing around with the airports and flight times – there was no direct flight for me. I met the crew at the hotel near the work site. The Tunneler paid for my gas. I appreciated that. The rest of the crew was already at the hotel by the time I got there.

The Tunneler was there, of course, as well as Hollywood and another guy from the Seattle area that I had worked with at Global - Stretch. I guess he was looking for a change too. The two assistant tunneling supervisors that were on the NYC job were there as well. A woman who worked with Ballard Marine

Construction on a fairly regular basis was there along with another guy I had not previously met. We all went out to dinner together and had a few drinks. It was good to get to know the crew a little.

The next morning, we drove to the jobsite to inspect the tunneling machine and the tooling set up. The tunneling hadn't started yet. We were there to make sure everything that BMC would be working with on an intervention was on site and ready to work. We were also going to enter the machine and get to the cutting head from the inside so we knew what we would be dealing with when we did do an intervention. Once at the job site we were directed to the TBM. It was out in the field fairly close to where it would start the tunnel.

We all walked up to it and looked at it. It was small. Very small. Wow. It was pretty cool looking, but I didn't see how an intervention crew was supposed to fit inside the thing. I think it was only six feet in diameter – maybe eight – or maybe it just dug an eight-foot diameter tunnel. After the concrete casing was in place and the tunnel was completed, I think it would have an inside diameter of six feet or less. I didn't know for sure. You'd have to ask the Tunneler. He's the guy who knows all about the TBMs and the tunnels they dig.

After looking at the front section of the machine, we looked at the rest of it. Several sections that would be attached to the rear of the first section, making the thing fairly long, were laying around in the field surrounding the Cutter Head. We inspected the back piece – where we would enter the machine during the intervention. There was a pressure hatch on it – like on a submarine - that was only about two feet in diameter. We couldn't tell what the inside looked like until we opened the hatch. It didn't open easily, but after a bit of a struggle we got it open. We all looked inside. If you think the machine looked small from the outside, you are in for a shock.

The crawl space on the inside was *really* small! Even for a crawl space it was small. The diamond-plate floor panel that we would be crawling on (on our hands and knees!) was only eighteen inches wide or so. When I got down on my hands and knees inside, I could arch my back and hit the equipment attached to the top. At each joint of the sections, we would have to wriggle through the space. Or at least I would have to.

I am a little chubby and it was a tighter fit for me inside the machine than most of the others. Hollywood is a couple inches taller than I am, but he is skinnier too. I think he fit in there okay. One of the assistant supervisors was several inches shorter than me and skinny, so he had plenty of room. He was raised in Superior, Montana but lived north of Seattle now. The woman wasn't small, but she was smaller than me and fit in the machine okay also. The other assistant supervisor was more my size and had the same issues I did. He lived in Bellevue and rode motorcycles too. He also enjoyed the same kind of dive bars that I did. Stretch was quite a bit taller than I am and a couple inches taller than Hollywood. He had a little trouble fitting into the work space along with those of us who were on the bigger side.

After crawling through a couple of the rear sections, we returned to the front section which included the cutting head. It wasn't attached to any of the rear sections yet. We all had to crawl in from the rear and out the front through the cutting head to where we would be working on changing out the cutting teeth. I barely fit through to the outside. I had to bend and flex in ways that my body hadn't in quite a long while. I almost got stuck once and the only way I could get out the front was to fall out on my head. That would be quite messy once the machine was underground. I was thinking to myself that I would rather not do that.

The Tunneler got a giggle or two out of my struggles and agreed with me that, on this project at least, it might be better if I filled the position of Chamber Operator – which was what the crew who stayed outside the cutting head was called. I was happy with that. I didn't need to be one of the CAWs even though their hourly rate was higher. When I worked on the project in New York, I made more as a "Chamber Operator" just because we worked longer hours than the CAWs did. It was all pretty physical work and I enjoyed doing the support stuff for the CAWs. I didn't need to be under pressure – pressurized – to like the work. It wasn't the "pressure" of diving that made working underwater fun – it was being under water. This tunneling stuff was all in the dry – even though we could get soaked – so it made no difference to me whether I was pressurized or not.

After we were done inspecting the TBM and crawling in and around it, we went back to one of the equipment warehouses on site that held the replacement cutting teeth and the tools we would use to change the teeth out. We picked up the teeth and fit the tools to them. We talked about how we would transfer them from the back of the TBM up to the cutter head. They were heavy and it would be quite a chore to transfer the new teeth to the front of the machine and bring the used teeth back. It was fun looking at all that stuff and getting our hands all over it. All said and done, we spent a couple days doing that.

I didn't know when the actual tunneling would start on this project. I kept my ears open, but never heard about any interventions. I have no idea whether or not any interventions were done on that job, but I didn't have anything to do with them if they were. I don't know if I was working on something else or if the Tunneler had other people he needed to keep working go there without me. It didn't matter to me one way or the other, that machine was a little small for me anyway.

The Tunneler had told me before, that many times tunneling jobs were done without any interventions. It was quite common for the original cutter teeth to last the whole job – especially if the ground being tunneled through was fairly soft. He did a lot of work on tunnels all over the world and many of them never had any interventions. Interventions were one of those things that just had to be planned for whether they were needed or not. It did make sense to get that stuff all straightened out before the job started rather than have to do it all in the middle of a job if an intervention was needed, but hadn't been planned for.

I heard about several tunneling jobs going on around the states and a couple overseas that BMC was doing the intervention plans for – it was the Tunneler who did all that. It involved a lot of writing. Basically, he had to put together operations and safety manuals for each job. There were many jobs that only he went on and they never needed any interventions. He said I was on his list and I told him I would gladly work on any projects he needed me for. I think BMC was bidding on other SAT work also and I told the Tunneler that I would be available for that kind of work too. He was more or less in charge of the Hyperbaric side of BMC, not just the tunneling. I didn't work with BMC again until the following summer.

*   *   *

In the spring of twenty-sixteen, the Tunneler called me to see if I was available to work on an intervention for Bertha in Seattle. He said it would start in July and last two or three weeks, but there would be a week or so of work in June to make sure all the equipment was ready to go. I was currently working on the Olmsted Dam project but would be home before the intervention in Seattle was due to start. I told him I would be happy to work on that project. I would be a Chamber Operator and trainee assistant supervisor. I thought that would be fantastic and interesting. I had wanted to get on that project as did almost all the divers in the Pacific Northwest.

During my break from the Olmsted project in June, I went over to Seattle to help get Ballard's equipment ready for the intervention. The job site was near pier forty-six – a little south of the Ferry Terminals - in Seattle. I met the Tunneler, and most of the people I had worked with in North Dakota at the job site. There was a young woman there too, one I had not met before. She was from Sedro-Woolley – way north of Seattle but south of Bellingham. She had worked with BMC and the Tunneler on several projects over the past few years, but I had never worked with her. I don't think she had worked for any dive companies in the Pacific Northwest other than Ballard Marine Construction.

We had to fill out a bunch of paperwork for STP – the company that was running the SR-99 tunnel project. We had to get badges which we were required to wear whenever we were on the job site. We had to get parking permits for a garage STP had rented. No parking was allowed on the actual job site. We had to show our original certification cards for CPR, OSHA, and the other required courses for working construction in Seattle. It took hours. We rotated through; some of us working on Ballard's equipment while others were getting permitted.

We went over all the equipment – the SAT system, compressors, generators, compressed gas bottles, and the DART. The DART is a hyperbaric shuttle used to transport CAWs between the pressurized work area at the front of the TBM and the SAT system where the CAWs would be living for up to twenty-eight days if the job were done in SAT mode. It was basically a Deck Decompression Chamber on wheels.

Seattle can be a very wet and rainy place. It wasn't actually raining the first couple days we were working, but it had been raining the few days before. There was lots of mud; wet, slippery, slimy, sticky, beige mud – like what you see at lots of construction sites – all over the place. Of course, it stuck to our boots and anywhere else it could get. It was kind of a mess and not real conducive to getting work done. Mud seemed to be a huge part of this Tunneling work.

We spent about a week getting everything ready. When we were finished, I drove back home to Helena to spend the remaining part of my break with my wife before returning to the dam project in Kentucky. I spent the last half of June and first half of July working my shift at Olmsted for Global. When my hitch was over, I returned home only to head back to Seattle shortly after arriving.

I got home from Kentucky on a Sunday and had to be in Seattle the following Wednesday morning. My wife wasn't super happy about the short time off, but by now, she knew what my work schedules – or lack there-of – were like. She also knew that the Seattle tunnel project was a pretty big deal and was excited for me to be a part of it. I drove over late Tuesday night so I could spend as much time at home with my wife as possible. I really had no idea how long I would be in Seattle. I might have to go back to Kentucky again right after finishing up the intervention.

This time we were doing the actual intervention on Bertha. The first part of the job would be to inspect the cutting teeth and see how many needed to be replaced, and how much work there would be to refurbish the cutting head itself. Sometimes there was structural damage that needed repairing – that could turn into quite a bit of work. These first inspections would determine whether or not we would be working in SAT mode or just doing SUR-D-O_2 shifts. The surface decompression would be much less expensive for STP if there wasn't too much work to do.

The decompression is done inside the TBM itself. There are four areas in the tunnel and TBM that are important to the intervention crews. These are the Cutting Head and space in front of it, the Tool Room which is just behind the Cutting Head, the Work Room – behind or next to the Tool Room, and the Personnel and Tool Locks. The front three areas are pressurized to whatever pressure is needed to keep the area in front of the Cutting Head stable so the CAWs can safely work there. The Tool lock is a small chamber that tools and parts can be transferred from the non-pressurized area of the TBM to the pressurized spaces – usually the Tool Room. The Personnel Lock is a small chamber that allows us to pressurize and decompress workers who will be working on the Cutter Head – it is usually attached to the Work Room. The Work Room is where the CAWs prep for the work and also clean themselves up as much as possible before decompressing out.

If the work is done in SAT mode – the CAWs don't decompress inside the TBM. Instead, they transfer through the locks into the DART which is then transported outside the TBM and existing tunnel back to the SAT system on the job site. The CAWs would then transfer into the SAT system and live pressurized just like the SAT divers do for up to twenty-eight days at a time. If there is a lot of work at higher pressures to be completed, this ends up being much more cost effective than decompressing the CAWs after every work shift. SAT crews can work in eight or twelve-hour shifts and you don't have to waste time decompressing in between shifts.

After the first team went into the Cutter Head and made their assessment, it was determined that this intervention would not need to be done using SAT. Too bad, so sad for all the divers in the Pacific Northwest. For me it didn't make much of a difference. I would be working a twelve-hour shift minimum anyway. On this intervention I was to be one of the actual Chamber Operators running the compression and decompression of the CAWs. I would also learn all about the paperwork the supervisors and assistant supervisors had to fill out. The Tunneler oversaw everything and worked very long hours on this project.

While I was working on this project, I was staying with my best friend from high school. He lived in Marysville and had a spare bedroom he let me use. I appreciated his hospitality more than he knows; I am sure. My typical day started at six a.m. with a drive down I-5 to the parking garage south of pier forty-six, where we would all get on a school bus that took us to the work site near the mouth of the tunnel. We would meet at BMC's chamber Conex boxes to get our assignments and paperwork for the day. One of the crew members would stay "topside" outside the tunnel where we had a Deck Decompression Chamber set up in case any of the CAWs had hyperbaric issues after working their shift. That station had to be manned the whole time we were working. The rest of us would walk down the concrete-lined tunnel to the actual TBM.

This tunnel was HUGE! It was a very large concrete tube and it was dry – nothing like the tunnel we worked on in New York City. The main reason for this was that the conveyer system that removed the spoils from the Cutter Head was enclosed rather than open like the one in NYC. I liked this system a lot better. There was a lot of lighting in this tunnel too, so it wasn't dark and dank at all. Did I tell you it was huge? It was the largest TBM in the world at the time it started drilling this tunnel. The outside diameter of Bertha was fifty-seven-and-a-half feet. The inside diameter of the tunnel - the part we saw as we walked towards the TBM - is fifty-two feet. That may not sound like a whole lot, but it's about the height of a five-story building! When we got to the TBM we had to climb twenty-five feet of ladder to get us to the deck where we could thread ourselves through to the front of the machine. It was like walking through the engine rooms of a ship, or maybe the utility tunnels underneath a building. You had to watch your head to keep from bumping it on low-hanging steel structure and piping.

Once we got as far forward as possible, we had to climb up another ten or fifteen feet to get to the pressure locks that we used to press and decompress the CAWs. The work space was quite cramped. The lighting wasn't as good at the front of the TBM as the tunnel behind it either. It was dark and hot. I don't remember what color the steel was painted but I have a memory of everything being brownish and dark green – I don't know why that is. I am fairly sure it was painted white for the most part. I just perceived it as dark and brown. There was probably a lot of that marine anti-rust red paint splashed all around, also the Oxygen bottles we used for the decompression were dark green.

Once we were up front, we would have a quick turnover with the nightshift. They would give us their notes on what they had gotten accomplished during their shift. The chamber operators would show us where the current occupants of the decompression chamber were in their decompression and we would take our spots for the day.

As a chamber operator, my workspace was very small. I couldn't stand up in it. I couldn't even sit in a chair in it. The space was only about four feet high and about seven feet long by five feet wide. I, and all the other operators, had to crawl into the space and check all the valves and gages on our hands and knees. Once everything was checked out, I could sit back and watch the gages. We had a couple cushions to sit on while we were at our post. It was not very comfortable. There were three of us chamber operators and we would take turns watching the decompression.

We had other jobs to perform as well as running the decompression. We had to change out the oxygen bottles. They were located on a level below our work station and back at the end of the TBM. The oxygen we used was medical grade and brought to us in sixteen-bottle racks. All the bottles were connected to a "spider" – a bunch of tubes going from the bottles to a valve that we could attach a regulator to. When a bottle was empty, we would have to run down to the rack, close the empty bottle, then open a full bottle. We usually had to do that several times per shift. There was a davit – a small crane – on the deck where the racks were that we used to swap out the racks of oxygen. The fresh racks were brought down to the TBM when we needed them and we would swap the empty rack for a full rack. That happened a couple times a week.

The chamber operators were also the workers who had to press tools and new cutter heads into the CAWs. We also had to decompress the used cutter heads and tools out of the tool chamber. That process worked just like any med-lock or tool-lock on any chamber used in SAT diving. It was a smaller lock – chamber section – that had a hatch on both ends; one for us and one for the CAWs. We would make sure the lock was "on the surface" – meaning it was depressurized – then we would open our hatch and load in whatever the CAWs needed. Next, we would close our hatch and "send it down" - pressurize the lock to the same pressure as the guys in the Tool Room. At that point they would open their hatch and remove the equipment we had sent to them. They would replace it with the worn tools and pieces then close their hatch and signal us – usually with a couple taps – that the lock was ours and we could "bring it back to the surface" - depressurize it. That would take place quite a few times during a shift.

When I was supervising, I wouldn't have to crawl into the chamber operator space. Yay! Instead, we had a "Dive Control Station" set up with two-wire radio communications – just like on a dive station – that we could talk to the CAWs with. We also had video so we could see inside the pressurized spaces. The supervisor also had a radio to communicate with the TBM support crew. We had to let them know when the CAWs were ready to have the Cutter Head rotated into a new position to allow them to change more cutter teeth. If there was an issue with the TBM or the ability of the support crew to maintain the pressure inside the work area, they could let us know so we could get our crew out of danger.

Just like in New York, there was a space in front of the cutter head that had been coated with bentonite to help keep water out and pressurized air in. It's just a slurry and not a super reliable pressure wall so the danger of collapse and catastrophic loss of air pressure was always a concern. Of course, we had a system and a plan to deal with those kinds of incidences. It was the supervisor's responsibility to keep an eye on the pressure as well as direct the CAWs in their task. The supervisor was also responsible for giving the decompression schedules to the chamber operators, although the Tunneler was always on top of that and had the schedules ready for the supervisor at the beginning of each shift.

A team of Compressed Air Workers consisted of a crew of three. Two of the workers would climb out into the cutter head area where they would change out the cutter teeth. The third member would remain in the Tool Room to transfer tools and cutter teeth between the workers and the Tool Lock. They all locked in and out together. If one had an issue that required decompression out of the work area, we would decompress the whole team.

We had a Diver EMT in the TBM who had their own space where the CAWs were checked out before and after each pressurization. The DEMT would also perform first assessments on the CAWs if they got injured on the job. In fact, they were the first medical check for any of us working inside the TBM if we got hurt. Mostly all that happened was bumped heads on low-hanging structure. There were a few cuts and scrapes also. The DMT was an employee of BMC, not the main contractor of the job. We required a med tech who had hyperbaric training.

We were fortunate on that job that we didn't have any hyperbaric issues. We did have a few other minor medical issues, like small cuts and pinched fingers; nothing too serious though. The biggest health issue we had was colds or flu. The cramped, warm, humid spaces were a perfect environment for the spread of colds and flu. If one person came down with a cough or sniffle, it wasn't long before several other people caught it. I was lucky that I never got sick. I don't get sick often, thankfully. A couple of the CAWs got sick enough that they couldn't be pressed in. A couple of the topside crew became ill, but not bad enough to interfere with their work. Other than that, we didn't have any issues getting the job done.

I don't remember how many runs we did, but we changed out thirty-three cutter teeth. That doesn't sound like many. If you don't realize how much work it is to change the teeth out, then you might think the job would only last a couple days. The thing is, these cutter teeth are large round discs of steel. They weigh something like fifty or sixty pounds each. To change one out, the first thing to be done is getting it located. The TBM support crew has a map of the Cutter Head and they rotate the head around to the point where the disc that needs changing is in position.

Once the CAWs have located the correct disc, they clean it off with a pressure washer. The cutter teeth are held in place by bolts. Removing these bolts is often the toughest part of the job. Hydraulic tools are utilized, if needed, to remove the bolts. If the CAWs are lucky, the bolts can be removed with just a wrench. That is not a common occurrence, however. Breaker bars and extensions are often needed to get the job done. Any of you who have done any mechanic-ing will know what I am talking about.

The next step is removing the worn disc. Sometimes they slip right out, other times a special tool is required. Occasionally that special tool is a crowbar. If a special tool is required to remove the worn disc, it is usually needed to put the new disc in place. When the new disc is finally in position, the bolts are installed and torqued. Damaged bolts are replaced with new bolts. It usually takes two workers to handle this job.

At this point the team is ready to move on to the next disc that needs replacing. If the next bad disc is on the same radial arm of the Cutting Head, the CAWs just find it and start the process all over. If it is on a different radial arm, all three crew members must move back into the work room, seal the hatches, unlock the Cutter Head, and inform the supervisor that they are in position and ready for the rotation of the Cutter Head. The supervisor contacts the TBM support crew leader and lets them know that our crew is ready for the Cutter Head rotation.

There is a special lock inside the Work Room that must be unlocked for the Cutter Head to rotate. The CAWs always take the key to that lock in with them so they can personally lock it to prevent any movement of the machine. That is the TBMs form of Lock-Out-Tag-Out. No actual tags are used, but everything is logged and the CAWs are the ones who actually do the locking – holding their own safety in their own hands. When the intervention is complete, it is vital that the key is returned to the TBM support crew. Without it they cannot operate the TBM.

* * *

Before we were finished with the Bertha project, Jay Dee Contractors needed us to do an intervention on one of the Northgate Link tunnel boring machines. The Northgate Link tunnels were a pair of tunnels that were being constructed for Sound Transit and would connect Northgate to the U-district going underneath the University of Washington campus. These tunnels were being dug by twin TBMs named Brenda – for the northbound rail, and Pamela - for the southbound rail. These tunnels were quite a bit smaller than that being dug by Bertha. Their outside diameter was just twenty-one-and-a-half feet while the inside diameter of the concrete tunnel is just under nineteen feet. These tunnels were also dry and well lit, so quite a bit different than the cold, wet, muddy tunnel we worked on in New York City.

The crew for this project was split off from the crew working on Bertha. I was working as an assistant supervisor under the supervisor raised in Superior, Montana. He lived north of Seattle but south of Marysville. Sedro Woolley was also on this project. We were all on the day shift starting early in the morning. In an effort to save gas and have a more enjoyable commute, Sedro Woolley would meet me in Marysville. She would get in my car, then we would drive to Superior's house and pick him up. From there it was another half-hour drive - at least - to get to the work site at the north opening of the two tunnels. There was a parking lot across the street from the work site which was very convenient. We usually listened to Rammstein during the commute. It got our blood pumping for the day.

As at the other projects, we would meet the rest of the crew at Ballard Marine Construction's DDC outside the tunnel. We would gather our paperwork for the day and head down to the TBM. On this tunnel during this intervention, the TBM was a couple miles down the tube. J.D. Contractors had a rubber-tired train that we would all board – more or less like the one in NYC – and it would take us to the backend of the TBM. It wasn't the most comfortable ride, but it was better than walking!

No SAT interventions were planned at this site, so there was no SAT system here; just the DDC set up. We did have light-weight dive helmets designed in Switzerland to test out though. The Tunneler was working on a breathing supply system that would keep the CAWs from breathing the atmosphere in the Cutter Head area. He was doing this in preparation for jobs he had coming up in the future.

The helmets were nice. They were extremely lightweight compared to other dive helmets. The regulators breathed easily also. They were still a little bulky and had an umbilical going back to the entry lock area. The Compressed Air Workers didn't like the inconvenience of having a helmet on their heads, nor did they like having to worry about their umbilical. The system worked though, and would be very good for working in possibly toxic environments or where CAWs might need to breathe a helium mixture in a SAT situation.

We didn't have any issues completing the intervention on the Northgate project. It didn't take us long either. I was glad to have another tunnel project under my belt. I also enjoyed being able to tell my friends and family in Seattle that I had been involved in those tunnel projects – something they could actually see. It is rare for my friends and family to be able to see the projects I have worked on since most of them are underwater in places where the public can't get to. It is one thing to hear about a project, but a completely other experience to see it finished. I wanted to go through the tunnels after they were completed, but never have. Maybe someday.

* * *

The last tunneling project I worked on was in Egypt - Ismalia, Egypt – just outside of Cairo. The Egyptian government and military had contracted some French company to bore six tunnels under the Suez Canal – three here in Ismalia and three up north at Port Said (pronounced sah-EED). One tunnel at each site would be for trains and the other two would be for automobiles. This was to increase access to the Sinai Peninsula and tie the two parts of Egypt closer together. I think what the Egyptian government really wanted, though, was better military access to the Sinai and other parts of the Jewish and Arab world. The project was being overseen by the Egyptian military.

I had been contacted by the Tunneler in October about this project. My part was due to start the week after Christmas. This gave me enough time to work out my Olmsted schedule with North Sea. He was more than happy to accommodate my scheduling needs. I would be home in mid-December and be able to spend Christmas with my family.

This job was going to be done in the SAT mode. I was going over as a SAT supervisor. The Tunneler had asked me if I knew anyone else who might be available to go on this project as surface support. He preferred workers who had gone through a dive school, but that wasn't absolutely necessary. I talked to my friend, Billings, from dive school. He had graduated from Highline in eighty-five, but only worked one season in the dive industry. He was now living in Helena just a few miles from me. He was self-employed, so could take time off whenever he wanted. I told him this would be a great opportunity for him and he could make some pretty good money. He agreed to go when the Tunneler needed him – which would be in a couple weeks.

The second day after Christmas I flew to Seattle. I met a couple of the guys I had worked with on the Bertha project at SeaTac airport. They were both from Post Falls, Idaho. I had agreed to check a bag from Ballard Marine Construction stuffed with tools and equipment as one of my personal bags. That way they could save a little money on sending needed gear to Egypt. I had no issues with that – I usually travelled fairly light so never used my second bag option anyway.

We landed at the Cairo airport on the twenty-ninth of December. There were Christmas decorations here and there. Mostly lots of Santa Claus stuff. I heard a couple people point at me and say "Baba Noël" and smile. I didn't know what they were saying at the time, but later found out they were calling me "Father Christmas." I have been called that by kids in the states, so that was nothing new. I still got a kick out of it though. It actually helped when I went through customs. The agent looked at me, smiled, said something followed by "Baba Noël" and waived me through without checking any of my bags. I wasn't smuggling anything, but it was nice not to have to open all my luggage and answer questions about it.

One of the guys from Post Falls was detained because we had a bunch of dive equipment, tools, and gages. He was having some communication issues. I went over to see what the problem was. I told the customs agent that it was all for SCUBA diving and that we had come over to do some exploring of the Red Sea. The agent smiled and nodded at that and told Post Falls he was good to go. We were there on tourist visas rather than work visas.

When we got outside the airport, we were swarmed by guys offering us rides; each one trying to outdo the other in price. We had reservations at a hotel in Cairo and they had a shuttle. I told everybody we were waiting for the shuttle and wouldn't need their services. That didn't deter them much. One of our crew came over wearing camouflage pants an Army-green t-shirt and carrying a military rucksack – not smart attire for going into an Arab country as an American. A couple men with cameras approached him and asked if they could take a photo with him. I told him not to do it, but he didn't see any issue. I tried to tell him that they thought he was either military or mercenary. He didn't believe me because they said they loved Americans and wanted a photo with one. They wanted photos with us all because we were all together and had all these big duffle bags with us. I told them no; we didn't want to be in any photos. A couple of my crew thought I was being silly, until we got to the hotel.

We all loaded into the hotel shuttle when it arrived. It took us to a hotel adjacent to the airport. At the entrance to the hotel, we were stopped by guards dressed in full military camo carrying m-sixteens. There was a steel gate across the hotel driveway. One of the guards had a German Shephard dog, obviously trained to sniff out something. Another guard had a mirror on the end of a chromed metal rod that he used to inspect the undercarriage of the van. The guard with the dog circled the van, then had the driver open the back hatch. The dog sniffed all our bags. A third guard asked for all our passports, inspected them, and diligently compared the photographs to our faces. He handed our passports back to us after he was satisfied that our faces matched the photos. After the inspection, the gate was opened and the shuttle moved on up to the hotel. There were concrete pillars out front of the hotel entrance. They were there to keep a vehicle from smashing through and into the hotel lobby.

There weren't any military-style guards inside the hotel, but they did have security dressed in suits and I could see a couple of them were carrying concealed pistols. This hotel had an x-ray baggage checker that we had to put all our bags through to enter the lobby. We had to pass through a metal detector to get to the inner doors. Our bags met us on the other side of those doors. From there we went to reception, to check in. We had to present our passports, which they scanned and made copies of. Reservations had been made and paid for each of us. We each got our own room. That was nice. A big white-flocked Christmas tree stood in the middle of reception. It was covered in silver decorations. A Santa Claus and some reindeer were around the tree and there were festively-wrapped packages under the tree. One of the girls behind the counter smiled at me and asked if I had come to deliver gifts to the children of Cairo. I smiled and said I hadn't, but would spread good cheer if I could.

The next morning, we met a driver of a shuttle who would take us to the hotel in Ismalia; where we would be staying. Ismalia is about an hour drive across desert east of Cairo. It is right on the Suez Canal. There was no issue or inspection leaving the hotel in Cairo. The road to Ismalia is a normal four-lane highway with sand on either side as far as the eye can see. It was hot, even with the air-conditioning in the van.

Our driver seemed like a nice guy. He was Egyptian, from a small town on the southern side of the Sinai Peninsula. He was in Cairo for work because the money was better there than what he could make in his home town. He had a wife and a couple children at home he was supporting.

When we arrived at the hotel in Ismalia, we were again stopped by a steel gate and armed guards dressed in camo. They were also carrying m-sixteens. One had a dog and another had the mirror at the end of a metal stick. We had to go through the same routine here as at the hotel in Cairo. This hotel was on a much bigger plot of ground though. We had to cross a small canal just to get to the entrance gate from the main road. After passing inspection and going through the gate the driver took us on up to the hotel. The driveway was about a thousand feet and led to the hotel on the right side and a large parking area on the left. There were concrete posts in front of this hotel also. We had to put our bags through the x-ray machine here and walk through a metal detector to get in – just like the other hotel. By this time, I was figuring that must be the way it was at all the hotels here in Egypt. They were having issues with terrorists on the Sinai, just across the Suez from us, so I suppose something like this was to be expected.

This hotel was regally grand. It was on several acres and there were several parts to it. The main hotel was a huge building – seven stories. It had two restaurants and a bar in the main building on the ground floor. There was also a spa and workout room. There was a hair salon and a little shop as well. The reception area was big too. This place was more of a resort. It had separate cabins – cabanas - to the north of the main hotel. There was a large pool in between the hotel and the beach. Yeah, it was on the beach. It was on Forsan Island. That is why we had to cross a canal to get to it. This place was amazing. There was an outside bar and restaurant in between the pool and the beach with a paved area used as a dance floor and for shows – like belly dancing.

The Tunneler was already here at the hotel when we arrived. Superior and a few other crew members were also here. They had been working on getting the equipment ready for the interventions. After we checked in, we met with the Tunneler and he explained as much as he could about the hotel and the job. We were advised not to leave the grounds of the hotel during our off-time. It wasn't necessarily safe for Americans or Christians we were told. Funny, I thought, for a place that had Christmas decorations all over. The main restaurant of the hotel - where we would eat most of our meals - still had Christmas decorations up (they left them up until January sixth - the Epiphany).

The company that hired BMC was paying for all our hotel accommodations and meals. We ate breakfast and dinner at the hotel restaurant – it was buffet, but also had a menu we could order from. I usually ate the buffet. Several times a week they would cook on a grill outside and offer up a Bar-B-Que, some Chinese dish, or some Arabian specialty – like shawarma (that was absolutely delicious!). All the food was great and there was lots of it. Every morning there were several different types of pastries along with all the regular breakfast staples; eggs and omelets to order too. I had to watch myself so I wouldn't get fat – well, fatter anyway. Ha!

Most of the crew was staying in the main part of the hotel. I, and three other guys were staying in one of the cabanas. The cabana had four bedrooms, a bathroom, kitchen, and living room – are you kidding me?! It was just like a little house on the beach with a great view of the Suez Canal. It even had a little patio with a couple deck chairs facing the canal. Wow! This was awesome.

At the beginning we were only working day shift and only eight or nine hours a day. We had enough time to relax around the hotel and enjoy some of the amenities. The outside bar had hookahs and lots of different flavors – they call it "Shisha" (SHEE-shah) - there. I wasn't a smoker, so never partook. Billings tried it several times and a couple times I took a puff just to see what it was all about. It didn't do anything for me, and being a diver, I have a hard time polluting my lungs. I did enjoy grabbing a drink or five at the bars though! Prost! Or as they say in Egypt: Fe sehetak!

Every morning after breakfast we met the van out in the hotel parking lot. The driver would take us to the worksite about nine miles away – a fifteen to twenty-minute ride if the traffic was not bad or a train didn't slow us down. The worksite was at the entrance to the tunnels half-a-mile or more from the edge of the Suez Canal. We couldn't see the canal from the worksite which was on the outskirts of Ismalia. We were definitely on the edge of the desert. There was sand everywhere. Most of the buildings were made of concrete, brick, or stone.

The entrance to the worksite looked like an entrance to a military base. The worksite was enclosed by a mason block wall. A bar gate blocked the entrance. On either side of the entrance there was a C-shaped pile of sandbags about four feet high with a fifty-caliber machine gun mounted on top. Two or three guards dressed in camo and sporting m-sixteens were positioned behind each pile of sandbags. There was a guard shack by the gate and more than six guards dressed in camo. A few of them had m-sixteens. One of them had a dog and another carried the mirror on a stick.

The van was subjected to the same type of search performed by the guards at the hotels. The members of our crew that had been in Egypt for a while had company badges with their photo, name, and the name of the company we were working for on them. The rest of us who were new had to show our passports and give our names to the guards – they checked the list to see if we were on it. The guards went through all the backpacks of us new guys. After all that, some laughs, and a couple "Baba Noël" jokes, we were waved on through. So far, everybody I had met spoke English.

Our next stop was at a grouping of small buildings where all the main offices of the people in charge, the engineers, and the project officials were. The Tunneler had to meet with some of the people inside. He took me in to meet some of the people since I was going to be a supervisor and I might have to talk with them later on. I would also be required to go to some of the planning meetings – especially when we were going to start doing the interventions using SAT. There were also some temporary buildings – more like sheds – next to the offices that the subcontractors could use as an office if they wanted. One of those was assigned to BMC. The Tunneler was using it for equipment storage.

The rest of the guys had gone on to the area where we would be working. When The Tunneler and I had finished with our meetings, we got a ride out to our area of the worksite. There were eight Conex boxes set up on a freshly-poured concrete pad. The pad was large – fifty feet by a hundred feet or more. On the left half of the pad, four of the Conex boxes were set up in a C formation with the opening facing the road we had just driven up on. The fifth Conex was just to the right of the C, parallel to the box it was next to. Inside it was a SAT chamber. About eight feet to the left of the fifth Conex was another Conex that contained the LST station for the SAT chamber. Just to the left of the LST box was another Conex that contained a DART – the DDC on wheels (this one was on train wheels). About eight feet to the right of the DART box was the last Conex. It contained a DDC and a small office used as a medical office. It was set up exactly like those BMC had back in the states. It might have even belonged to BMC, I don't remember.

The first four Conex boxes were supplied by the main contractor. The first one sat perpendicular to the road and was a guard shack manned by at least two Egyptians in uniform, but not camo. The second and third boxes were parallel to the road and set back a whole Conex box's length from the road. One was set up for the Tunneler's office. There were three tables set up inside to be used as desks – one for the Tunneler, one for an English guy we were working with, and one for a representative from the company doing the tunneling. The third box butted up to the office Conex. It contained a bathroom with a shower at one end. It had a little refrigerator, coffee pot, and microwave. It was the crew lounge. The fourth Conex was perpendicular to the road and formed the last part of the C. It was set up for our techs to use as a work shop. All our tools and spare parts were in it. The SAT system was supplied by a German company who had workers already on site. They had been doing interventions for some time, but – for some reason or another – didn't seem real interested in doing the SAT work.

None of the equipment was set up and ready to go. We didn't even have all the parts we needed. One of my first jobs was to go through the chamber, the LST shack, and our equipment, to see what we were lacking and what needed to be put together. There was a lot of work to do to get this system up and running. The SAT system had been supplied – not to us but to the company in charge of the tunneling by the German company. Supposedly it was ready to go and just needed to be hooked up to gas bottles to be functional. Ha! What a Laugh! It was missing almost all the regulators and only one or two of the hatches actually sealed. The DART didn't even line up to the SAT chamber. Crazy! I can't believe the main company signed off on the system before we got there. Obviously, whoever had inspected it had no clue what they were looking for. They probably just saw a big tank, some gages, and plumbing, then figured it was good to go. I would bet they had never even seen a SAT system before. Oh well, it was my problem now. Well, mine and the Tunneler's problem anyway.

Egypt is NOT like America by any stretch of the imagination. It's not even close to European either. The place is great, and I really enjoyed my time there. It has a lot of very interesting history that is easily accessible. But doing business or getting supplies? It is a completely different world. There are no superstores like Home Depot or Lowes. I think Walmart may be there, but I never saw one. To find tools and equipment – especially commercial dive gear and high-pressure equipment – we had to go on missions of discovery; starting with the phone. We would make calls to people claiming to be dealers and/or distributers only to find out, when we met them, that they truly had no idea what we were even talking about. When we did finally find someone who could supply us with what we needed, their inventory would be extremely small. Of course, I didn't expect it to be as easy to find equipment there as it was in the states, but I didn't really expect it to be as complicated as it was either.

It took us a good week to get what we needed. The Tunneler had to get his crew to bring as much equipment with them when they came over as they could get past customs. That was more complicated than expected because anything that looked like it could be used to build bombs or weapons was highly scrutinized. The customs agents had never seen anything like the equipment our crew members were bringing over, so of course, not all the stuff made it through customs. My friend, Billings, came over a few weeks after me and helped carry some of BMC's supplies with him. He didn't have any issues getting through customs.

We had some help from the French (not much) who were running the project for the Egyptian military. A little more help from the Italians; who were operating the TBM for the French. The Germans, who were doing the majority of the interventions for the Italians, were a help, but also a hindrance. I think they looked at us a little like we were trying to steal their work. The Egyptians helped as much as they could; and, ultimately, they were who we depended on mostly. They had to okay everything anyway. None of those groups were as safety-conscious as we were, though.

It took us over a week to get enough equipment together to make the system functional. It wasn't perfect, but it was operational and safe. I did get to see quite a bit of Cairo as we were out scouting for and procuring equipment. I enjoyed that quite a bit. I even got to eat at a few restaurants outside of the hotel. The Tunneler took me and a couple others to a Shisha café or two also. I didn't smoke, but they had interesting beverages – no alcohol though.

An interesting thing about Egypt is that there are no bars or taverns outside of the hotels. Even most restaurants didn't serve alcohol. There are night clubs and dance halls, but they are all located inside one hotel or another. I don't know if that is an Egyptian thing, or if it happened after the government was taken over by the muslims. One political issue going on while I was there was that the muslim government advisory committee of ethics was trying to make belly dancing illegal. Most of the Egyptians were against this because they considered belly dancing an important part of their history and culture. There was even a world-famous belly dancing school in Cairo. I was told by several belly dancers that Egyptians have been belly dancing for over ten-thousand years. Wow! There were even five different styles of the dancing; who knew?!

Anyway, one of the most critical tasks we had to perform was transferring the SAT workers from the living chamber to the TBM and back. This was to be done using a DART – the DDC on wheels. We had to ensure the DART would work as a transport vessel. We also had to ensure that it would match up to both the habitat and the TBM's personnel lock. There was a lot of finagling and adjustment to get the DART to line up perfectly with the living chamber. It had to be lined up perfectly so the joint wouldn't leak when it was locked on. We had to do the same thing on the other end – down in the TBM. We ran a few dry runs with the DART getting it to the TBM. It was quite a process.

The first step was to lock the DART onto the SAT chamber – the habitat. We pressed a test subject – one of our tenders – into the system. His task was to open the hatches between the habitat and the DART to make sure that it all worked like it should. Then we had him close the hatch on the DART. We would add a little pressure to the DART hoping for a seal on its hatch. When that was successful, the test subject would close the habitat hatch and we would vent the air out of the TUP (Transfer Under Pressure) space. The TUP is the little tunnel formed when one chamber is locked onto another. When the TUP was at surface pressure, we would disconnect the DART from the SAT chamber.

The next step was to roll the DART away from the habitat and hook it up to a crane with a four-point sling. The crane would lift the DART and place it on the back of an equipment truck designed to drive into the tunnel. There was a special set of tracks and locking mechanisms on the deck of this truck. We locked the DART onto the tracks. Then we placed ratchet straps over the DART and tightened them to prevent any unwanted movement. When we had the DART locked in place, the truck was driven to the TBM. This was quite a trip. Our work site was alongside the tunnel access about five hundred yards from the access entrance. The truck trip consisted of the drive to the access, a hair-pin turn, followed by another five-hundred-yard ride down the access to the tunnel entrance where we were stopped for an inspection. It didn't matter that we had gone through an inspection check just to get onto the worksite; now we had to go through another check before entering the tunnel. We had to go through this inspection when we walked into the tunnel as well.

The inspection here wasn't as intense as the other checks. There were no dogs, no mirrors on sticks, and the guards weren't carrying m-sixteens. They just did a quick look around and through the vehicle, checked our ID badges, and looked through our bags if they felt like it – which wasn't often. After passing inspection, we continued our trip down through the tunnel to the TBM – that was about a mile. At the TBM, the truck driver drove into a space designed for it. There was a lifting system – operated by the TBM support crew – for raising the DART up into the TBM.

Slings would be lowered to us and we would hook them up to the DART. Once that was done, we would undo the straps and pins securing the DART to the truck. The lift system would then lift the DART about twenty feet into the belly of the TBM. Next, floor plates with tracks on them would be folded down into place under the DART. After those were secured, the DART was lowered onto the tracks and hooked up to a little electric pusher. The pusher moved the DART several hundred feet to the end of the tracks that were on an elevating platform towards the front of the TBM. Here we secured the DART to the elevating platform and placed hand rails around it. The platform would raise about ten feet to the level of the personnel lock. Once there, we locked the elevator in place. We unlocked the DART and rolled it forward to lock it onto the personnel lock. If that all went well, we would pressurize the personnel lock until it equalized with the pressure inside the DART. If no leaks were detected, the Compressed Air Workers would open the hatches in the DART and move into the personnel lock. The return trip was a process exactly opposite to getting into the TBM, except we didn't have to be inspected on the way out. The whole process took over half-an-hour. Of course, the company wanted us to do it as quickly as we could.

Finally, at the end of the first week of January, we pressed in our first SAT team of Compressed Air Workers. All three of them were divers; two of ours and one Italian. Neither of our guys had been in SAT before, but both were experienced divers and had many TBM interventions under their belts. I didn't know anything about the Italian other than the Italians running the TBM telling me he was qualified and certified to do the job. I think the Tunneler was pressured into putting him on the SAT crew. It was good for inter-company relations anyway.

The SAT set up was by no means perfect. It was small. It was difficult to keep the humidity as low as it should be. The hot water for the showers didn't always work as well as it should have. Sometimes we didn't have as much water as we required either. Our guys had never been in SAT before, so didn't know enough to complain about anything. That was nice for us. I felt sorry for them, though. The Italian never complained about anything either. I don't know if he knew things weren't exactly right, or if he just wasn't the type to complain. He was a hard worker and really helped our guys in the system. I was glad to have him in there.

Once we started the SAT operations, we needed another SAT supervisor and SAT Tech. The Tunneler was having a hard time finding anyone willing to work on this strange project in

Egypt. I called some of my friends in the industry and made a few recommendations to the Tunneler. He hired two friends of mine, a supervisor from southern California who was living in Austin, Texas; and a SAT Tech from New Orleans. They both came over to Egypt to work the night shift. I was very happy to get these two guys working with us. The supervisor is a great guy and the SAT Tech is very good. He made lots of improvements to the SAT system and finally got the humidity issue under control. I'm not sure they were happy with me talking them into joining us, but I was happy they had come to Egypt.

The first SAT run on the project had a storage depth of five-point-five Bar (one-hundred-eighty-two fsw) and an excursion depth of five-point-seven (one-hundred-eighty-eight fsw). It lasted thirty-five days including the three-day decompression. It was a little longer than the recommended run of twenty-eight days, but the job requirements from the main contractor deemed it necessary. We only had one completely functional chamber so we had to bring the whole system up to swap out teams. Our initial plan was to use the DDC in the medical van to decompress the teams, but we didn't have a habitat control system for it and there were no bathroom facilities in it either.

This tunneling project was different than the other interventions I had been on. The forward progress wasn't shut down for any length of time. Of course, they shut down the TBM while we were in the Cutting Head replacing worn discs. We didn't work a twenty-four-hour cycle, instead the TBM operators had a schedule of worn discs to replace. They would shut down for the time it took us to replace those discs. When we finished, they would start drilling again. We didn't replace discs every day either. It might be a day or two in between interventions sometimes.

There were two tunnels being drilled at the same time – one for east bound traffic and the other for west bound. After the automotive tunnels were finished, a third tunnel for trains was to be drilled. While I was there, we were tasked with changing the worn discs on one machine and a German team was tasked with taking care of the other TBM. The Germans were still doing their interventions without SAT. They were working at the same pressures as we were. Their Superintendent just didn't see the same need for Saturation operations that the Tunneler did.

At one of the meetings, the German in charge of his project told the Egyptian military commander in charge of the whole project that a certain number of hyperbaric incidents – the Bends – were expected and acceptable. I couldn't believe my ears. I tried to explain that there was no excuse for any hyperbaric incidents when we all – even the Germans – had the equipment, training, and means to prevent them. The odd thing was, most of the German CAWs didn't have a problem with it either. I think one or two of them got bent every week while I was there. When one of them got bent, they would get treated and sent home for two weeks; after which they would return to work on the TBM – just for a chance to get bent again. Insanity, or stupidity? I didn't know which. Really it just came down to saving money being more important than the safety or health of the employee.

The SAT operations didn't make it perfect for our crew either, though. It was expected that their work shift would be six to eight hours, maybe up to ten if the extra time was needed to meet the daily work goal. It was supposed to be understood that twelve hours was to be the maximum work day – including the travel time from, and back, to the habitat. A couple times we were coerced into working fourteen or fifteen hours. I voiced my opposition to no avail. The weird thing to me was that when the time for prayer for the muslims arrived, the job was shut down for the fifteen minutes that it took the muslim workers to do their thing. I was never in the tunnel when the drilling was going on and forward progress was being made, so I do not know if the TBM was shut down for prayer time during those operations.

After I had been there a few weeks, we had another turnover of some of our crew. Our incoming crew included Sedro Wooley – one of the women that the Tunneler had on his crew list. Her arrival caused quite a stir amongst the muslims on the job, starting at the top. There were no issues with her getting into Egypt nor any issues at the hotel. A few of the people at the hotel had a hard time understanding why a woman would want to work in construction, but that was about it. Getting onto the jobsite was another story.

She rode in the van with the rest of us to the worksite for her first shift. The Tunneler had done his due diligence submitting all her paperwork and certifications to the command ahead of time like he did for every one of his crew. He was told all was in order. When we arrived at the gate, however, you would have thought we were trying to smuggle drugs or something onto the site. We were held at the gate for over an hour while the guards made calls and waited for approval to let her enter the work site. When the approval finally did come, we had to take her to the command center and introduce her to the head of the project as well as the other company heads.

They all made a huge deal about a female doing this type of work. We were told that she would be expected to work just like the men and if she couldn't, she would not be allowed back on the project. She was also told and retold about the dress code. She wasn't allowed to wear shorts and she couldn't wear tank tops. They wanted her to wear long sleeved shirts, but we finally got them to agree to allow her to wear t-shirts as long as the sleeves were at least four inches long. Also, they wanted her to keep her hair covered with a hijab. It didn't help that she was blond. We got them to agree to just wearing her hard hat or ball cap at all times. We were all supposed to wear hardhats while we were working anyway, so she was used to that.

When she was working inside the TBM, she did well – as she always did. Most of the guys from all the other crews really liked having her around and many went out of their way to help her out – not that she needed it. Sedro Wooley is not a big girl, she is trim and athletic, but not muscley, so might appear that she wasn't strong enough for many of the tasks we were asked to perform. That was by no means the case though, and she proved that several times when she out-worked a couple of the men on the job. They, of course, didn't appreciate that much; especially when their fellow crew members gave them a hard time for being outdone by a girl. After a couple weeks, she was accepted as one of the regular crew.

After the first SAT was completed, we brought the living chamber back to the surface – that was we depressurized it. We gave it a good cleaning and New Orleans completed some modifications to make it more comfortable for the next crew getting pressed in. That was all accomplished within two days and we were ready to press in the second team.

The second crew consisted of Sedro Wooley, Superior, and another guy from the Seattle area. None of them had been in SAT before. I went over all the SAT procedures with them. I had worked with all of them before and knew that there was no reason to be concerned about their performance. The biggest worry, as always with people new to SAT, was how they would deal with being locked in a chamber with other people for a month. It turned out that none of them had any issues with that. I wasn't really expecting any issues as I had run all of them through the chambers on Bertha and the Northgate tunnel.

About half-way through the second SAT, it was past time for me to return home. The visas that we had entered Egypt on were good for four weeks. I had gone way over that. That wasn't a huge deal. It just meant that I couldn't re-enter Egypt without paying a fine. I was happy to do that. I didn't know how much the fine would be, but I could pay it at the airport on the way out so I wouldn't have any problems upon my return. To pay the fine, I had to go to the office of the military running security at the airport. The guards acted like it was a big deal and that the fine would be very expensive. I was escorted to the office by a couple armed guards and sat down to wait in a waiting room outside the commander's office. There were a couple other people ahead of me, presumably waiting for the same thing.

After half-an-hour or so, I was summoned into the commander's office. He looked at me, smiled, asked if I had enjoyed my time in Egypt. I told him that I had. He then asked if I wanted to return. I answered that I did and I really hoped that my overstay of my visa wouldn't cause any problems with that. He replied that it wouldn't cause any issues that couldn't be cured by money. I smiled and wondered how much it was going to cost me. He looked at my passport and visa. He asked when I thought I might be returning. I told him that I hoped to return in four to six weeks. He punched some numbers into a calculator he had on his desk. He looked up at me and said it would cost me four hundred pounds. Four hundred pounds?! Holy shit!

I was trying to do a quick calculation of English pounds to US dollars in my head, when he reiterated that it would be four hundred pounds Egyptian. Oh, yeah, I had forgotten that the Egyptians called their currency pounds and not dollars. Whew! Four hundred Egyptian pounds worked out to about twenty-two US dollars. What a relief! I didn't have any ones, so gave him a twenty and a five. He had no US dollars and I told him I didn't need any change. He was happy with that. He stamped my passport and visa with the appropriate stamps guaranteeing my ability to return to Egypt whenever I pleased, as long as I was out of the country for at least one day. I thanked him and went on to my gate to wait for my flight. Billings and I returned home without any issues.

*   *   *

I only had a week at home before I flew to Singapore to attend a class to get certified as an IMCA SAT Supervisor. The class was taught by the same instructor that I had taken IMCA LST and Surface Supervisor classes from in Louisiana. Those classes had been paid for by my employer, Global Diving and Salvage, but they weren't paying for this class. They had already paid for my SAT Supervisor class to get me certified by the Diver Certification Board of Canada (DCBC) but that didn't qualify me for all the jobs an IMCA cert would. I had held the Association of Commercial Divers International (ACDI) cert for several years, but the only place that was any good was in the United States – nobody overseas recognized it. I figured it would be a good investment in my career, so I was paying for this class myself. The management at Global had told me they would help me with the experience needed to get the certification.

The class lasted two weeks. It was fairly intense, but a lot of fun. There were six other students in the class from all over the world. It was great fun to reconnect with the instructor. He took me to a couple of his favorite restaurants and pointed me towards some good tourist destinations. The food was great and the sights were fantastic. It was quite expensive, though. Their laws were quite restrictive too. It is against the law to have chewing gum let alone chew it. The penalty for drug dealing is death. They take crime and punishment quite seriously there. I didn't break any laws and had a good time. I was glad to get home though.

In April I went back to Egypt to continue working on the tunneling project. Billings didn't return with me for personal reasons. Everybody wanted him to return, but he had other things to do. The Olmsted Dam project hadn't started up for the year yet, so my jobs weren't conflicting with each other. That kept everybody concerned happy. It was good to get back to the crew in Egypt. All three of the team in SAT were German. We also had a cat. A large, long hair, female calico cat had started hanging around our Conex boxes. There were dogs running around the site and occasionally a cat here and there. Our crew felt protective of this calico and started feeding her, so of course she stayed. I think she had at least two names, because we couldn't agree on one – cats don't pay any attention to a name anyway. Some of the crew called her Nefertiti, the rest of us called her Cleopatra.

A week or two after adopting us as her caretakers, Cleopatra gave birth to seven kittens. We set up a den for her - made up of a cardboard box and towels - in our crew lounge Conex box. Everybody kept a watchful eye on her and made sure she had plenty of food and water. We even set up a litterbox for her since she would be spending the nights inside the Conex while she was caring for her kittens. Before that she had just hung around outside mostly - except when she had the urge to jump on somebody's desk and take a nap. We had air conditioning in our Conex boxes and I'm sure she was much more comfortable inside during the hot days.

After a couple weeks, we entered our crew Conex/breakroom to find the cats were gone from their box. Everybody freaked out a little and started looking all over for her. It was funny to see a bunch of big, burly diver-types scurrying around and worrying about a litter of kittens. After about ten minutes, one of the guys called from the bathroom saying he had found them. Cleopatra had moved her brood from the cardboard box into the shower pan. She and her kittens were moved back into her box. Later that day she moved the whole bunch back into the shower pan. For the next couple days the crew played a game of hide and seek moving her back and forth.

On the third day of game play, she secretly moved her kittens - one by one - into the tool shed and hid them under the large toolbox we had in there. One of her kittens gave away her new hiding spot by mewling. By this time, Cleopatra had been leaving her kittens alone while she roamed around outside. The little kitten must have become lonely or hungry. When her family had been found, we knew we had to move them back to the breakroom. The tool room contained too much toxic and dangerous stuff for the kittens to get into.

It was a pain to get her out from under the toolbox, but we did it. We returned her to the cardboard box in the breakroom. Shortly after being relocated to the box, she started carrying her kittens – one at a time – back to the tool shed. Holy smokes! We put a kibosh on that move. She was moved back to her box again and the doors were closed. The next morning, we found that she had moved back to the shower pan. At that point we decided to just leave her there. It must have been cooler and more comfortable for her and her kittens in the shower pan. Score six for Cleopatra and zero for us. At least we knew where she was and didn't have to worry about the wild dogs snacking on her little ones.

As the kittens got older, some of our crew started worrying about what was going to happen to them. One of the guys looked into what was required to take the cats back to the states. It turned out all that was needed was a check-up and documented clean bill of health from a veterinarian. I told my wife about that and she wanted me to bring Cleopatra home with me. I would have liked to do that, but Cleopatra was a feral cat and disappeared a few days before I left Egypt. She hung around until her kittens were eating the food supplied by our crew, then she was gone. I thought that was a little funny, but feral cats may be less family oriented than house cats. I don't really know. Two of the kittens had died when they were only a few days old, but the rest were healthy and were all taken back to the states by members of our crew. New Orleans took two of them. Austin took another. I didn't take any, we already had two cats at home.

There were no real issues during my second hitch in Egypt. Everything went pretty much as planned. The Germans were doing more of the interventions than we were. I think we were going to put more Americans in SAT after I left, but I don't know whether or not that happened. My second hitch was only five weeks or so. By the time I got home, the job at Olmsted Dam was getting ready to go. Work was winding down for us in Egypt and I wasn't required to return. I kept in touch with the Tunneler and he assured me that when the next project came up, he would let me know. Sadly, that was the last tunneling project I ever worked on.

* * *

Thoroughly Dehydrated The End of it All

I started working regularly at Olmsted Dam on the Ohio River for Global Diving and Salvage as of the fall of two-thousand-fourteen. The work was somewhat seasonal – the season being from sometime in mid-May through mid to late December – just before or after Christmas and maybe into January depending on the weather. I didn't want to work the whole year on that job as some other people did. Remember, I like a day off for every day I work. Luckily for me there was another supervisor, a friend of mine – North Sea - who felt the same as I did. He was getting ready to retire, but not quite there yet. He wanted to make a little more money before finally retiring.

North Sea and I had agreed to a schedule of four weeks on with four weeks off. That was agreeable with the management. I think the crew enjoyed the change as well. Some of the crew worked the whole season. A few of them were already living in the area. A few others moved to the area – families and all – after getting hired on for the whole season. If I had known in the beginning how long the job was going to be, I think I might have purchased a house in the area. Houses were inexpensive and quite a bit cheaper than a hotel. Of course, Global was paying for the hotel, so that didn't cost me anything anyway. A house might have been a good investment though.

We worked ten hours per day, five or six days a week at Olmsted. Usually, Monday through Saturday every week was the norm. Once-in-awhile, the construction needs determined that we not work on Saturday. We didn't work on holidays – like Memorial Day, the fourth of July, or Labor Day - either. I was the swing shift supervisor for Barge Number One. Swing shift worked fewer Saturdays than day shift did.

With all this time off so far away from home, I got bored. I love motorcycle riding and the Bible Belt was a part of America I had not explored on a motorcycle. All these free weekends were just begging me to go riding. I thought I might purchase a motorcycle and keep it in the area. I could store it in one of the crew's garages during the times I wasn't in Kentucky. I started looking around for a good deal on a bike I would enjoy.

In the summer of two-thousand-fifteen, I found a good deal on a two-thousand-two BMW R1200 CLC. It was a BMW designed for the same market as Honda Goldwings and other long-distance cruisers. It wasn't the long-distance cruiser I was looking for, but I really liked the BMW R1200C. I called my wife and asked if it would be okay with her if I bought it. She told me we could probably afford it. So, I bought it. It was electric blue and chrome. It had saddlebags and a rear trunk. It had ABS brakes, cruise control, a radio/CD player, power ports, and a fairing. It was not the style of motorcycle I would normally ride. I liked bikes without all that extra fluff. I was not a fan of fairings – windscreens – and all the techy stuff didn't belong on a motorcycle if you asked me. It was still fun to ride, though.

Global was paying our airfare to get to and from the job. I asked them if I could just take the money and get myself to and from the job. They asked why, and I told them I would rather drive than fly. They said they wouldn't give me the money for a plane ticket then, but they would pay me the mileage rate to and from the job. They would not pay for a hotel during travel though. That would be on me, as would all my meals. They had looked at a map and discovered that it was one-thousand-seven-hundred-twenty-three miles from Helena, Montana to Paducah, Kentucky. They also figured it would take me two or three days to make the trip. It only took me a day-and-a-half.

It was a win for me, because I liked riding better than flying. To fly, my wife and I had to get up at four in the morning to make the flight leaving at six. Even though Helena is the state capitol, there are not many flights in and out. If I drove, I could leave anytime I wanted and I wouldn't have to wake my wife early to drop me off at the airport. I also spent quite a bit less money on gas than what Global paid for mileage. It was a win for me all around. It was a win for Global also, because the mileage expense was about half what an airline ticket for me cost.

From then on, I drove myself back and forth from the start of the season until my hitch just before Thanksgiving ended. When I worked in December, January, or February, I flew. I really enjoyed the riding and it was great to have a motorcycle to ride during my off-time in Paducah. Heading home, I would take different routes and a few days to see different sights and visit family. I put a lot of miles on that motorcycle. In June of two-thousand-sixteen, I traded the BMW in for a two-thousand-sixteen Indian Chief Darkhorse; one of my favorite motorcycles ever. I rode that thing all over the place.

*   *   *

We did a lot of diving on the Olmsted project. When Global first got the contract for the diving, it was for inspections and to assist the pile-driving crews when needed. There wasn't going to be any sort of regular crew, because there wasn't going to be any regular diving. The idea was that there would probably be about a hundred dives a year – if that – and they would be done in one or two-week spurts. The project was designed as a diverless "in the wet" construction project. The Germans had built a dam in the same manner previously with good results.

I always loved it when I heard "diverless" on a project that would require divers here and there. Often, it meant that no dive plan had been made and there would end up being way more diving than if the project had planned diving work. By two-thousand-thirteen the prime contractor realized that it was more cost effective to have a dive team on site and ready to go all the time. There was a lot of standby time for the crews then, but that changed dramatically in the following years. By two-thousand-fourteen, there was enough work to keep two dive crews on site - one for dayshift and the other for swing shift – for the whole work season. A dive crew consisted of a non-diving supervisor and six diver/tenders.

Global was having a little trouble keeping a supervisor for the swing shift. I don't really know why; it was a pretty nice job. It was Army Corps of Engineers though, so there was a *lot* of paperwork to do and keep track of. Also, we had to have a DSO (Dive Safety Officer) in the dive shack with us most of the time. I suppose that bothered some of the supervisors. Maybe they didn't realize that the DSO was there just to observe and had no real power – even though some of them thought they did. Most of the DSOs didn't know as much about commercial diving as they thought they did. To be a DSO you only had to go to a four-week class in Florida – put on by the ACoE – that was just an introduction to diving and commercial equipment. Some of the DSOs were SCUBA divers and knew a little more, but not much.

I got along with most of the DSOs well. The easiest thing to do was make sure they had a connection for their computer, answer a few questions they might have, then ignore them for the most part. I always tried to have them on board for our daily meetings where I lined out the work for the day. That way they would have an idea of what was going on and leave me alone to do my job. I did have an issue with a couple of them over the course of the job, though.

The first time was in two-thousand-twelve, my first time on the project. I told you about that one a couple chapters ago. The second time was over my use of Nitrox. Nitrox is a mixture of Oxygen and Nitrogen - usually made up of more than twenty-one percent Oxygen. Normal air – like we all breathe on this planet – is made up of roughly twenty-one percent Oxygen, seventy-eight percent Nitrogen and one percent other gases; like Argon, Carbon Dioxide, Helium, Radon, et al. Nitrox is sometimes called "Enriched Air" because of its higher Oxygen content. The prime contractor had decided that we should use Nitrox on our deeper dives in order to lengthen our bottom times.

The working depths on this project ranged anywhere from ten feet to over seventy – when the river was at high water. Most of our diving was done in the twenty to sixty-foot range. Of course, if we were diving at less than thirty-five feet, we could dive all day. Deeper depths required less time to keep us on the No-Deco tables. The ACoE was adamant that we didn't plan any dives requiring decompression. That meant that diving anything deeper than fifty feet would really limit our bottom time. That was, unless we were utilizing Nitrox.

I was a certified Nitrox SCUBA diver and had taken advanced classes in Nitrox diving. I had been using Nitrox in commercial diving here and there since the late eighties, so I was well-versed in its use. Seattle and the other supervisors – including myself – conferred and decided that a mixture of thirty-eight percent Oxygen would best suit our needs on this project. Global sent a Nitrox generator to us and we made our own mix on the dive barge. We trained several of the crew in the operation and calibration of the machine.

For many reasons, we kept our max dive times under four hours. We were constantly fighting current, which tired out the divers faster, so I limited my divers' bottom times to three hours. That meant that I would go through three divers on a typical day. The ACoE required us to use the USN revision six dive tables which had a no-d limit of one-hundred-twenty-five minutes at forty-five feet, and only ninety-two minutes at fifty feet. I always included a safety factor of three feet when calculating depth, so that meant that even at thirty-seven feet, I was limited to a bottom time of two hours – unless I used Nitrox.

I used Nitrox on almost all the dives over thirty-seven feet; even if I was planning on keeping the diver down less than two hours. One of the main reasons for that was because there was a lot of stuff in the water that the divers could get fouled on. I didn't want them to be concerned about having to do any in-water stops or run them on a Sur-D-O_2 if they did run into complications. I wanted them, and myself, to have plenty of time to get themselves off the bottom. Most of the other supervisors only used the Nitrox when diving deeper than forty-five feet; and sometimes not even then.

Anyway, one DSO must have had an issue with Nitrox. I don't know what it was, because he never really said, but he gave me shit for using it almost every time I did. I tried to explain my reasoning to him, but he would not listen. He hassled me about it for several weeks. When I wouldn't bend to his will, he went as far as to report me to the upper management for using Nitrox when it wasn't required. I talked to Global management about the issue and they told me I was the supervisor and as long as I wasn't endangering the crew, I should run the deck how I saw fit.

The prime contractor management called me in for a talk because of what the DSO had told them. Because I was on the swing shift, I had to go in early to make the meeting. Several of the head foremen were there when I walked in. The head guy asked how I was and if I was having any issues with my crew. I told him everything was fine. Then he asked if everything was okay, why was I using Nitrox so often. I told him it was for the safety of my divers. I talked to him about the depths we were working, the tables we were using and why it was safer to use Nitrox to extend the bottom time rather than falling back on surface decompression to prevent hyperbaric trauma. After my explanation, he told me to keep doing what I was doing. He wanted to preserve the safety record of the job. He also said he would have a talk with that DSO and reiterate that he was there to observe and not to control anything. I thanked the head guy and went to work. On my next hitch, that DSO was no longer on the project. It seems I wasn't the only supervisor he was bothering.

Another issue I had with a DSO was about our Bailout Bottles. This DSO had just completed the ACoE introduction to diving class in Florida. He was excited to demonstrate how much he now knew about diving. He diligently inspected the dive gear we were using. I don't have any issues with that and I applaud anybody who takes their job seriously – especially when it comes to safety. The way he went about it was not appreciated, however.

He came on board like he knew everything. When he saw something we were doing that didn't jive with his training, he loudly announced that we were doing it wrong. On top of that, he wanted us to stop doing things the way we were and start doing them the way he wanted. I had several talks with him to explain why we did things the way we did. After a little while, he came around for the most part. One thing he would not let go was the way we used our Bailout Bottles.

He noticed right off the bat that we wore our bottles upside down. We do this for several reasons. One is so the valve doesn't bang on the back of the dive helmet. Another is, with the bottle upside down, we can easily reach the valve handle to open it when we need the bailout. That raised another concern this DSO had with our practices; we leave the Bailout bottle shut off. One of our pre-dive checks is "off at the bottle, on at the hat" for the valve line-up on the bailout system. We do this so our Bailout Bottle doesn't accidently drain while we are working. That happens more often than you might think. He wanted the tenders to open the valve on the bottle before the diver went in the water.

Another issue he had was that we didn't require a pressure gage on the bottle. A couple of the guys had gages on their bottles, but most did not. None of our company-supplied-bottles had a gage on them. As far as I was concerned, I didn't like having a gage on the bottle. The gage requires an extra hose on the equipment which just adds one more item of our gear that can get fouled on something, trapping the diver on the bottom. I saw it as more of a safety hazard than a safe practice. I always required the bailout bottle to be gaged before each dive, so the diver knew what was in the bottle before the dive. There was no need to check it during the dive, as long as the bottle valve was closed. There are pressure gages available now that screw into the first stage. That type might be okay, but the diver can't see it while the bottle is being worn anyway, so what is the point? Besides, I have seen those little gages get snapped off during a dive, resulting in the draining of the bailout that cannot be stopped. I don't like 'em.

To me, it should be left up to the diver to decide how the Bailout Bottle is worn. It is personal dive gear and as long as it all functions the way it is designed, then the diver's preference and comfort are what is important. I have always preferred to keep my equipment to a minimum of what was needed. Even when SCUBA diving. When I started SCUBA diving, I didn't have a pressure gage on my bottle. Instead, all my bottles had J-valves on them. That is a type of valve that kept a five-hundred psi reserve in the bottle until the reserve valve was opened. That way I knew when I had to open the reserve, it was time to go back to the surface. I didn't have to keep checking some gage.

I went round and round with this DSO for days. I didn't make the changes he wanted and told him that he did not have the authority to require me to force my divers to make those changes. When he found that he wasn't getting anywhere with me, he went to upper management. Not just my upper management either. He talked to, called, e-mailed, and texted all the upper management; his bosses, my bosses, as well as the prime contractor's lead management. He didn't get any support except from his own bosses. He made enough noise, though, that his bosses talked with the prime contractor and my superintendents.

A meeting was called between all the management, the concerned DSO, and myself. He explained what he thought the issues were and why I should force my divers to do what he demanded. After he was done, I went through all the reasons the divers should be allowed to continue the way we had been wearing our equipment. I also went on to explain why our way was safer than the way this DSO thought things should be done. At the end of it all, it was all decided in my favor except for the pressure gauge issue. After that, we were required to have some sort of pressure gage on the bottles; the style was left up to the diver. The company rigs were all fitted with the little gage that screwed into the first stage on the regulator yoke. Win some lose some, I guess. That particular DSO didn't return the following season and I never saw him again.

*　　*　　*

The Olmsted Dam project was an amazing construction job in many ways. It had many issues; as many government projects, as well as any large construction projects do. Time and cost overages are all too common. This project was first approved in nineteen-eighty-eight at a projected cost of seven-hundred-seventy-five million US dollars. It was also projected to be completed by nineteen-ninety-eight. Ha! Sorry. The project ran into many, many issues; funding – or lack thereof – being a major issue. Construction finally began in nineteen-ninety-five. It was finally completed in two-thousand-nineteen at a cost of over three billion US dollars. Ouch. It was good for us though! We made a pretty good living for several years off that project. Thank you, US taxpayers! It was the longest and largest civil works project ever completed by the Army Corps of Engineers.

As I stated earlier, this project was originally designed to be done without divers. Well, they would have divers do inspections here and there to monitor quality and progress. No construction was going to involve divers, though. Locks were constructed first and completed in two-thousand-two. After that, the rest of the dam was constructed. It was described as an "In the Wet" construction process, where no cofferdams or river diversions were utilized. The dam is just under half-a-mile wide. Next to the Lock are five Tainter gates – radial arm gates used to control water flow – and about fourteen-hundred feet of wicket gates that utilize a crew in a boat for operation – and a permanent weir on the Kentucky side. Concrete shells and wicker gate bases were cast on the beach and placed in the water one at a time. Thirty-two pre-cast concrete sections were placed – that included twelve wicker gate bases and four other types of shells. There were also about three-thousand-three-hundred twenty-four-inch-diameter round piles driven to attach the concrete sections to the river bottom. A lot of boring stuff to talk about, but kind of interesting if you think about it. I just wanted to give you an idea as to the immenseness of the project.

There is so much involved in such a massive project as this, that it is hard to comprehend – even when you are working on the project. We did a lot of diving that was required, but wasn't part of the actual construction. If it wasn't done, though, the construction couldn't happen. One of those jobs was the cleaning and repair of the submerged tracks of the skidway. The skidway was a two-rail track leading from where the shells were cast on the beach down into the water deep enough that the shell could be picked up by a huge catamaran crane barge built specifically for this job.

This was usually one of the first tasks we would perform at the start of the season. During the off-season – winter and early spring – the river would change a lot. It would get really high from the snow melt. That would increase both the volume and the velocity of the water moving downstream. All that flowing water would bring all different kinds of debris with it, from trees to anything you could imagine. This stuff would get caught up and entangled in all the different parts of the project. One of our jobs was to clean this stuff away.

The skidway tracks were placed directly on the ground out of the water, but raised off the river bed several feet where it was underwater. It was the perfect trap for logs, trees, and other debris. Often debris would damage the tracks when it made contact. Not only would we have to clear the debris, we would have to make repairs on the tracks. This often involved the removal of the damaged pieces – usually utilizing a Broco torch. New pieces would either be bolted or welded back on.

Often the flooding river would bring in a lot of silt that would have to be removed from the tracks. We would do that with either a water blaster, an airlift, or a combination of the two. Sometimes there was so much silt to remove, it would take us several days. The first couple times we did it, the project manager would ask us to do the inspection just a day or two before the tracks were needed. We informed him that there was more than two days-worth of work to be done and we didn't get the tracks cleaned and repaired in time to meet the scheduled deployment of the concrete shell. After that, management would have us do the initial inspection at least a week before the tracks were needed.

We also had to clean silt and debris from the Tainter gates and their tail races. There were five of those gates. It often took us a couple weeks to get all the debris removed from them. We would do that work in between the work we did assisting the piledrivers drive sheet-pile and the round foundation pilings. We got to do a lot of different tasks on this job. We all enjoyed the diversity of tasks. The divers gained lots of experience utilizing many different types of equipment making them better equipped to work on future projects of all kinds.

The conditions varied quite a bit as well. Visibility could be anywhere from twenty feet to complete black-out conditions. The current we worked in varied from half-a-knot to as high as four knots. Of course, nothing could be done when the current was over two-and-a-half knots, but it took us a while to convince the prime contractor of that. They tried many different ways of enabling us to work in higher currents. Sheet-pile walls worked the best, but the diver had to be fairly close to those, so they weren't very practical.

Some engineer also designed a chain curtain. It was a large horizontal metal rod with anchor chain hanging off it. A crane barge was required to hang it in the water upstream of where we were working. It was not practical, because it had to be close to the diver work area, didn't slow the current much, and added to the material in the water that a diver could get fouled on. We didn't use it often. We finally got the management to agree to standby days if the current was over two-and-a-half-knots.

*   *   *

Safety was a major concern on this job. Things have changed a lot in the dive industry from when I first started. We had many safety protocols to follow. The ACoE required that we have a designated tender dressed in and ready to go during the whole time we had a diver in the water. What they wanted – but didn't require – was a diver sitting in a chair at the dive station fully dressed in with the dive helmet on the diver's lap. While that may be practical in the navy or the army, it is not practical on a construction job.

Of course, we had a standby umbilical with a dive helmet on it at the dive station. There would also be the bailout bottle, weight belt, and any other equipment required by the standby diver ready to go. One of the crew was designated the standby and should be ready to jump in the water at a moment's notice. Often the standby diver would work the deck dressed in his dive suit – either a wet suit, dry suit, or hot water suit, but that wasn't always conducive to the work being done on the deck. I didn't require the divers on my team to be wearing a dive suit when they were the standby diver. What I did require was their guarantee that they were willing to jump into the water, if needed, regardless of what they were wearing.

The ACoE also required that we run safety drills and document them. We would have to let the DSO and the Emergency Response Team know when we were going to run a drill. We were required to involve everyone on the site just like it was an actual emergency. Since everybody knew it was a drill, everybody was prepared for it beforehand. To my way of thinking, that was not a true representation of an emergency. Of course, I realize that running through drills is good practice and gets everyone acquainted with the process and equipment used. However, I also think there is value in running surprise drills, when everyone involved thinks it is an actual emergency. Management must be informed of surprise drills as well, otherwise there would be other issues involved that I wouldn't want to get into.

I ran the safety drills a couple times a year as required by the ACoE; the kind where everyone knows it's a drill and is prepared for it. I also would run sneaky unscheduled drills a couple times a year to keep the dive crew on their toes. When I wanted to run a sneaky drill, I would have to tell the DSO and he would let the upper management of the project know what was going on. No one else would know though. That way, the ERT would also react to it as if it were a real incident. The upper management liked that I ran these kinds of drills.

Anyway, on one of my hitches, we hadn't run a drill in quite a while. I was about two weeks into my hitch and I noticed the standby dress was getting lax. Granted it was in the middle of the summer and the weather was hot, but still, the standby diver needed to be ready to go at a moment's notice. Sedro Woolley was just finishing up her dive. Earlier, I had informed the DSO that I would be running a safety drill at the end of Sedro's dive. He had informed the site management and let them know it was one of my sneaky drills. No one else knew.

Bottom times were running about two-and-a-half- hours and we were diving Nitrox. At about two-hours-and-fifteen minutes I shut off the deck comms – I should let you know that we had diver's comms on a loudspeaker out on deck so the surface crew could hear what the diver was saying at all times. So, I shut off deck comms just long enough to tell Sedro Woolley that I wanted her to say she was fouled, followed by a statement that she was feeling faint and seeing spots, then go silent. I also wanted her to feign unconsciousness when the standby arrived and just be as limp as she could be. Then I turned the deck comms back on.

A few minutes later, Sedro Woolley said she was fouled. I asked her what she needed and she asked us to come up on her hose. The deck crew did and immediately felt that she was fouled. At this point she said she felt like she wasn't getting any air. Shortly after that she said she could see spots, then drifted off. She was a great actress. At this point I yelled to the deck crew that we needed to splash the standby and retrieve an unconscious diver. I informed the DSO of the situation and I announced over the jobsite radio that we had an unconscious diver emergency on Dive Barge One.

To my amazement, the standby, who was wearing work clothes – steel-toed boots and all – threw on his bailout, put on the hat, quickly checked by the tenders, and dove into the water. He was at the diver in less than twenty seconds. Wow – that was awesome! When he reached the diver, he communicated that her umbilical was wrapped around a pile, but he had freed it. He relayed that the diver appeared to be breathing but was unresponsive. He clipped her harness to his harness and instructed the deck crew to come up on both umbilicals. When he got to the surface and next to the barge, our retrieval davit was already deployed and the standby attached the diver to it and the deck crew got the diver on deck. The whole operation took less than one minute. I was thoroughly impressed.

As soon as the deck crew got the diver's helmet off, she smiled at them. I went out on deck and congratulated the crew on a job well done. About a minute after the diver was on deck, the ERT arrived at our barge with their boat, ready to transport the diver to the beach. At this point everybody was informed it had just been a safety drill. The next step is for everybody to critique the drill and fill out an assessment. My deck crew was congratulated by the management on an excellent performance.

I was so impressed with the standby diver's performance that I offered to let him skip his work dive, but still receive his wet pay if he wanted. He told me that he would just as soon make the regular work dive that he was scheduled to do. I told him I was sorry his work boots got wet, but he told me he was fine with that and positive that they would be dry by the time he finished his work dive. I thanked him for doing his job well and without any complaints.

*   *   *

As a Dive Supervisor, I have always been picky about who I had on my crew. One of the nice things about inland diving, as opposed to offshore work, is that if you have a bad crew member you can send him away and get a replacement fairly easily. When I worked a lot in Montana – earlier in my career – it was harder and I might have to finish the week out with a less-than-ideal crew member. In areas where lots of divers lived – Seattle, L.A., the Gulf coast – replacements could be had in less than a day.

The Olmsted project was a little remote – diver wise – like Montana. It would typically take a week to get a replacement – at least two or three days. The crews on this project were large for an inland job; non-diving supervisor and six deck crew that were diver/tenders. Management at Global knew that I was particular about who I had on my crew. We both wanted crew members to get along with each other and work well together. We also knew that unscheduled crew change-outs took time and cost money. We wanted to minimalize that. I tried to make it easy on management by assessing my crew and assigning them to a list I had at the end of each of their, or my hitches. Along with placement on the list, I would include an evaluation of their work ethics and habits and describe their strengths and weaknesses.

I put all crew members I worked with (including supervisors) on a four-tier list that I emailed to the job superintendent, the project manager at Global, and the office back in Seattle that handled crew member assignments. I figured that was the best way to keep everybody happy and working well together. I rarely told the crew where they were on the list and I never told any one crew member where other members were on my list. I didn't like kiss-asses and brown-nosers at all – those people were always at the bottom of the list.

The first group was Group A. These are crew members who work hard, are willing to learn, have good attitudes for the most part, get along well with others, are honest, and don't complain often. This category was my "will work with anytime, anywhere" group.

Group B has characteristics similar to the first group, but less time in the field. I would always prefer to work with well-experienced hands, but I also liked helping new people improve their knowledge and skills to make themselves more valuable crew members. This category was my "will work with anytime, anywhere as long as they are not the only ones on the crew" group.

The third level – Group C – was my "will work with if I have to because people in the top two groups aren't available" group. Some of my close friends referred to this bunch as my "will work with in a pinch" group. People in this group were capable divers and decent workers. They may not have as good an attitude as others. Maybe they don't work as well with others. They might not have the most positive attitude. Some of them were people I just didn't mesh with and they didn't mesh with me. That's okay, you're not going to get along with everybody – even if they are good workers. I would work with these people, I just preferred not to.

The last group – the bottom of the list – Group D, was my "No Way, No How!" list of crew. These are people that I could not stand to have on any job of mine. They didn't practice safe work practices. They didn't listen to me when I asked them to do things or tried to teach them how to do things. They might have really bad attitudes. They were consistently dishonest or stole things. They liked to cause excessive drama on the job, or maybe they liked to get into fights on the job. They weren't willing to take care of their fellow crew members when needed. Lack of respect for fellow workers – no matter what their position was – is a big issue for me. I really don't like the caste system in any work or society. I know people need to start at the bottom and work their way up, but they don't need to be disrespected while they are doing that. There weren't very many people on this list. I'm a pretty easy-going guy for the most part and willing to give anyone a chance – even if other people didn't like a crew member. I always had to see for myself how a person worked – or didn't – and how they got along with other crew members. I wouldn't prejudge anyone on rumors or hearsay.

Global management was pretty good about making my crew up with people I liked to work with. They even told me they liked getting feedback about the crew members. They had a policy for having all the crew members go through an evaluation every six months, but that rarely happened. Usually, a crew member had to request an evaluation as a first step in moving up the ladder or being considered for certain training or other jobs. I only had three evaluations in all the years I worked for Global Diving and Salvage.

*　　*　　*

In the fall – October to be exact – of two-thousand-sixteen, we reached a major milestone in the project; dive-wise anyway. We made the Ten-Thousandth dive of the job. Ten Thousand Dives! On one job. We made it without any major incidents also – no hyperbaric injuries, no cases of the bends, and no broken bones. Sure, we had a few scrapes and a twisted ankle here or there, but no loss of time accidents.

It was one of the guys on my crew, the swing shift crew, who got to make the ten-thousandth dive. He had been working on the project almost since Global started it. He was the guy on our crew that had been working on the project the longest. The other divers thought he deserved to make the dive, so were happy to let him jump rotation in order to do it. He was a diver from the Seattle area that had been working for Global quite a while. I was happy for him.

Global Diving and Salvage made a big deal of it. It was a good mark on their safety record. The prime contractor made a big deal of it too. It was a good shot in the arm for their safety record which they needed, because there had been a couple deaths on the project since its inception in nineteen-ninety-five. The Army Corps of Engineers made a big deal of it as well. Anytime the ACoE could get good publicity from this project they took it and ran with it.

The contractors all got together and had a big banner made. Group photos were taken of everybody involved standing behind the banner. The prime contractor put on a Bar-B-Que for everybody working on the project. All the heads of management made little speeches thanking everybody for their hard work and safe practices. It was a nice way for the management to show their appreciation of their employees.

After that many dives, you might think the project was close to being finished, but it was not. Seattle and the prime contractor management did some figuring and forecast that there would most likely be another five thousand dives before the end of this project. Wow. If that were the case, we were only two-thirds of the way complete. When I looked at what was left to do on the project, I had to agree with them. I wasn't on the project when it was completed, though, so I have no idea how many dives were made in total to complete that project.

* * *

The last dive job I ever went on was my first hitch of the season of two-thousand-eighteen at the Olmsted project. The day shift and the superintendent, Seattle, had started in April, I think. They usually started several weeks before the swing shift and got the ball rolling. I went out the last week of May. I was all set to do a five-week hitch so I could have the whole month of July off. I had a couple motorcycle rides planned that I wanted to make in July and another at the end of September. I had my schedule worked out with North Sea and okayed by Global management.

I rode my Indian out to Paducah, Kentucky, arriving at the hotel the Sunday before my first shift on Monday – as was normal for me that time of year. The weather was good and I was having fun. We were off to a good start. Before my shift started on Monday, I had to go through the standard safety protocol meeting, get a piss test, get a breathalyzer, and sign all the documents stating that I understood all the safety protocols and the site etiquette – speed limits, parking, and that kind of stuff.

It was good to see the crew again after our long winter's nap. Some of the crew had worked other jobs, and not all the people I had expected to be on the job this time were there. Global had made a few personnel changes – they did that every season. Divers got moved around both by choice and by decree of Global's management. I liked everybody I had on my crew, they were all good workers and good divers.

The river level had been going down from the spring run-off high, and the currents were diminishing. One of the factors was the amount of water coming down the Mississippi. More water in the Mississippi slowed the current of the Ohio. Montana had a good snowfall and all that melting snow was filling the Missouri River, which flowed into the Mississippi River. In fact, people along the Mississippi were worried about flooding because of the volume of water flowing into it from the Missouri. That was one of the reasons we were getting a slightly delayed start. Often, we started in March or April.

The weather in the Paducah area was very nice. I was getting a decent motorcycle ride in every morning before my shift started. A decent ride for me was at least a hundred miles. I often went to some little town nearby for a burger and a milkshake before heading to work.

The dive work was a little slow on the uptake this spring, so we weren't working Saturdays yet. We started by doing the initial inspection and repair of the skidway tracks. There was a little silt to remove along with one piece of a tree. About three repairs to the wing guides on the track needed to be made and we were done with that project. The second week I was there, we only worked a four-day week.

Thursday we were informed that we would not be working Friday, Saturday, or Sunday. That was great for me, because it meant that I would have a three-and-a-half-day weekend to make a motorcycle trip somewhere. I looked at the weather for the weekend and it was forecast to be sunny and warm all through the southern states. Awesome! I had a couple friends in Alabama that were due a visit.

I called them up and one was free for the weekend and said he was game for a little riding. Yeehaw! Sweet Home Alabama, here I come. I left for the ride down to his place Friday morning. I arrived at his place in time for a Bar-B-Que dinner. I had a great weekend riding around southern Alabama with him and his brother-in-law.

Around noon on Sunday, I left his place; heading back to Paducah. I wanted to get a good night's sleep and be ready for my shift Monday afternoon. I never made it out of Alabama, though. Somewhere north of the Haunted Chicken Ranch, my bike went into high-speed wobbles with tank-slappers and I remember thinking "this is going to hurt." I woke up a month later in the University of Alabama Birmingham Hospital, paralyzed from the chest down. I spent another month in the hospital after that, before returning home to Helena, Montana.

That was the end of my dive career – forced early retirement. I miss the diving and tunneling jobs. I miss working with all my friends. I miss all the motorcycle riding. I miss riding all over the country spending time with my motorcycle buds. I miss being able to visit all my family spread all over the place.

I went through a pretty dark time right after my accident. My wife did everything she could think of to keep me healthy and keep my spirits up. I tried to make things easier, but I know it was difficult for her. She convinced me to go to a week-long program put on by EmpowerSCI in June, two-thousand-twenty-two. That experience turned my mindset around one-hundred-eighty degrees. After that experience I wanted to finish the book I had started four years earlier – **WET PAY**. Before I could finish that book, though, I was compelled to write another book; the story about my motorcycle accident including my experience with the EmpowerSCI group – What the HELL Happened to Me?! I had to get that story off my chest.

Now, I spend my time writing; and irritating my wife. We welcome our friends and family to visit whenever they can. It is great for me when they do. It is fun to talk about the good old days. I keep in touch with many of them. I like hearing what projects they are working on and where they are travelling. All I can say at this point is stay safe and breathe deep. And remember: Aqua Omnia Praebet – Water Provides Everything!

* * *

The End – Finally!
but there are more stories

Afterword

First of all, I want to Thank you for reading my book or books if you read both. Secondly, these books are by no means complete accounts of my thirty-plus years in the Dive Industry. I worked on so many jobs with so many different people that there is no way I could write a readable book and cover my whole career. I worked with many fabulous people and if you don't find yourself mentioned in any of the stories or if you remember good stories that I didn't include in either book, that doesn't mean I don't remember you or the story. I did so many jobs that worked out just the way they were supposed to with no issues at all. Successful jobs like those do not make for very exciting or fun reading. Unfortunately, the stories that make good reading are usually about episodes we would rather not happen during a dive job. Diving has been described as "hours and hours of boredom marked by moments of sheer terror." It's the "sheer terror" that makes a good read.

If you don't find yourself in my stories, please don't feel slighted. You can be sure I remember you and your work ethic and performance. You were part of the "hours and hours of boredom" that make for a successful career in diving. I thank you for helping me have and long and happy career.

sam humphrey

Acknowledgements

I would like to thank my parents, again, for bringing me into this world and putting up with me and all the headaches and heartache I am sure I caused.

I would like to thank the LSTs – George, Bud, Pat, & Riley - and the Supervisors – Chris, Jon, Marc, Mark, Mike, Herb, & Bruce - who taught me things and pointed me in the right direction.

I would like to thank Marty Fortney, again, for all his help with editing, and his support.

I would like to thank all my friends who keep in touch, keep me going, and remind me of the good old times – Byron, Dack, Jon, Chris, Dubby, Brent, Dennis, Pete, Randy, Heg, Melly, Ballard, Landon, Chad, Cofelt, Mike, Emily, Justin, Marty, Gina, PapaLar, Baldhead, Doug, Joel, et al.

I would like to thank my sister – the one who ripped my earring out – for always being so supportive, positive, and loving.

I would like to thank my wife, Cindy, who keeps me going and without whom, none of this would be possible.

About the Author

sam humphrey

Sam was born in 1961. He started swimming before he could walk. He took a SCUBA Diving course in 1978 while he was in high school in Bellevue, Washington. He joined the U.S. Navy in 1979 in hopes of becoming a diver. That didn't work out for him. He was released from the navy in the spring of 1983. In the fall of 1983 sam enrolled at Highline Community College to get on the waiting list for the Underseas Technology program developed and run by Maurice P. Talbot. Sam was accepted into the program in the fall of 1984. He graduated from that program in the spring of 1986. This is when his actual career as a Commercial Diver started. Sam was mainly employed in the Dive Industry until the spring of 2018 when his career was cut short by a catastrophic motorcycle accident that left him in a wheelchair and forced his retirement. Sam now lives in Buffalo, Wyoming and spends the majority of his time irritating his wife and writing both non-fiction and fiction.

About the Illustrator

Joel P Rabe

Joel is a self-taught artist who developed the basics of art through the public school system with additional education at the college level in Commercial Art. Growing up in the Pacific Northwest and Alaska has inspired him to capture the outdoor lifestyle through his artistic endeavors. Expressing himself through humor has always been in his nature. He tends to lean toward cartooning, but realism is a close second in his artistic style. His preferred mediums are Pen & Ink, Pencil & Water Color, and Carving; although he works in many other mediums as well. Joel's artwork has been featured in **The Spokesman Review** and **Liberty Lake Splash** newspapers and featured on the cover of the **Spokane Coeur D' Alene Living** magazine. He has also been featured on television. He ran a successful art business – Davinci Painting – from 2002 to 2016; working in both residential and commercial sectors. His work included, but was not limited to, design, faux finishes, murals, sculpting and carving. He believes "We should use our creative gifts to make a difference. Art should evoke positive emotion."

Other Books by sam

What the HELL Happened to Me?
My physical and mental struggles after a catastrophic motorcycle accident and ending up a paraplegic in a wheelchair, Cindy's absolute dedication and her unwavering devotion, my family and friend's loving support, the skills and patience of most of the staff I have had in the various medical facilities - it all adds up to one stunning story of horrible luck, remarkable resilience and a heart warming relationship that binds it all together.

NET PAY:
Stories from my Career as a Commercial Diver
A semi-biographical collection of stories told from my point of view. These are funny, exciting, and sometimes horrifying true tales of my experiences working above and below the surface of the water. The jobs were on dams, bridges, in rivers, lakes and the oceans.

What is a Woman?
A somewhat humorous but completely honest answer to the question: "What is a Woman?" The answer includes a biological definition as well as a spiritual description.

Cafe' leBug
A book about Bugs: Insects, arachnids, myriapods, crustaceans, worms, etc. This book is aimed at a younger audience to introduce them to the life around them. It is made up of one-page descriptions of some type of bug with a full-page photo or illustration of the bug being described. The description includes the taxonomy of said bug. It is a fun little book that will educate the reader about the world of entomology.

Look for these Soon to be Published Books by sam

Non-Fiction:

Completely Drenched:
Even More Stories from my Career as a Commercial Diver
A collection of stories taken from the many exploits of sam and his fellow divers. These stories are in not particular order and aren't included in the first two volumes - WET PAY and DRYING OUT.

Shootin' the Breeze:
Stories from sam's life on a Motorcycle
A collection of stories from sam as he grew up with motorcycles. Like his previous books, these stories are all true. Some are funny, some are sad and others are harrowing. Sam started riding powered two-wheelers when he was nine years old.

Fiction:

If Two are Dead
A story about friends, love, life and the consequences of betrayal and thoughtlessness. It is sometimes sad, sometimes funny, and sometimes terrifying.

Reviews of WET PAY

Dear Aunt S,
Thank you very much for the wonderful book! I started reading it yesterday and it is fantastic! I'm interested in getting my SCUBA certification, and I really enjoy the real-life accounts in the book.
Love, M
* * *

You do a great job describing the life of a diver and how commercial diving works. I think it's a great book for spouses and people that are not directly related to the diving industry.
This is an excellent book for both commercial divers and non-divers alike. I have been a commercial diver for over 27 years. The author explains every part of commercial diving in excellent detail. Even if you have no knowledge of diving, Sam makes it very easy as he explains every part in detail. I Highly recommend this book
B H
* * *

You don't have to be a commercial diver to enjoy the book. [It] Gives a good view on the life and career of a diver, from the tough times in the beginning and the more exciting jobs to be had in the future.
H S
* * *

Awesome true story of Sam's diving career. If you are interested [in] diving this book will keep you reading. And if you are thinking of diving as job this is the book to read.

D K

* * *

I read Sam Humphrey's book "Wet Pay" and enjoyed it immensely! Well written and very conversational; good easy read and strikes home in many ways. Thanks, Sam! Of course, Amazon has to sell more stuff, so they teased me with another of his books ("What the Hell happened to me"). I took the click bait and ordered it. It is also well written, but took me a while to get through. Not because of the author's words or style, but because it was so emotional for me. I had to give it a couple of days between many chapters (Parts), due to its powerful story. I just finished it and couldn't recommend it more to everyone. Just be prepared.... If you have ANY empathy, you may cry like a baby like I did!

B M

* * *

Great read and all true...well... as best as divers can recall. Highly recommended especially if you know Sam and some of his fellow divers mentioned in the book.

M R N

* * *

There have been few times where I chuckled aloud while I reading a book. This is one of them. Granted I am in the same industry that Sam was, so it struck a lot of chords. Great writing and easy to keep reading. Looking forward to more books from Sam.

L E

* * *

If you are thinking about becoming a commercial diver, give this book a read. It will help you out. And for those that don't know what a commercial diver does this is full of good info and fun stories. Easy read too.
J H
* * *

I enjoyed all the stories Sam wrote. I never really realized what jobs these commercial divers do; the author takes you all over the US on his adventures of different dives; He has a wonderful sense of humor and explains what each job entails. Sam is a great writer and you just want to keep reading this book - it's a great read Also recommend reading his first book "what THE Hell happened TO me?"
J K S
* * *

I enjoyed this book and am hopeful that Sam gets busy with a sequel. It is funny and sad but mostly it is entertaining. I enjoyed reading about his dives from the beginning to well into his career. I hope you read it. It was hard to put down.
M F
* * *

Reviews of What the HELL Happened to Me?!

Motivational and uplifting. Great read for anyone with disabilities.
A C

* * *

One man's Triumph to Live. Sam is an inspiring writer he takes you with him on his journey, you want to fight for him, cry, laugh. This book will make you think about life and how to fight through Sam will bring you into his struggles and his life to survive such a horrendous accident. The book draws you in to actually feel you are there. Sam I'm inspired by you don't give up write more books that's your new chapter in your new life. Thank you Sam.
K F

* * *

Inspiration. Amazing story. The author tells a detailed story of the daily struggles of being a paraplegic that goes unknown for many unless you have been involved with someone affected by a tragedy. Read in a day. Couldn't put it down.
M S

* * *

Loving life to tragedy and back! I wanted to read this book about a friend I had lost and then found again. I met Sam while serving with him in the Navy aboard the USS Robison DDG 12. We became great friends. He was a big part of my life until he married and was moving to South America. I lost him for many years. One evening I found him on FB and called him. He told me of his tragedy and we started up where we left off. His book tells of his views on life and his tragedy to his recovery of being paralyzed. What a story. It is easy to read and hard to put down. I would recommend it.

M F

* * *

What a wonderful story of a tragic event. Sam is an amazing guy. Enjoyed the book. Sam has a way with words that keep you interested. He writes of his story in a way you feel you were there sharing his pain.

D K

* * *

Truth, honesty and triumph. This is a wonderful book from love of living life to the fullest to a great tragedy and pain and then finding that love can bring back living life to the fullest again. I am thankful Sam and Cindy have one another and continue their love to persevere to accomplish great things. I don't believe I have ever read a more honest heart felt book. Thank you Sam, for laying your feelings and fears out there to help others.

V W

* * *

Brutal honesty. Sam shares his catastrophic life altering experience. The lows and highs. The good and less than good medical care services. The challenges of being a patient. His wife dedication and advocacy. Lack of services. Lack of supply access. Insurance!
B D

* * *

Great read. I like the way Sam told his story; he holds nothing back. I love that Sam included pictures of what his life was like before and after. I found it to be a great read.
T R

* * *

Story of hope in very difficult change in life. I appreciate that Sam shared this story of his adjustment to life after his motorcycle accident. It is inspirational to others dealing with hard situations.
M

* * *

Great story Great guy. Sam's book is an easy, great read. It's like he's sitting there telling you his story. He and Cindy are truly an inspiration to many.
B W

* * *

A story of life when it takes a different direction. A hard story of life and the right attitude; a short and a very interesting read. Thanks for taking the time to write your story
VJ S

* * *

From the exhilaration of riding motorcycles to learning to live after a tragic accident. I really felt like I could see the amazing views and feel the love of motorcycles as described by the author. His heartbreaking tragedy gives us a real-life prospective of a paraplegic. He describes the struggle of learning to live with the changes from helpless depression through recovery for him and his wife. A very good story.
A C

* * *

Story of amazing resilience and recovery! Loved the entire story. Sam has been through some terrible and sometimes wonderful times while recovering. His story is an inspiration.
J C

* * *

sam in Mark V Gear summer 1985

sam getting ready to dive in the Persian Gulf 2012

sam in front of SAT 1 2005

sam in front of LST panel 2007

www.ingramcontent.com/pod-product-compliance
Lightning Source LLC
Chambersburg PA
CBHW020242010526
44107CB00039B/1467/J